The Effective Organization

This book is about organizations and the management of events that affect them. Specifically it explores how organizations or, more precisely, organizations through people, manage the complexity of the events that may be part of their interactions on any given day. Events can be small and local in scope like a sales transaction, a ritual or an awards ceremony, or grand in scope and scale like a sales campaign or a battle or war. Organizations are expected to manage a variety of events but sometimes events expected to be a path toward success and achievement lead to the organization's ultimate collapse or ruin. It's impossible to think of an organization that doesn't think, plan, organize or manage people and operations because of events.

Dennis W. Tafoya (Ph.D., University of Michigan; M.S., University of Pennsylvania) is President of CompCite, a research organization located in Devon, Pennsylvania. He has more than 35 years of teaching and research experience in business, government and university settings. His current projects examine the design and use of strategic operational practices and the quantification of performance across different settings.

The Effective Organization

Practical Application of Complexity
Theory and Organizational Design to
Maximize Performance in the Face
of Emerging Events

Dennis W. Tafoya

Routledge
Taylor & Francis Group

NEW YORK AND LONDON

First published 2010
by Routledge
711 Third Avenue, New York, NY 10017, USA

Simultaneously published in the UK
by Routledge
2 Park Square, Milton Park, Abingdon, Oxon OX14 4RN

Routledge is an imprint of the Taylor & Francis Group, an informa business

© 2010 Taylor & Francis

The right of Dennis Tafoya to be identified as author of this work has been assserted by him in accordance with sections 77 and 78 of the Copyright, Designs and Patents Act 1988.

Typeset in Sabon by RefineCatch Limited, Bungay, Suffolk

Library of Congress Cataloging-in-Publication Data
Tafoya, Dennis, 1947–
The effective organization : practical application of complexity theory and organizational design to maximize performance in the face of emerging events / Dennis Tafoya.
    p. cm.
  1. Organizational effectiveness.   2. Complex organizations.   I. Title.
  HD58.9.T34   2010
  658.4'01—dc22   2009050160

ISBN 10: 0–415–88035–1 (hbk)
ISBN 10: 0–415–88036–X (pbk)
ISBN 10: 0–203–85007–6 (ebk)

ISBN 13: 978–0–415–88035–0 (hbk)
ISBN 13: 978–0–415–88036–7 (pbk)
ISBN 13: 978–0–203–85007–7 (ebk)

There is a saying that when the student is ready the teacher will appear. I've been fortunate to have several appear. Three who have been most instrumental are Nolan Kaiser, Robert Norton and Peter Orlik.

CONTENTS

FIGURES AND TABLES

FIGURES

TABLES

PREFACE

This book is about organizations and the management of events that affect them. It differs from other books related to the topic in three ways: first it presents new approaches to the study of organizations and organizational behavior. The book's new typology of organizations offers a progressive way to classify all organizations into one of four types. This schema is unique, efficient and robust.

Second, the book illustrates the use of complexity theory as a tool for organizational research. Complexity theory is widely used in the physical and natural sciences but there are relatively few examples of the theory's application in the social sciences. The material in this book reflects a concrete example of the theory used to examine and explain phenomena in the social sciences, specifically behavior in organizations, using both experimental and quasi-experimental research methods.

Finally, both academicians and practitioners alike will find numerous analytical guides and materials for use in conducting research or studying aspects of organizational performance. The illustrations and materials used in the book can serve as templates for examining an organization's past, current or future performance or potential, or as a point of departure for the design of one's own research efforts. This makes the material useful to those who study organizations or are seeking ways to improve organizations of which they are members.

The book is divided into four parts. The first part focuses on the nature of organizations and strategies used to shape performance. The six chapters in this section present new and unique ways of looking at and thinking about organizations, specifically how they are designed, developed and used to achieve a mission. The first chapter is an overview of a new model of organizations and each of the following four chapters focuses on one of the four types of organization that make up this new model (i.e., the "enterprise," the "community," the "group/team" and the "individual contributor" organizations) and how each functions.

The first part of the book provides a framework for the book and discussions regarding the relationship between organizational structure and the management of events. People who decide if an organization's performance is successful, that is, if it meets their needs, are its "stakeholders." Stakeholders, then, are those with a stake in the organization's operations and results. The book's second part moves from a general discussion of organizational theory to specific treatment of key factors likely to affect organizations and their stakeholders. In Part II, organizational performance is examined in terms of two topics: the events that organizations are expected to manage to achieve their mission, and the different risk exposures, threats and vulnerabilities that can interfere with or result from the management of those events.

"Organization" is a term people use to describe efforts aimed at directing or controlling behavior. When used as a term or process it reflects activities like planning, the use of rules, procedures or evaluations as a means for seeing that people behave, act, do things the way the organization's leadership, management or membership wants them to. "Self-organization" is a special term used to refer to behavior or acts people construct on their own, without the direction of others be they a boss, manager, leader or group. In the book's second section, information provided explores ways in which organization and self-organization emerge vis-à-vis the management of events.

Material presented in the second part of the book examines the dynamic tension created when attempts to manage or shape organizational performance in the pursuit of a mission is contrasted against managing risk, threats or vulnerabilities. Readers are presented with materials illustrating how an organization's pursuit of a mission by team members or opponents, friends or foes, collaborators or enemies ultimately translates into the action of individuals who define performance in their terms, to meet their needs.

Part III brings material presented in all previous chapters to a new focus: discussion of types of things done to get the performance needed from people or the organization as a whole. This discussion begins with an examination of fundamental practices and procedures used to achieve missions, goals and objectives. This section has three general themes:

1. Ways organizations can maximize efforts to achieve their vision and/or mission (a must);

2. Strategies for managing risk, threats and emerging vulnerabilities (a preferred result); and

3. Ways to contribute to the organization's growth and/or general well-being (a desired end).

This section tackles some of the most difficult topics people can expect to handle in their efforts to shape organizational performance. Material presented in this section may not provide all of the answers one needs for questions like "What should an effective organization look like?" or "How can the members of our organization develop a 'sense of urgency'?" but what is presented can stimulate thinking about the strategic use of people, processes and materials to maximize individual and organizational performance.

Part IV summarizes material presented and reviews different ways to use complexity theory to address other organizational issues. Material presented in this section reflects on two themes. The first looks at ways academicians and practitioners can use the content to meet their research or problem-solving needs. For example, the new organizational model, the typology of events and the new treatment of results (as products, outcomes and impacts) offer clarity and precision when designing, developing or seeking to improve an organization or its performance. Regardless of a reader's need or interest, these materials offer new ways to think about old topics and are flexible enough so that they can be quickly applied to any number of different situations.

The conclusion also contains a review of ways complexity theory can be expanded to examine other questions in the social sciences. The contribution and use of this theory in the natural and physical sciences is extensive and well documented. The examples, studies and illustrations used in the book demonstrate the potential application of complexity theory for applied and theoretical research in sociology, anthropology, communications, psychology, economics and political science, or, just in ways of thinking about making an effective organization. It's hoped, however, that the book's contributions are not limited to academic areas for *The Effective Organization* was written to help those in all organizations, whether military, law enforcement, religious, governmental or the like, interested in devising ways to maximize their performance.

ACKNOWLEDGMENTS

Much of this book is based on observations and data collected over several years. During that time I've had the opportunity to work with a number of people whose help or comments have made direct contributions to my thinking or sheer willingness to carry on with the project; they are, in effect, also representative of the types of effective organization described in the book. For example, I'm not sure how often authors name their favorite book store but I'd be remiss if I didn't acknowledge The Penn Book Center @ 34th and Sansom in Philadelphia for the many ways they helped me and my research efforts. The PBC, an independent bookstore on the perimeter of the University of Pennsylvania campus, is an excellent illustration of the quality of service/help provided by the effective organizations described in this book. Their creation of a special section devoted to complexity theory to support my research efforts is more than a way to encourage the sales of more books; it reflects the sense of urgency about meeting customer needs one finds in effective organizations. The staffs' efforts always produced books and materials as I needed them. The organization and staff serve as fine illustrations of the enterprise and team organizations discussed in the book.

In the book the healthcare industry is featured as an example of the ways different organizations can merge and function as part of a single system and the contributions of Dr. Daniel Will of the University of Pennsylvania's Scheie Eye Institute and Dr. Sara Slattery of the Internal Medicine Department at Penn Medicine proved to be excellent illustrations of that phenomenon as well as important individual contributors to my research efforts. Dr. Will was willing to handle general questions on healthcare delivery systems or specific topics regarding the function of surgical teams or ways in which technology and process are used to meet patient needs. Dr. Slattery's competence and attention to detail separates her from most one encounters. Our discussions of healthcare delivery, ways to maximize office procedures to meet patient needs or even my questions regarding biology and medicine vis-à-vis complexity theory are greatly appreciated. Both illustrate the ways competencies and operational practices combine to produce an effective organization.

Liz Beckius, Culture Program Manager at Best Buy Co., was always willing to see value in the project. Her help finding material related to Best Buy programs proved invaluable, particularly as illustrations of complexity theory in business and industry. It's easy to hold Best Buy's operations and personnel in high regard and Liz is an excellent illustration of the levels of performance one learns to associate with the organization.

Laurie Gripshover, of The Resourceful Coach, is a fine illustration of how competent individuals with a keen sense of urgency can work to define, build and operate an effective organization. What separates her out for me now, however, is the fact that despite the obligations associated with her own business she always found the time to carefully read, think about and comment on any material I asked her to review.

Organizations that exist primarily in pursuit of a mission versus profit or monetary goals, classified as "community organizations" in the book, are one of the four types of organization discussed. Schools, religions and charitable or special-interest organizations are examples and Ken Klippen is an example of an individual with strong interests in two such organizations. His willingness to candidly discuss his role and perspective as a lobbyist for a special-interest group and his religion provided valuable perspective on types of organizations.

The same is true for John Garvey of the United Auto Workers union. Unions like the UAW are their own organization but they also exist as organizations within other organizations. John's comments helped illustrate how unions, as an example of the "community category," emerge and function to meet the needs of both the union and those in the organization the union works to represent. Moreover, like others in organizations classified as "communities" John illustrates how this type of organization's pursuit of a mission is embedded in the efforts and energies of the people who make up the organization.

Nina Connor made herself a regular and ongoing source for insights into operations of a number of the community organizations with which she is involved. Her willingness to listen and comment on my thoughts or to complete surveys and questionnaires has made her a good friend and valued professional.

Professor John Tropman at the University of Michigan found time in his roles as dean and professor to make the kinds of contribution to the book that expand its potential in both academic and non-academic arenas. He made himself available to read and discuss ideas and materials related to the project which, in the end, helped define the value of the project for me and others. I am indebted to him.

Jay Tolson, retired CEO of Fisher & Porter, a manufacturing organization, has been a long-time supporter of this project and me. He always found time to meet and could always identify just one more test for the algorithms or models associated with the project. His willingness to support, encourage and generally help me has proved invaluable from the first time I met him. I doubt that I could ever repay him for the help (or lunches!) he has provided. He is a mentor and model of the ways people can extend their competencies beyond their immediate role or position.

Nancy Gripshover is perhaps the single most significant contributor to this effort. Nancy's support, encouragement and unselfish willingness to help me have proved invaluable to me and the development of this material. Somehow she always found time to complete "yet another questionnaire" or read just one more page. This book couldn't have happened without her.

Finally, is a core group of people who provided substantial support to the processes associated with this project. Sally Frazier, whose efforts extended beyond that of an executive secretary to include continuous support and encouragement for me and this project never stopped. Sally always found a way to contribute without ever seeing it as anything more than "doing her job."

Cathie Orlowski, a long-time friend and associate at Intel Corporation, has been engaged in some facet of this project from the start. Her willingness to read and comment on early versions of the manuscript or to search out materials or people needed was always valuable and appreciated. Our work together goes back many years through which time she has made contributions to me and my work. I can never thank her enough.

Sue Delaney is a fine person, academic and team member. Her willingness to take on extra work and to struggle through the earliest pages of material that became the book proved inestimable in my efforts to produce this final document. She is a wonderful blend of the competence, determination and reliability one always looks for in people and only finds in a few. She is a great team member and a valuable asset to this project.

Finally, I want to acknowledge the support provided by some key people at Routledge, a division of the Taylor & Francis Group. I wrote this book with the idea in mind that it would be a tool for people in all types of organization. If that is achieved it is due in part to the efforts of John Szilagyi, my editor, Sara Werden, my working contact in New York, Gail Welsh, my copy-editor, and Gail Newton, the production editor who keeps us all on schedule. John's and this team's support illustrates for me Routledge's willingness to explore new ideas or to keep important ideas outlined in the past available to readers and researchers. (Routledge's recent publication of Karl Popper's classical work from the 1970s, *The Two Fundamental Problems of the Theory of Knowledge* is an example.) Routledge is a fine illustration of the effective enterprise outlined in the book and John, Gail N., Sara and Gail W., the enterprise's professionals whose guidance and support help the organization achieve its vision and mission.

PART I

Complexity Theory and Organizational Design
A Structural Model of Organizations

CHAPTER 1

Complexity Theory as a Tool to Aid Understanding of Organizational Performance Management in Effective Organizations

Events are the focal point of every activity in an organization. Stores focus on the sales event, doctors the surgical event or patient meeting, educators on a lecture (teaching event), politicians on campaign events, even subversive groups on terrorist events. Events are the means through which organizations achieve their mission.

The route to appreciating the role of events in organizations begins with understanding the manner in which they are constructed—how organizational events emerge from thoughts, ideas and plans to influence the behavior of people and other organizations. Organizations are not simple, discrete entities and variation among different organizations is almost limitless but there are certain common themes one can attribute to all organizations.

Complexity theory is a useful tool to systematically organize and describe the emergence of events associated with organizations across a wide variety of settings. The focus here centers on examination of how and why behaviors used to manage events emerged and the ramifications of the management strategies used. Complexity theory is a means for the systematic study of organizations from a common perspective, from those elements common to all organizations: the people, processes, materials and culture that give rise to an individual's or group's collective behavior. Complexity theory is a means for understanding why an organization exists, its purpose or mission and how it uses structure and processes to increase the likelihood events are managed in ways that achieve the mission.

The relationship between an organization's vision or mission and the behavior designed to achieve them is not a straight path. Despite best efforts to shape performance, ultimately what happens at "the event" rests on the actions of people: the individuals or groups expected to manage the event. In other words, when one encounters poor customer service that behavior is not simply an instance of "people trained to provide quality service who don't" but, rather, of "people trained to provide quality service who *choose* not to provide quality service." Something in the organization's design and/or development opens the door for individuals to act on their own or, in the language of complexity theory, to self-organize a response to the event at hand.

Team members, for example, may be coached to be supportive of the team, but they form cliques and may even try to exclude other team members from participation. Managers are instructed to be fair and objective professionals, yet they may discriminate and/or display favoritism or bias when hiring or promoting employees. Employees are taught to think "safety first" if there is fire in the building, but people have been known to disregard their own safety and rush back into a burning building to see if everyone got out. Successful event management is only partially within the organization's control: the organization's membership is comprised of independent, free-thinking people who combine what the organization expects with their own bias, perspective, skills or needs.

THE PROCESS OF SELF-ORGANIZATION

There's no consensus on a specific definition of self-organization or the related concepts of complexity and emergence.[1] We view self-organization as a useful tool because it offers a uniform way for examining how people, acting alone or with others and without direction, can construct a response to events that emerge around them. Take a familiar concept like customer service. Organizations teach people how to provide the levels of service they expect. Nevertheless, despite the training, there is often little consistency in the service provided.

The amount and type of service provided can vary from person to person. Some people take it upon themselves to "go the extra distance" to meet a customer's need. They provide "value-added service." It's more than expected. Others, however, deviate from what is acceptable. Instead of providing "quality customer service," the employee may provide the minimum or may be rude or simply ignore the customer. Again, the individual chooses to behave in this manner.

The challenge self-organization presents those in organizations is that sometimes it can be desirable, of potential benefit, and, at other times, a potential liability for the organization and its membership. Or, as economist Paul Krugman framed it, self-organization "is something

we observe and try to understand, not necessarily something we want"
(Krugman 1996: 6).

FEATURES AND BENEFITS ASSOCIATED WITH THE STUDY OF
SELF-ORGANIZATION IN COMPLEX SOCIAL SYSTEMS

Complexity, according to Scott Camazine et al. (2001), is a relative term.
Systems, like organizations, are complex, not because they involve many
behavioral rules and large numbers of different components, but because
of the nature of their "global response" to their environment (Camazine
et al. 2001: 11). It's the nature of the organization, the system, as it
appears to others, given its macro properties. An organization's complexity is not found in those elemental properties that define it for those
walking the corridors of its buildings or watching its commercials on
television, or listening to the speeches of its leaders. An organization's
complexity is reflected in the thoughts, values and ideals of its stakeholders; it's the whole package, just as a sentence is more meaningful than
the individual words that form it (Polanyi 1974: 184). When looking at
the organization as a whole, systemically, complexity gives an observer
a sense for what the organization is, what it looks like and, very importantly, what it stands for. This is particularly clear when the observer
compares what the organization sees as important with what he/she
believes is important. In other words, complexity is a way of gaining a
perspective of what the organization is that one can't get by merely looking at the organization at its lower levels (e.g., Polanyi 1974: 181–207).

Typically, organizations move from their lofty, sometimes idealistic
and often vaguely defined vision or mission statements to action through
the formal and informal use of processes, such as planning, communication or evaluation. Processes stimulate behavior or shape it after it emerges.
For example, a local government may see protecting the public's welfare
as part of its mission. Since roadways fall under the local government's
control, government leaders may structure the mission of internal departments, like the highway patrol, as an extension of the overall government's
mission. To achieve this mission the highway patrol may have goals:

1. to make sure speed limits are maintained; and
2. that vehicles on the road meet state safety standards.

Moreover, to maintain speed limits the highway patrol might use monitoring activities to see that drivers "behave as expected." These activities
might include conducting a number of patrols, setting up and managing
speed traps, isolating high accident areas or similar actions that can help

the police department achieve its mission. Table 1.1 summarizes the elements of this type of planning process.

The process of achieving an organization's vision and mission, however, is not straightforward. Those in organizations also have to deal with the emergence of unplanned behaviors and events. These may or may not help the organization achieve its vision or mission and, in some cases, may obstruct its efforts or, worse, potentially harm the organization.

As Table 1.2 illustrates, unplanned behavior or performance, even if well intentioned, can be hazardous for organizations for several reasons.[2] For example, unplanned or spontaneous behaviors may put the organization or its membership in jeopardy. The employee who first

Table 1.1   Guiding the Emergence of Planned Activities: The Foundation for Expected Performance and Behaviors

Vision: where we see ourselves (e.g., 5–7 years in the future)

Mission: what our aspiration must be to achieve our vision (e.g., over the next 2–4 years)

Goals: benchmarks in key areas to achieve the mission (e.g., for quality, productivity, people)

Objectives: quantitative benchmarks to achieve each particular goal

Activities (performance and/or behavior): measurable tasks and activities to achieve each objective

Table 1.2   Unplanned Behavior or Performance

UNPLANNED RISKY BEHAVIOR OR PERFORMANCE	UNPLANNED NEGATIVE BEHAVIOR OR PERFORMANCE
• Attempting to put out fire • Intervening in a robbery • Coaching co-workers/team members in work processes without authorization • Speaking in public on/about the organization without authorization • Saying "the customer is always right" without authorization • Whistle-blowing to help "eliminate a problem" • Challenging a leader's direct orders • Changing an agreed-upon plan without client authorization	• Rude treatment of a customer • Challenging an aggressive driver • Attempting new production processes without authorization • Offering contrary and unauthorized interpretation of a situation • Challenging medical or other professional advice • Unauthorized discussions with a competitor, enemy, opponent • Unauthorized interpretation of a rule, doctrine, policy

attempts to put out a fire before setting off an alarm or leaving the building may be performing a noble act, but it could put the employee's or others' lives in jeopardy. The same is true for the person who intervenes or attempts to prevent a robbery. These are dangerous events.

Compare the list of behaviors in Table 1.2 with those in Table 1.3. Rude treatment of a customer, co-worker or supervisor is seldom prudent behavior. These behaviors can put people or the organization at risk of retaliation. Retaliation also is a possibility for whistle-blowing, challenging an aggressive driver, or ignoring medical or other professional advice someone has received. These behaviors can reflect feelings of self-righteousness, a sense of authority without merit or, simply, poor judgment. So, on one hand emergence is the process of transforming the organization's mission into action; into behaviors or performance. However, emergence also applies to a second group of behaviors—those that are not planned, directed or controlled. For example, Table 1.3 has a list of common but unplanned and often desirable behaviors and events that might occur. Both lists illustrate an important point: behaviors have an effect on people. The effects may be direct or subtle, they may affect people emotionally or physically but they have an effect.

The potential value in understanding the role of self-organization in organizations increases when one is willing to look at the organization's elements (e.g., people and events) systemically. For example, when is poor customer service, service that is contrary to what one has been taught to provide, not just a single incident but reflective of a pattern of behavior? Or, on a broader, community level: when is speeding, drug use, theft, aggressive behavior or anti-social acts, either by an individual or a group, an example of emergent wide-scale patterns of behavior? The difference between something being a one-time occurrence and something reflecting a pattern of behavior is significant. One-time occurrences or single acts may be random and spawned by any of a number of factors. Repeated

Table 1.3   Unplanned Desirable Behaviors

- Employee displays problem-solving initiative (deliberate)
- Hitting a home run in baseball (random)
- Receiving an unsolicited monetary gift (random)
- Receiving a "pat on the back" (random)
- A promotion (random)
- The opposing team fumbles the ball (random)
- Bringing in a treat for those at the office (deliberate)

acts or actions illustrate that a number of factors also may spawn behavior patterns which, in turn, make it possible to identify thresholds associated with the underlying nature of the self-organization process.

Table 1.4 contains illustrations of times when self-organization can be beneficial and other times when it can be risky for the individual, group or an organization. The issue for those managing organizations is: how does one reduce or manage the risky incidences of self-organization and capitalize on, and perhaps even encourage, positive self-organizations? The process can be tricky since self-organization rests in the control of the individual and not the organization. The same behavior that "stimulates innovation" may also be "contrary to policy" or "lead to more problems and expenses" for the organization. Moreover, since self-organization in social systems cannot be prevented, it is very important that processes are in place to observe, analyze and maximize the likelihood that positive self-organizations emerge more often than negative ones.

FUNDAMENTAL CONDITIONS NEEDED FOR SELF-ORGANIZATION TO OCCUR

Complexity theory is a tool we're using to examine emerging performance, particularly the type of performance defined and organized by

Table 1.4   Ten Reasons Why it's Important to Understand the Role and Process of Self-Organization in Organizations

SELF-ORGANIZATION CAN BE BENEFICIAL	SELF-ORGANIZATION CAN BE RISKY
1. It can stimulate innovation.	1. It can challenge established patterns.
2. It opens the system.	2. If unchallenged it can give the impression there are favorites.
3. It can lead to relaxed attitudes toward change.	3. Some self-organization may put people in danger, at risk.
4. Observing self-organization can give us clues about process problems, about training problems.	4. It may be contrary to policy.
5. It can position "ownership" on the lower levels.	5. It can lead to more problems, expenses.
6. Observing self-organization can give clues about recruiting problems.	6. It can lead to division within the organization.
7. It can lead to cost savings, problem-solving.	7. It can lead to formation of sub-groups.
8. Self-organization can be a natural process element that's been overlooked.	8. It can undermine leadership.
9. It can create shortcuts, improve efficiencies.	9. It can lead to delays, obstructions.
10. It can stimulate initiative, growth.	10. It can confuse stakeholders regarding who's in charge, what to expect next time.

people without the direction or instruction of others; in other words, performance or behavior that is self-organized.

This focus on human social organizations differs from research that has examined complexity and self-organization in natural, physical or biological systems. These studies offer relatively neat, clean examples of complexity theory and self-organization at work. Adam's book, *Mathematics in Nature: Modeling Patterns in the Natural World* (2003) is filled with examples of self-organization in nature. He covers cloud patterns, formation of sand patterns and dunes or the formation and dispersion of waves on the water. It's an interesting introduction to the observance and measurement of complex physical phenomena in everyday life.

Also of interest are the studies of biological systems. The foraging behavior of ants or honey bees (Seeley 1985, 1989) or predator/prey studies (Segel and Jackson 1972) which illustrate complexity and self-organization in biological systems are very interesting. But, while there's value in using studies of natural systems as a guide for studying human systems, they are only useful to a point: human organizations, like political systems, religions, businesses or military units, are fluid, dynamic systems and are not bound to physical or biological blueprinting like ant colonies or beehives. Bees and ants don't have free will.

Table 1.5 illustrates some differences between the study of complexity and specifically self-organization in human and natural systems. The table illustrates that there are real benefits to understanding the differences between the human and natural systems since they have a number of common features and even where the two processes differ widely there's potential value in the comparison. For example, spontaneous self-organizations are evident in both natural and human social systems. There are also ways to map the self-organizations and to note key thresholds in each. Consider the number, variety and complexity of thresholds in human decision-making associated with taking action. When a human reaches a threshold they make a decision—for example to continue or not or, simply, just to value the threshold or not. An animal's behavior is not guided by the variety of thresholds reflected in human decision-making and that is an important distinction.

Examining processes in both human and natural systems can tell us something about the underlying nature of the system studied. When conditions are right for spontaneous self-organization to begin, that implies that the self-organization was "pushed" from the system. Again, this is a difference between human and natural systems. Natural systems appear to need the self-organizations that occur to materialize as a logical part of the system's evolutionary cycle. Cell mitosis in biological

Table 1.5 The Differences in the Emergence and Manifestation of the Self-Organization Process in Natural and Human Social Systems

NATURAL SYSTEMS (e.g., physical and biological)	HUMAN SOCIAL SYSTEMS (e.g., organizations, institutions)
• Self-organization can begin in a spontaneous or controlled fashion.	• Self-organization can begin in a spontaneous or controlled fashion.
• There's an obvious end or terminal point.	• The process's "end" can be difficult to isolate.
• The process's form and format are fixed; they are restricted within the context in which they appear.	• The process's form and format are fluid. The process can transcend boundaries as it unfolds.
• It requires no (cognitive) competencies.	• It can require formal competencies.
• It requires no capacity to strategically use history.	• History may be a guide.
• The results are "predictable."	• Results can be elusive.
• The results are knowable.	• Results spawn products, outcomes, impacts.
• The time to fruition is "predictable."	• Time to fruition is variable.
• The threshold appearance is "predictable."	• When threshold appears is unpredictable.
• Self-organization's "temporal nature" tends to be predictable in the organizational context.	• Self-organization does not appear to follow a defined timeframe.
• Self-organization may be strongly dependent on certain conditions (e.g., temperature, volume, velocity).	• Conditions may or may not lead to self-organization.
• Self-organization process tends to be "wired"; one "knows" what to expect.	• Self-organization is susceptible to conditional vagaries (e.g., if communication or information requirements are insufficient the self-organization may not materialize or may be ill defined).

systems is an example. Cells in biological systems have to divide and become a finger, nose or heart. There is no choice making. Humans make choices; they choose to be aggressive or nice or to innovate or create. Both cell mitosis and human choice-making are instances of a system "pulling" the self-organization to the fore, but that's as far as the similarities can be carried.

There's an identifiable terminal point for self-organizations in natural systems that may not be evident in human, social organizations. For example, when do road rage, union formation or an act of heroism end when they've begun as self-organized processes? Clearly, the group forming the union can begin to formalize the nature of their organization, but have the momentum, values or ideas that drove the unionization effort ended? (Or, for that matter, when is an organization "finally" formed?)

Is road rage only defined by the expression of rage? What about the pre- and post-rage sentiments? Perhaps road rage is the center of a distribution of rage sentiments that have at the apex overt behaviors of a particular type. If this is the case, when does the process end? Axelrod's (1984) study of cooperation is an illustration. Axelrod documented the formation of cooperative behavior of participants engaged in studies he conducted. But does cooperation end when the cooperating parties separate, say to go home for the night? Or, rather, is there perhaps some unspoken agreement that says, in effect, "we'll pick up co-operating from here, once we get back together" so that what's constructed when people agree to cooperate is a "state of cooperation" that may continue after the immediate activities that define the cooperating event end. If this is the case it may say something about the results associated with the self-organization of cooperative behavior. As the number of people engaged in working together increases, the number and complexity of products, outcomes and impacts associated with the results of their interactions can increase dramatically.

What about the person who takes it upon herself to rush into the burning building to see if co-workers need help getting out? No one told her to be heroic. Can someone tell her when it's time to stop being heroic? Has the tendency of being heroic always been part of her makeup and simply on "standby," ready for action? And, will it be available tomorrow should another event needing a heroine arise?

The time of year, temperature or humidity must be within certain parameters for self-organizations to occur within some natural systems. These conditions are like a toggle switch, not signaling a start or finish point but rather a threshold marking when it is "OK" to start or "time" to end. Human social systems aren't bounded by these types of thresholds, or at least not in the same ways. Try telling someone who is angry to stop being angry or who smokes to give up the habit. The thresholds may mark points of ascent or descent but not beginning or end points.

Self-organizations in natural systems tend to materialize within a format that is fixed: ant and bee foraging behavior *has to happen* within the contextual environment of the nest or hive (otherwise, it's just eating). This is because foraging behavior is for the benefit of the colony and not the individual ant or bee. So the colony, per se, is a parameter that defines the format around the search effort. Human social systems, in contrast, are mobile and dynamic. If the setting is not right, move to one that is. If the people aren't right or cooperative with your efforts, find some who are. If the time is not right, delay until it is. These aren't options for natural systems. Failure to operate within certain parameters may not only result in an ill-conceived self-organization effort but, in the extreme, damage to the organization (e.g., colony) as a whole.

Natural systems have no established capacity for the strategic use of history; in fact, history can make only marginal, if any, contributions in natural systems and certainly, as far as we know, no contribution based on conscious deliberation. In human social systems, however, those involved in self-organizations either may use direct historical referents or, if none exist, tangential or cross-over referents by searching for parallels possibly associated with former experiences.

Because self-organizations often *have to happen*, the processes and results associated with them are generally predictable. In natural systems, results are "predictable" in the sense that they are seemingly programmed to unfold in a particular way. What is observed couldn't be anything else because the system and its elements do what they are designed to do. So, it's possible to talk about what to expect about the process or results of self-organization with some measure of certainty. Schrodinger (2006: 76–85), for example, is careful to distinguish between natural systems that are highly predictable and human social systems that lend themselves to limited predictability. Boundaries surrounding the results associated with human self-organizations are complicated by the range and variety of results possible.

Regardless of the type of social organization examined, the focus of all effort expended is measured in terms of results. But the term "results" is a broad and sometime vague concept. We break down results into three categories. The first of these are the *products*, the observable results of one's efforts. Products are the things one is expected to produce when doing one's job, the ways one behaves when performing a service, the decisions one makes, the actions one takes, the behaviors one displays associated with a task, assignment, job, etc. They may be tangible or as intangible as a process (e.g., service or information exchange) or effort (delivery of a product) but they can be observed and measured.

Products can be good/bad, well or poorly done, done "as expected" or "less than expected," etc. They can be designed to help humanity, to save lives or to terrorize communities or individuals. The most significant characteristic of products, however, is the notion that they are only a means to an end. As such, products are meant to reflect the organization's:

1. mission, philosophy, ideology, values;
2. activity, capability, capacity, competency; and
3. intentions, directions, objectives.

The real effect of organizational effort lies in the next two result categories: outcomes and impact.

Outcomes are a consequence of *products*. In many ways, the relationship between products and outcomes is a classic stimulus/response model. "'X' happened and 'Y' is an outcome." There may be more than one outcome associated with a single product and, like products, outcomes can be good or bad, desirable or not, etc. A *desired outcome* is the immediate conclusion of the product, when what is observed is what was expected.

Impacts are the end result of the *products* and *outcomes*. Once they emerge their presence can be long lasting and can unfold in other areas (i.e., not originally associated with the products or actions taken in the first place.) Impacts, either good or bad, are the *real* payoff of results. A desired impact is one that benefits the organization in a particular way and attempting to produce a desired impact is the cause, basis, antecedent, motive or rationale for activity, action or effort. Impacts may be tangible (e.g., increased market share, defeat of an opponent), intangible or abstract (image enhancement, creation of an emotional state like fear, satisfaction or happiness).

Results can be examined in terms of products, outcomes and impacts for both natural and human systems but only human systems think and act in terms of these distinctions. For example, the relationship between work and leisure in human systems is a classical relationship studied in both economics and sociology as a means for explaining why people work. That is, one works so that one doesn't have to work, so that one has "time off" from work. It's a relationship between products ("work") and impact ("free time") that doesn't exist in non-human systems.

Another important distinction between self-organization within natural and human social systems is the extent to which key thresholds are "predictable." Thresholds play an important role in the self-organization process. These thresholds are most notable because they mark a point where critical decision-making occurs in this behavioral change process. The individual considers the trade-offs associated with following or deviating from the norm, and then acts. The individual either performs at the norm or moves from it.

It's what Tim Harford refers to as people behaving rationally. "Rational people," he writes, "respond to trade-offs and to incentives. When the costs or benefits of something change, people change their behavior. Rational people think—not always consciously—about the future as well as the present as they try to anticipate likely consequences of their actions in an uncertain world" (Harford 2008: 4, 9–10). Non-human systems don't reflect the same profiles. Moreover, our approach extends Harford's notion to include human actions in a "near certain world": a world where the use of rules, norms and laws defining how one should behave are used to reduce or eliminate ambiguity.

To illustrate this, consider Figure 1.1. In it there are four critical thresholds, two on the ascent and two on the descent from the norm. Thresholds mark the individual or group's progress, they reflect the processes followed, and they reveal the implications associated with reaching and crossing each threshold. They also signal the inherent complexity associated with progress; everything changes as one moves further up, or down, the self-organization lines.

A final point regarding thresholds and the distinction between self-organization in natural and human social systems is that it's not possible to predict accurately when the thresholds will appear in human social systems, how long, if at all, one can "linger" at a threshold, and the time

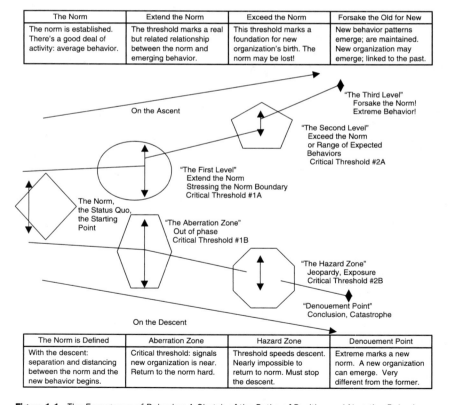

The Norm	Extend the Norm	Exceed the Norm	Forsake the Old for New
The norm is established. There's a good deal of activity: average behavior.	The threshold marks a real but related relationship between the norm and emerging behavior.	This threshold marks a foundation for new organization's birth. The norm may be lost!	New behavior patterns emerge; are maintained. New organization may emerge; linked to the past.

The Norm is Defined	Aberration Zone	Hazard Zone	Denouement Point
With the descent: separation and distancing between the norm and the new behavior begins.	Critical threshold: signals new organization is near. Return to the norm hard.	Threshold speeds descent. Nearly impossible to return to norm. Must stop the descent.	Extreme marks a new norm. A new organization can emerge. Very different from the former.

Figure 1.1 The Emergence of Behavior: A Sketch of the Paths of Positive and Negative Behaviors.

between thresholds. In human systems, thresholds are predictable; the difficulty is predicting when they will emerge. This isn't the case in natural systems.

Most natural systems cannot tolerate variability. The self-organization may be spontaneous at the start but after that the temporal nature is predictable, almost routine. Self-organization in natural systems may be strongly dependent on certain conditions (e.g., temperature, volume, velocity) such that when the conditions are met one can expect the next step to occur. This is because natural systems tend to be "wired" to behave in certain specific ways. Again, the self-organization process may be spontaneous when it starts, but participants in natural systems have defined roles, processes unfold in established ways and, so, progress moves toward a definable end, all things considered.

THE CONDITIONS FOR SELF-ORGANIZATION IN HUMAN SOCIAL SYSTEMS

Organizations like retail stores, schools, military units, sports teams or even terrorist groups are the focal point for discussions in this book for several reasons. First, we're familiar with these types of organization. We belong to or are influenced by many of them every day. They also are good places to see examples of two types of behavior: that which is a result of another's direction, instruction or guidance and behavior constructed by individuals or groups without the direction of others.

Behavior constructed by individuals or groups without the direction of others is of particular interest because it reflects a decision to behave in ways that may be contrary to what the organization's leadership or supervision wants or expects. This is self-organized behavior, a very specific phenomenon occurring in a specific place under particular conditions. Consider the employee trained to provide a high level of customer service who chooses instead to be rude. The decision to construct a rude response in this instance is an example of self-organized behavior; it is contrary to what the organization's supervision wants or expects. So is the decision by a group that decides, on its own, to demonstrate dissatisfaction with management through a "work slow-down" or strike. The organization's leadership didn't OK this action and it probably doesn't support it; the organization's membership took it upon themselves to behave this way.

Behavior, whether by an individual or group, is self-organized when it meets certain criteria. These include the following:

1. *The behavior is a product of localized interactions.* A localized interaction implies that an organization's participants involved

in self-organization activity tend to focus their interactions among themselves (Camazine et al. 2001: 488; Sole and Bascompte 2006: 14). Certain conditions can create the opportunity for localized interactions. Sometimes localized interactions stem from the nature of work done, for example, when people work together on a committee. Other times simple geography is a factor. People who do the same type of work typically work in the same locality, talk with each other and, consequently, share ideas, opinions and beliefs with each other. These "localized interactions" are an opportunity for self-organization to occur.

2. With localized interactions there is a reliance on *local information* (Camazine et al. 2001: 12). Those engaged in localized interactions talk to each other and share information. They can create their own language (e.g., specialized or technical), slang, their own rules for interaction or expectations for how information is managed at this level.

3. *An absence of well-defined top-down control* is a feature stressed by many who study behavior or performance in self-organized systems (Camazine et al. 2001; Holland 1998; Johnson 2001; Krugman 1996; Sole and Bascompte 2006: 14). This criterion implies that the emergent behavior is not a result of being told what to do or because of a blueprint prepared by others. Control in this instance is defined at the local level, through localized interactions.

4. *The self-organized behavior forms patterns*, again without external guidance (Camazine et al. 2001: 12). Pattern formation signifies several things about the self-organization process. First, pattern formation is an indication that the observed behavior is not a one-time phenomenon; it's probably happened several times before. The identification of a pattern also associates an element of predictability with the behavior. Identifying the pattern implies one should be able to predict the occurrence of future incidences of the same behavior or performance. Finally, identification of a pattern increases the accuracy or validity of any classifications of the behavior or performance observed. The patterns that form are not restricted only to the behavior but also key features or characteristics of behavior occur repeatedly and form their own patterns.

5. *There is variability among elements within the organization.* The relationship between "variability" and self-organization

means there is a level of inconsistency, unevenness, discrepancy or perhaps even contraction within the organization (Sole and Bascompte 2006: 14). For example, one factor that influences self-organization in a fast-food restaurant is variability in management. One manager does things differently from another, perhaps is more permissive or relaxed about company policy. Variability can also be observed when key policies or procedures are incomplete or missing, a condition likely to occur in many new organizations. Missing policies, procedures or rules create variability because there's a lack of consistency or gaps in the ways things are done or what's expected of people. People can use the resultant variability to fabricate solutions or to fill gaps that meet their needs or benefit them in some way. So, if there's a fire and no one has received training in ways to respond to the fire this is an opportunity for the individual to create his/her own response.

6. *There is evident use of positive feedback* regarding actions and this, in turn, can lead to the development of rules for the self-organizing system. Negative feedback "plays a critical role, providing inhibition to offset the amplification and helping to shape [behavior] into a particular pattern" (Camazine et al. 2001: 16–21, 489). Positive feedback, in contrast, reinforces the likelihood that the same behavior can be repeated in the future. If, for example, a local government's budget doesn't allow for monitoring traffic on weekends, people who speed (self-organized behavior) on the weekends without being caught also may be expected to speed on following weekends.

7. *Adaptations.* There is unevenness in the adaptation process within organizations (Sole and Bascompte 2006: 14). The need for adaptation implies that change is occurring within the organization. Some change is easier to incorporate into the organization but both change and capacity to adapt to change create pressures within the organization. If the adaptation process is uneven or in flux it can be difficult to think about or react to the process with confidence or a sense of certainty. Uncertainty in this instance can create stress points, which in turn can lead to the development of thresholds, defining entry points and sometimes even enabling self-organized behavior.

8. Finally, *there is the capacity for change.* "The capacity to respond to changing conditions on an evolutionary time scale is obvious from micro-evaluation to macro-evolution" (Sole and

Bascompte 2006: 14). However, the simple capacity for change is not the important element when discussing the self-organization process. Rather, the *range* of the capacity to change is the salient feature needing to be examined. Organizations with a limited capacity to tolerate change are less likely to foster self-organization. For example, organizations that have a restrictive environment defined by extensive rules, procedures and practices experience less change and, in all likelihood, fewer opportunities for self-organization.

These rules or criteria for self-organization provide a useful way to summarize and introduce the material presented in the following chapters. In those chapters, complexity theory generally and self-organization in particular are used as tools for better understanding organizations and behavior in organizations.

Sometimes the discussions examine how the organization's environment facilitates or inhibits the self-organization of unwanted behavior or performance. In these instances, this places an emphasis on isolating factors serving as conditions for behavior to occur and other times on how an environment may define parameters for behavior when it occurs (Ashby 1962). The contribution of structural and operational practices discussed in the following chapters, for example, demonstrates use of conditionality and constraints to maximize control and better define an organization's environment.

CHAPTER 2

The Structural Makeup of the Complete Organization

There are reasons we join the organizations we do. Think about your "social self," the person who works, studies, lives, prays and/or plays in the context of others. You engage in these activities in a number of different organizations. In fact, it's virtually impossible to imagine anyone who is not part of or affiliated with some organization. Sometimes we're born into these organizations, like the religions, cultures or the political parties we support, and other times we voluntarily join them, like sports clubs or places where we work or live.

This chapter focuses on how organizations seek to manage participant behavior from the moment they enter until they leave (and sometimes after that). The chapter begins with a look at reasons why people join organizations because this sets the stage for control to occur and it is where the relationship between organization and member begins. The relationship we have with organizations is dynamic and always fascinating: "Come join us and stay (as long as you fit in)."

ORGANIZATIONS EXIST TO ACHIEVE A VISION AND MISSION: WAYS TO ATTRACT AND CONTROL MEMBERSHIP PERFORMANCE

The variation among organizations seems unlimited but certain themes are common to all. Whether they are designed for a short term, e.g. to raise funds or to solve a problem, or for the long term, e.g. to disseminate a religion, to make a profit through the sale of merchandise, or to overthrow and form a new government, all organizations exist because of a vision and to accomplish a mission. The *vision* is the concept, anticipation, theory or idea the organization's leadership has that separates where it is now from where it wants to be in the future. The vision is an ideal that points the way or provides direction, for example, for the next three to five years; it's the foundation for the organization's mission.

The *mission* is the translation of the vision into something tangible. Mission statements typically look out one to three years into the future and present a measurable dimension to the organization's vision. To be the "best," or the "premier provider of," or the "industry leader," or "the authority," or "to change the way things are" are representative phrases one might find in a mission statement. Combined, the vision and mission serve to indicate both a reason and target for performance and sometimes a way for attracting others to help.

Performance goals, objectives and activities turn the vision and mission into reality. *Goals* are measurable targets, quantifiable summary statements that define *what* must be accomplished to achieve the mission. *Objectives* are the things done to accomplish each goal. Objectives tell something about *how* the goals will be achieved. *Activities* are the day-to-day things *done* to accomplish an objective. Activities are the substance of events. These include things like the making of a product in a factory, the consulting service of a marketing manager, the sales transaction in the retail store or the religious leader conducting the funeral service. Activities point to where the organization's efforts are either successful or not.

Table 2.1 illustrates the inter-relationship between the vision, mission, goals, objectives and activities for three different organizations. In this example the organizations have a unique, dependent relationship with each other. So, apart from illustrating the differences among the vision, mission, goals and objectives as organizing devices, the information in this table also illustrates how the vision, mission, goals, objectives and activities of different organizations can contribute to competition and conflict among organizations, even when such competition or conflict may seem illogical.

For example, one expects the mission of the terrorist organization to bring it into conflict with the airline and security organizations. It is the nature of this organization to be an adversary of the other two. Sometimes, however, even organizations that should be collaborating may find that their missions can bring them into conflict with their own partners. The airline and security subcontractor's missions, for example, may create unwanted tensions between them. One organization struggles to meet customer needs by making sure planes arrive and leave on schedule while the other creates potential bottlenecks and departure slow-downs as it struggles to make sure the environments on the ground and in the air are safe. Each is trying to achieve its mission but it's obvious that in terms of the big picture, effective organizations must consider the visions, missions, etc. of others as well as their own.

Table 2.1 The Strategic and Tactical Use of Organizing Elements for Three Organizations with Dependent Relationships

ELEMENT	INTERNATIONAL AIRLINE	TERRORIST ORGANIZATION	SECURITY SUBCONTRACTOR
Vision	Be the largest international airline in the world	Our enemies are in disarray	All flights are without security threats
Mission	Be recognized as the primary airline for international travel	Launch a terrorism program in our enemy's major cities	Stop threats to airlines at target airports
Goals	• Establish flights to major international airports • Set competitive pricing • Offer the best service	• Threaten the security of one international flight • Promote worldwide media coverage of our activities	• Set up a security process at all airports • 100% passenger screening • 100% baggage screening
Objectives	• Ensure 98% on time departures and arrivals • No lost luggage • Fast turn-around of planes	• Recruit supporters committed to the cause • Build a core of elite fighters • Build a security system to avoid detection	• Hire staff needed • Secure the best equipment • Ensure staff can use the equipment
Activities	• Fast boarding of passengers • Handle luggage fast • Prompt, courteous service • Work with regulators	• Train supporters • Conduct six successful attacks • Surveillance	• Train staff • Test staff competencies • Evaluate security processes • Surveillance

Organizations communicate their vision, mission, goals and objectives to motivate and focus interested stakeholders—people with a stake in the organization's purpose or activities. Since the vision is a sense of where the organization is headed, communicating the vision can be a useful tool in drawing people to, or motivating those in the organization. This can be true whether the vision is clear and direct ("Defeat the Nazis") or vague and imprecise and left to the membership to define for themselves ("Achieve world peace").

The "vision" is the least tangible of the strategic tools used to direct and control the organization or its membership. Visions can range from those relatively simple to state and understand to some that are vague and, sometimes, even purposefully imprecise. For example, the vision statements, to "rule the world" or to "find a cure for breast cancer" are clear, despite the magnitude of their scope or the effort it might take to achieve each. On the other hand, some that are equally easy to say are more complex and difficult to understand. For example, vision statements such as "to eliminate prejudice" or "to ensure that everyone is happy" leave one wondering about how something as pervasive as prejudice can be eliminated or what is meant by "happy."

Some organizations want an inherently ambiguous vision statement. A terrorist organization's vision of a world free of all infidels leaves it up to members to decide what that world would look like and, sometimes, how to achieve the vision. Everyone in the terrorist organization creates his/her own path toward achieving the mission, thus making each person an individual contributor and a sub-organization within the larger organization. This way there is no "one" organization per se; there is a composite, perhaps a blend of people moving toward some vision.

Regardless of its clarity, having a vision is a standard organizing device for all organizations. Visions say something about the organization vis-à-vis the outside world. "We not only march to a different drummer; we're headed in a different direction." Competing visions can emerge within a parent organization under the right conditions. Crime and terrorist organizations, for example, exist within a larger organization— a national government. It is their different visions that bring them into conflict with the parent organization. Each organization has its own vision for its future and the visions often are not in harmony. In very closed organizations like a secret society, it is an accepted practice to restrict communication of the "real" vision or mission to a privileged few members. These organizations wait for the initiation of new members to introduce them to the organization's mission.

Good mission statements put the vision in perspective; they add clarity so people have a reference point to use as they organize for achieving the vision or doing their work. Mission statements with timelines help people know where they are, given the time remaining. A good timeline helps participants anticipate if and when skills and competencies or operational processes need to change to accommodate new development or growth.

Sometimes the organization's leadership thinks it has communicated the vision and mission when it hasn't. Throughout the 1980s and 1990s it was fashionable to print vision and mission statements on the backs of calling cards, on stationery or weekly bulletins, assuming that "if we print it they will understand." Going through the process of developing and posting a mission statement should be more than a perfunctory act. Unless the organization doesn't see a need to communicate its mission, that is. A terrorist organization, for example, needs people who will act in ways the organization's leadership needs them to act. The terrorist organization may not care what the bomber thinks or believes; it just needs a bomb to be detonated.

The strategic use of a mission is easy to illustrate using extremist groups like terrorists but it is also a popular strategy for political parties, religions, the smear campaign of a competitor, or a teenager's rallying cry against some other targeted opponent (be that a rival school, a teacher, or a perceived injustice). In each of these cases, activities are organized around such vague missions as "freedom," "individual rights" or "school spirit." Again, the instigators don't care what banner draws people to the organization's mission, just that once there those "called" do as they are told.

Part of the value of ensuring that the vision is clearly stated and communicated reduces the opportunity for members to interpret it in their terms. When left to their own devices, people without a stated mission or direction will construct one for themselves. The solution for making the vision and mission meaningful is to integrate them into the goals and objectives associated with ongoing activities. The assumption is that if you achieve your objectives, you'll achieve your goals, and if the goals are achieved, the mission is achieved and, finally, the vision is achieved.

To use goals and objectives in this manner two things are required. First, the critical relationship between the vision and mission must be clear and the tasks and activities people are expected to do must match the organization's needs. Second, the activities needed to complete each objective must be presented in a measurable form. Presenting goals, objectives and activities in a quantifiable format helps followers know what is expected of them and reduces the ambiguity associated with phases like "how much," "how often" or "how well."

PUTTING THE VISION, MISSION, GOALS AND OBJECTIVES IN PERSPECTIVE: GIVING MEANING TO THE ORGANIZATION FOR ITS PARTICIPANTS

Regardless of their role in an individual's life, all organizations have three things in common: they exist for a purpose; they have performance expectations for their participants; and they use specific tools to achieve their missions. People, on the other hand, join or belong to or interact with organizations because they meet or address a need. The result is a subtle but sophisticated relationship: our agreeing to be part of the organization means we will help (or at least not hinder) the organization's efforts to achieve that mission. From the organization's perspective this condition for membership is more than just saying, "Here's what we believe," it is also a way of saying, "If you don't believe this, too, then don't bother to join us."

In many instances, especially for organizations that are part of our private lives, the mission or vision is like a magnet for membership. We join because we share the mission. We're drawn to a vision and want to be part of organizations with that vision. This is especially true of religious and political organizations. We'll do what we can to achieve the mission because we believe in it.

In contrast, when we belong to an organization because it pays us for our work or services, our reasons for joining the organization may have little to do with its stated purpose or mission. As long as we're paid, for example, we'll stay. It's not surprising that commitment to these types of organization may not be as strong as the commitment one has for the organization that one joins because the organization's vision or mission is seen as one's own, personal mission.

Sometimes tensions can develop between one's membership in private and public organizations. Conflicts surrounding "school prayer," abortion, military draft, ecological issues and even the chlorinating of water emerge when the missions (and values) of different organizations overlap. When an overlap occurs this can create tensions for the member to resolve. Recent conflicts between religious organizations and political candidates supporting abortion illustrate this point.

Think about organizations to which you belong. What are their missions? Are there any conflicts among them and, if so, how do you resolve them? How does the organization's mission define your relationship with the organization? Seeing a link between an organization's mission and behavior, where you work or a sports team that you're on, should be easy but what about the relationship between a political parties or religion's mission and your membership. Is your role active (on committees, raising funds, participating in demonstrations) or passive (voting when you have to or giving money when asked)?

Both private and public organizations have performance expectations for their membership but they can differ widely. Everyone who belongs to an organization is expected to "perform" in some way that contributes to the organization's efforts to achieve its mission or vision. In well-defined organizations expectations are captured in the job or task that must be accomplished. Giving the individual performance expectations is a way the organization lets the member know he/she has been accepted by the organization and has a role in the organization achieving its mission. They're also subtle tools used to shape and control behavior, however. "Successfully accomplish those tasks you've been assigned and you can belong to the organization. Fail to accomplish them and your membership can be in jeopardy."

Some organizations don't need your physical effort; just your money will do. Charitable and political organizations are famous for this type of performance expectation. "Honorary" membership to their board of directors or becoming a member of the "inner circle" can accompany the right financial contribution. The organization will find the people who'll do the work to achieve its mission; you're just expected to give money that will be used to pay the workers.

One final thought regarding the use of vision and mission, goals and objectives is that performance associated with each always needs to be evaluated. Membership is a two-way street. Just as the organization has expectations for its membership, the membership has its expectations too. Those who support the organization because they share the organization's mission expect the organization and its leadership to perform in ways that are consistent with its mission. Serious problems can develop when gaps open between an organization's leadership and membership.

When members sense their leaders have failed to perform or have behaved in ways that are perceived as inconsistent with the vision or mission, they may end or limit their support or, in certain instances, revolt. Martin Luther's challenge to Rome that his Church's leadership was not performing in ways that were consistent with the religion's mission is an historic example. Threats by the membership of some Christian churches to split from the main Church because of the ordination of female priests are a current example. If an organization's mission is to "make a profit" and it fails to do this often enough, more than just its membership may abandon its ranks. Other stakeholders, like customers and suppliers, may lose confidence in the organization's ability to perform so they, too, may no longer support the organization.

An army's poor performance can put whole nations at risk. The same is true for poor performance within a company. If the sales department fails to meet sales objectives, a manufacturing plant fails to meet production, or the fund-raising committee of a public radio station doesn't achieve its membership and contribution goals for the year, serious problems may develop. Lofty ideals expressed as mission statements are nice but performance counts.

Ironically, what makes evaluations so powerful is a feature often underutilized—the opportunity to open and maintain communication channels between those designing the work and those doing it. The "missed opportunity" associated with the use of evaluations occurs when evaluation practices are treated as one-dimensional events: performance is assessed and that's it! It's expected that the results of an evaluation will be communicated, but:

1. Do those being evaluated have the opportunity to communicate their thoughts?
2. Are efforts made to link the evaluation back to organizational goals and objectives or the mission itself?
3. Are the foundations for the evaluation, for example the work that was to be done, reviewed to see if changes need to be made in what is being done and, in turn, evaluated before the next evaluation occurs?

Adding just these three points increases the contribution of the existing evaluation and the potential validity of future evaluations.

A STRUCTURAL MODEL OF ORGANIZATIONS (CETI)

There's an old adage that for organizations to exist they need to make money. It's a logical conclusion. After all, how can any organization exist without funds? So the notion that money is a gauge of organizational effectiveness and longevity is true in many cases but certainly not all. Money is simple and straightforward but a more robust indicator is "performance."

Performance is an organization-specific concept. In fact, organizations exist to perform against the expectations of their stakeholders, people who have an interest, a stake, in what the organization does or its performance. Sometimes those expectations are tied to money while other times they can be tied to "saving souls," "saving lives" and even "taking lives." It's all a matter of stakeholder needs.

Table 2.2 illustrates some fundamental performance mechanisms matched against three levels of an organization's structure. Like most tools the usefulness of the people, processes and materials and environment outlined here are defined in terms of their capacity to fulfill the organization's needs. Looking at performance tools like these illustrates the relationship between performance expectations and different organizational levels. Strategic performance needs typically are addressed from the top of the organization, tactical needs from the middle regions or departments and functional needs by those operating at the lower levels.

Table 2.2 Minimal Performance Expectations by Organizational Level

	PEOPLE	PROCESSES	MATERIAL/ EQUIPMENT	ENVIRONMENT
Administrative level	• Leads the organizations • Prepares strategic plans • Prepares staffing plans • Company orientation • Reviews performance	• Prepares contracts • Negotiates contracts • Approves budgets • Approves policies and procedures • Approves vendors • Conducts audits	• Approves large purchases	• Implements health programs • Ensures safe, healthy environments
Operations level (plant/project)	• Recruits participants • Sets performance standards • Trains and develops • Performance evaluation • Disciplinary programs	• Prepares business plans • Sets policies and procedures • Prepares budgets • Recommends vendors • Manages complaints	• Purchasing programs, equipment, material • Inventories control	• Implements safety programs • Implements quality programs • Manages access
Individual participant level	• Works with team • Provides information • Meets customer needs • Manages customer complaints	• Does job as assigned • Suggests improvements • Follows processes and procedures • Follows policies	• Uses equipment as instructed • Maintains equipment	• Treats co-workers with respect • Respects privacy • Operates within safety and quality programs

Examining performance from this perspective also illustrates the relationship among the organization's key orientation devices: the mission, strategies, plans, activities and events. The need to accomplish its mission is realized through successful design and manipulation of strategies, plans, activities and events. No one of these is the sole driver of organization performance. Each must be used effectively to derive the maximum benefit possible. Too much emphasis on processes over other elements can lead to imbalance between a vision and final product or, conversely, building bureaucracies over operations can slow processes and potentially lead to imbalances in priorities, poor decisions or missed opportunities.

ORGANIZATIONAL STRUCTURE SHAPES BEHAVIOR

A quick Google search reveals a variety of approaches one can take to classify organizations and their structures. For example, the U.S. government uses the SIC, Standard Industrial Classification, as a means for categorizing organizations by the type of work or profession the organization reflects. Table 2.3 is a selection from the SIC. In addition to the government, many financial and accounting areas use the classification in the preparation of financial records or as a means for comparing organizations that provide the same types of product or services. Although still widely used by the government and others, the classification system shares a number of the shortcomings of many current classifications.

First, since it's largely used for matters related to economic issues it omits a lot of organizations that we might be interested in studying. It doesn't allow for the classification of government organizations at different levels (e.g., local vs. state), for religious organizations or purely social organizations like clubs, or fraternities or sororities or those tied to a social cause, like Greenpeace, the NAACP (National Association for the Advancement of Colored People) or the Southern Poverty Law Center. This is a major shortcoming.

A good classification system should be able to capture all types of organization. The alternative we offer allows for the classification of *any* organization and its comparison to any other organization. In this case organizations are classified in terms of one of four functional dimensions. We label these the "enterprise," "community," "team" and "individual contributor."

The classification scheme is also unique because it not only allows for the classification of individual organizations but the four functions used also reflect the makeup of every organization. That is, all organizations are a composite of these four dimensions with one more dominant than the

Table 2.3 Standard Industrial Classification: A Representative Illustration of the Division Structure

---

DIVISION A: AGRICULTURE, FORESTRY, AND FISHING
Major Group 01: Agriculture production crops
Major Group 02: Agriculture production livestock
Major Group 07: Agricultural services
Major Group 08: Forestry
Major Group 09: Fishing, hunting and trapping

DIVISION C: CONSTRUCTION
Major Group 15: Building construction, general contractors
Major Group 16: Heavy construction other than . . .
Major Group 17: Construction special trade contractors

DIVISION D: MANUFACTURING
Major Group 20: Food and kindred products
Major Group 21: Tobacco products
Major Group 22: Textile mill products
Major Group 34: Fabricated metal products
Major Group 35: Industrial and commercial machinery

DIVISION F: WHOLESALE TRADE
Major Group 50: Wholesale trade-durable goods
Major Group 51: Wholesale trade-non-durable goods

DIVISION I: SERVICES
Major Group 70: Hotels, rooming houses, camps and other
Major Group 72: Personal services
Major Group 73: Business services
Major Group 75: Automotive repair

---

other three. Figure 2.1 illustrates how typical organizations are classified using this process. This classification method, produced by examining the operations of several hundred organizations, suggests that these core dimensions unfold as the organization emerges and matures. An organization may be classified as a "community" in its early stages and evolve into an "enterprise" over time. When this happens it's significant for it signals both performance expectations and the means for achieving those expectations will change for the organization.

FOUR TYPES OF ORGANIZATION

The categories used here and outlined in Figure 2.1 are distinguishable from each other yet flexible enough to describe organizations regardless of their size, mission or the makeup of their membership. As a result, small and large for-profit organizations can be compared and contrasted, along

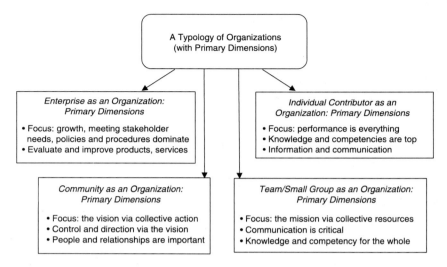

Figure 2.1 A Typology of Organizations (with Primary Dimensions).

with religious or military units, schools, stores, factories, athletic teams or social clubs and our smallest organizational unit, the individual.

A quick review of an organization's key features illustrates that the differences among these four classifications are not subtle. For example, most for-profit businesses are classified as enterprises and doctors, who might work for an enterprise, are classified as individual contributors. While doctors may have a for-profit business associated with their practice, it is the doctor's affiliation that defines whether or not they are independent agents or part of a larger organization. If the doctor is a member of a for-profit hospital's staff, the focus is on the hospital as an enterprise. If the doctor is a specialist in her own practice and/or key member of the hospital's staff, the doctor is classified as an individual contributor. In that case the doctor may be affiliated with an institution but if the doctor outlines her own performance regime, performance expectations and maintains a level of independence regarding when and how she works she's classified as an individual contributor.

The labels used profile the nature of the organization's inherent features; the things that can motivate or control how things are done, performance expectations or entice people to join the organization. Pacifists, for example, typically do not join the army or a terrorist organization. So the dimensions give us an idea of what to expect in certain organizations. But the dimensions also do so much more.

These dimensions help us understand what to expect from the organizations, particularly given the practices and processes that define them. Communication and information management practices are vital for success in some organizations while others concentrate on building relationships and still others on strictly evaluating or assessing products produced or services delivered. Knowing what practices are emphasized says something about the nature of the organization and may be used as a guide when attempting to uncover a particular organization's potential problems, weaknesses or vulnerabilities. For example, communication and information management are important skills for project teams, so if they're absent or poorly utilized, that may tell us a lot about the organization and its potential effectiveness.

The use of these four dimensions also offers a unique way to talk about the makeup of organizations. For example, if one takes the organizational profile C-I-T-E (Community, Individual, Team and Enterprise) we have a community-type organization with a heavy individual contributor component. Next, its team component makes its contribution to the classification and, finally its enterprise component completes the profile. This might be the profile of a small revolutionary group, whose members are linked by a common mission which is executed through the roles of strong, competent individual contributors. The terrorist organization's vision and the efforts of its membership typically will look very different than those of a for-profit enterprise, like an oil company or retail store, but very similar to those of key adversaries, like a military unit or hospital, which have the same classification, "community."

A big advantage this classification offers becomes evident when studying the performance of different organizations around the same event. Now different organizations can be compared in terms of their strengths and weaknesses, management effectiveness and even the way the organizations manage events given their operational makeup. The comparisons can be made without regard to how similar or dissimilar the organizations are in terms of size, purpose, financial well-being, organizing philosophy and so forth. For example, one can compare the performance of a health provider organization (e.g., a medical team), a police organization and a government agency (e.g., FEMA) vis-à-vis the same event (e.g., a hurricane).

AN INTRODUCTION TO AND SUMMARY OF THE FOUR ORGANIZATIONAL TYPES: PUTTING STRUCTURE AND PERFORMANCE INTO PERSPECTIVE

The first factor that defines an organization is its mission—why it exists. All organizations are described as being one of four distinct types. In each case the organization is defined in terms of the special features and characteristics that maximize performance to achieve its mission. The *enterprise*, for example, centers its activities on performance that achieves a mission defined by factors like growth (e.g., physical or economic), meeting stakeholder needs and managing risk. The enterprise's means for achieving its mission is by maximizing direction through structure and policies and a concerted effort to improve the products and services it offers.

This strategy doesn't emerge by chance; it is a focal point because the enterprise's stakeholders often have a choice regarding which enterprise they will support. If one enterprise doesn't meet their needs there usually is another, perhaps a competitor, that the stakeholder can switch to for need fulfillment. Table 2.4 lists different examples and enterprises along with examples of the other three categories for comparison. Commercial businesses like car dealerships and restaurants are good examples of enterprises. However, organizations like a manufacturing facility and even organized crime can be classified as enterprises.

Communities are a second organization type. The "vision" of "what we are striving for" is the community's primary focus. Any of the four types of organization can (and perhaps should) stipulate its vision for its membership but for the community organization the vision is *the* critical element. So, partially as a result of its orientation and partially because it's the nature of community organizations to be closed to outsiders or other influences, this organization exercises strong control over participants.

Religious organizations, public institutions like schools and government agencies, and social movements typify community organizations. These are organizations where people are important largely because they are the instruments for action. Participation in communities is not always a given. In some instances candidates need to prove themselves worthy or at least be willing to go through some type of initiation before becoming an active member.

Vision translates into mission statements for most organizations, and this is definitely the case for the *team* organization, the third organizational type. Team organizations exist to achieve a mission, be it to solve a problem in a manufacturing center (like a "skunkworks" team), to apprehend an assassin like a SWAT team or to win a game, like a sports team. A team's mission is always clear; it's the reason why the team exists. The obligation of team members is to utilize their skills to bring the mission within reach and then to achieve it. Communication and knowledge management are critical operational practices for the team. This is because of the often-specialized activities associated with the team's activities. In teams the mission is achieved through collective

Table 2.4 Type of Organization and Links to Internal and External Organizations

ORGANIZATION	TYPE C = Community; E = Enterprise T = Team; I = Individual Cont.	REPRESENTATIVE LINKS WITH IMPORTANT INTERNAL ORGANIZATIONS BY TYPE C = Community; E = Enterprise T = Team; I = Individual Cont.	REPRESENTATIVE LINKS WITH IMPORTANT EXTERNAL ORGANIZATIONS BY TYPE C = Community; E = Enterprise T = Team; I = Individual Cont.
Car sales dealership	E	Sales professional (IC), Parts dept (T)	Government agencies (C)
Fast food	E	Staff (I)	Government inspectors (C)
Automobile manufacturer	E	Factories (E)	Subcontractors (E)
Church	C	Committees (T), Pastor (I)	Special-interest organizations (C)
Car parts department	T	Dealership (E)	Suppliers (E)
Insurance company	E	Sales rep (IC)	Regulators (C)
Police	C	Officers (IC), SWAT team (T)	City government (C)
SWAT team	T	Police department (C)	Fire dept (C), City govt. (C)
Museum	C	Departments (T)	Thieves (IC; T)
High school	C	Departments (T)	School board (C)
Law firm	E	Lawyers (IC)	Judicial systems (C)
Lawyer	I	The firm (E), Support staff (T)	The judge (IC), Media (E)
Retail (bookstore)	E	Staff (IC), Authors (IC)	Vendors (E)
Trash collectors	E	Driver (IC)	Local govt. land fill (C)
Independent truck drivers	I	Driver (IC)	Unions (C), Regulators (C)
Professional sports team	E	Players (T), (IC), Coaches (IC)	Unions (C), League (C)
Recreational sports team	T	Players (T), (IC)	League (C), Sponsors (E)
Racing pit crew	T	Driver (IC)	Race track (E), Associations (E)

(Continued)

Table 2.4 (Continued) Type of Organization and Links to Internal and External Organizations

ORGANIZATION	TYPE C = Community; E = Enterprise T = Team; I = Individual Cont.	REPRESENTATIVE LINKS WITH IMPORTANT INTERNAL ORGANIZATIONS BY TYPE C = Community; E = Enterprise T = Team; I = Individual Cont.	REPRESENTATIVE LINKS WITH IMPORTANT EXTERNAL ORGANIZATIONS BY TYPE C = Community; E = Enterprise T = Team; I = Individual Cont.
Monks	C	Individual monk (IC)	Parent religious order (C)
Surgery team	T	Hospital administration (E), Doctor (IC)	Government (C), Drug suppliers (E), Vendors (E)
Medical doctor	I	Office staff (T), Associates (IC)	Regulators (C), Associations (E)
Restaurant	E	Cook (IC), Waiters (IC)	Local government (C), Vendors (E)
Gas station	E	Mechanic (IC), Owner	Local government (C)
International culture	C	Leadership (IC), Institutions (C, IC)	National government (C)
Township	C	Manager (IC), Departments (T)	Regulators (C)
Beauty parlor/spa	E	Ownership (E), Beauticians (IC)	Vendors (E)
Terrorist organization	C	Leadership (IC), Member (IC)	Affiliates (C)
Army military unit	C	Commander (IC), Platoons (T)	Opponent (C), Media (E), Contractors (E)
Congressman	I	Staff (T)	Political party (C), Opposition (C)
Senate/House	C	Congress (IC), Staff (T)	Political parties (C), Media (E)
U.S. Post Office	C	Mail carrier (IC), Sorters (T)	Regulators (C), Contractors (E)
FedEx delivery	E	Drivers (IC), Sorters (T)	Regulators (C), Airports (E)

action. However, because teams are small, knowledge and competency are critical resources the team needs to protect and nurture.

The *individual contributor* is the fourth organizational type. This organization received its name because of the prominent role key people have in the organization. These organizations often center on, depend on, look to, or otherwise follow a key figure. Sometimes, in fact, the term is used to describe one person who, while attached to or part of any of the other three organizations discussed, has what amounts to a stand-alone or key position in those organizations.

Individual contributor organizations usually operate as for-profit entities made up of professionals like doctors, lawyers or the skilled mechanic, waitress, carpenter or plumber. The individual contributor shares some of the characteristics of the enterprise without, necessarily, a strong use of procedures or other controlling and directional mechanisms one associates with the enterprise. The individual contributor seems more casual, despite the fact that the individual contributor's operations may be bounded by the formal directional mechanisms of other organizations or governing bodies.

The individual contributor can be a "stand-alone" personality or a leader of a small group or team, like the pharmacist in a drugstore or an employee who functions as an internal consultant within a large corporation. Knowledge and personal competencies are musts for this organization, again typically because of their limited resources, but information and communication practices are critical for extending the reach of this person's influence.

Table 2.5 provides a sketch of the four organizational types vis-à-vis other important operational elements. The table is self-explanatory but merits study as a means for understanding the relationship among the four organizational types. This is an especially important point given that the four labels used to define organizational types are meant to illustrate their primary feature. If an organization's primary purpose is "centered around a vision and achieving a mission or set of goals given the organization's vision" then that organization will be classified as a "community."

It's also important to understand the features of these different organizational types because in reality all organizations are a composite, in varying degrees, of all four types. Hospitals are a good example. The for-profit hospital itself is an *enterprise organization* but it has internal departments like "surgical" or "research" teams (*team organizations*). The hospital often has charitable auxiliaries (*community organizations*) that provide fund-raising or outreach activities and, of course, doctors or

Table 2.5 Four Types of Organization

	ENTERPRISE	COMMUNITY
Purpose	Achieve the organization's mission and goals by defining and maintaining the integrity of the system's elements and their inter-relationships.	Centered around a vision and achieving a mission or set of goals given the organization's vision.
Structure	Fixed elements (people, processes, materials, equipment, culture, management) with fluidity among the elements. Decentralized by function.	Ranging from perfunctory (e.g., leader to followers) to elaborate (e.g., executive, directors, mgmt, administrative, staff, etc.).
Processes and practices	Unobtrusive by design, dynamic in practice. Defined in terms of relationships among system elements. Evaluation, performance, direction and control, information management are key.	Both formal and informal defined in terms of rules and procedures, relationships, information, control and performance. Practices: direction and control, relationship, information management are key.
Drivers	Systems are largely passive; they exist as a descriptive referent to account for the elements of the system: the enterprise, departments or teams, and individuals. Performance is critical.	The organization sets the tone for: departments or teams and individuals. The organization is rule-giver, enforcer, standard-setter and evaluator via centralized leadership. Vision and mission are communicated from the top.
Time	Enterprises are "slaves" to time. Time is a central organizing factor and often a performance standard. Deadlines typically are hard and fast.	In many instances time is a general rather than specific referent. Time is a central organizing factor especially across broad timelines.
Challenges and threats	System components do not function as expected.	Other organizations that compete with or regulate the organization/ enterprise. Disruptions arising within the organization.
	GROUP/TEAM	INDIVIDUAL
Purpose	Centered around fulfilling a function that helps achieve the organization's mission. Structurally, a means for managing individuals around functions.	Centered around a task or assignment which, when successfully completed, meets the needs of the group or enterprise and/or team.
Structure	Nominal hierarchy, usually for functional purposes. Largely individual-driven given the organization's purpose.	Defined by expected behaviors (sometimes attitudes, opinions, beliefs) around defined activities.

Table 2.5 (Continued) Four Types of Organization

	GROUP/TEAM	INDIVIDUAL
Processes and practices	Open, perhaps not even defined or apparent. Processes are often defined in terms of process activities (e.g., evaluation or communication). Sometimes (e.g., sports) defined around rules, roles and relationships. Information, knowledge, evaluation, communication, management.	Specific in terms of tasks, performance and results. Knowledge, information, communication, relationship management.
Drivers	Departments, groups and teams define behavior in terms of their perception of what the organization's leadership expects or wants. They function at the discretion of the organization and for the organization's well-being. Peer pressure.	Individuals are members of the team and, in turn, the organization and system to the extent that 1. the task they perform or function they serve is of value to those entities and 2. the individual's performance meets expectations. Personal drivers include needs, wants and desires as shaped by competencies, attitudes, opinions and beliefs.
Time	Time is a benchmark for teams. They perform in terms of time; it's a referent point.	Individuals are often "time independent." They have the greatest flexibility with time vis-à-vis the other three. Even "deadlines" may "float."
Challenges and threats	Conflict with other areas within the organization (e.g., "turf wars"), others within the group or individuals. Failure to maintain competencies can be a threat with ripple effects.	Changing directions for the organization, changing competencies, or expectations, needs, wants or desires. Peer rivalries.

specialists (*individual contributors*) who may be part of the hospital or associated with it through their outside practices. Using this classification schema illustrates how the various sub-organizations line up and contribute to the overall organization.

A "community of monks" may be defined as a composite of the dominant "community" plus "group/team" branches plus some "enterprise" functions and some "individual contributors," perhaps as the heads of different departments or in key roles. By comparison, a local township office might be defined by a similar profile but, perhaps because of its role in managing local fees and taxes, the enterprise function has a higher placement in this particular organization's model. Here the township's profile might appear as a composite of "community" + "enterprise" + "group/team" + "individual contributor." This implies that the role of the group/team has more weight in the community of monks than the township office and in both the individual component has the least weight.

Understanding the component nature of organizations given these four dimensions is very important for accurately assessing an organization's performance and the threats, risks and vulnerabilities it may face. One might explain FEMA's failure to adequately manage the Hurricane Katrina/New Orleans catastrophe because its format was out of alignment with one that might have been more effective for a service organization. Service organizations often have a profile defined in terms of their vision and mission so they are labeled a community. These organizations have a strong group/team component to provide key transportation, housing, construction and needed healthcare services.

There's always some enterprise function in these agencies because of the large budgets needed to drive recovery efforts and, finally, there's a need for individual contributors, especially in program manager roles. However, FEMA's profile seems to have changed under the then-current Washington administration. FEMA's focus appeared to reflect a budget-conscious enterprise and the leadership role appeared to become more important as a political appointment (individual contributor) than a guiding role with experience managing this type of service agency. With changes in the organization's orientation and leadership roles its original focus on its vision (community) may have been displaced and, as a result, important organizational functions (group/team components) were slow to respond to the emergency.

Consider the information summarized in Table 2.6. This sketch illustrates the variable and dynamic nature of the individual dimensions when used to define a single organization. Each dimension contributes to the organization's makeup and function and, importantly, the organization's success or failure can be linked with the performance of each dimension. For this reason it is important that an organization's leadership knows the function of each dimension, its makeup and when and how to use the dimensions to achieve the organization's vision and mission.

The first two columns of Table 2.6 outline each dimension's function and how the function and element appears to others. The enterprise element, for example, operates to reduce risk for the organization as a whole and manages risk through its rules, policies and procedures and/ or structure. The table's last column is of particular note because it outlines consequences for the organization if, for example, a particular

Table 2.6   What the Dimensions of Organization Can Look Like in a Single Organization

THE DIMENSION	ITS ROLE AND FUNCTION	THREATS, RISKS, VULNERABILITIES
ENTERPRISE This is the organization's business center. The enterprise operates effectively to reduce risks and to accomplish its mission (e.g., to make money). The enterprise is used: 1. To add order, standardization 2. To provide guidance for external contact 3. To facilitate key processes 4. To introduce systemic change 5. To direct and fund the dimensions It's formed by: orders from "the top," committees, key staff, a "charter."	1. Define vision, mission, goals, activities 2. Rule-driven vs. rule-guided 3. Policies, procedures, operational practices in place 4. Structure in place 5. Enforces policies, etc. 6. Good management 7. Is profitable 8. Represents the organization to the outside	1. Poor vision and mission miss the marketplace, create vulnerabilities 2. Bias, poor standardization 3. Bureaucracy 4. Poor leadership, failure to design, introduce, enforce or maintain structure or rules (or biased in enforcing them) creating risk (e.g., accidents, missed goals, litigation, fines, turnover) 5. Poor execution and follow-through 6. Poorly designed and administered vision, mission, goals, practices, etc.
TEAM This is where work gets done. This is where people are managed. Where activities achieve objectives that achieve goals that achieve the mission that meets the vision. Teams are used: 1. To get things done re: vision, mission, goals, activities 2. To handle special jobs/projects 3. To manage people	1. Handle a particular scope of work 2. Achieve and push results 3. Design the work to be done 4. Get the right person in the right job	1. Treat a group like a team 2. Few meaningful evaluations 3. Participants lose sight of vision 4. Failure to audit performance 5. Special project teams aren't disbanded when project is finished. 6. Project results shared; integrated 7. Turf battles 8. Poor leadership and management
COMMUNITY If the enterprise is the brain, the community is the heart and soul. Community oversees the culture and rituals; serves as a bridge to link people. Community is used: 1. To support vision, mission, goals 2. As a haven, sanctuary, shelter 3. To manage, sometimes introduce change Leadership determines: size and role, cultural makeup, "authority," membership, rules and processes	1. Serve as a refuge 2. Interpret information 3. Orientations, mentor programs 4. Serve as "neutral" territory 5. Help maintain rituals and culture	1. Failure to offer and support programs 2. Sends out a "sink or swim" message to new people 3. Hires (or promotes) "friends" 4. Failure to recognize value of a "star." Communism and socialism are not "team" sports. Being on a team does not mean everyone is equal

(Continued)

Table 2.6 (Continued)   What the Dimensions of Organization Can Look Like in a Single Organization

THE DIMENSION	ITS ROLE AND FUNCTION	THREATS, RISKS, VULNERABILITIES
INDIVIDUAL CONTRIBUTOR		
1. Fits within the community, enterprise, team	Individual:	1. The individual or his/her job is not slotted appropriately to
2. Individual is used to: do one's job so that risk is managed, the enterprise accomplishes its vision, mission (e.g., makes money)	1. Is competent 2. Has a sense of urgency 3. Makes the right decisions 4. Can build relationships 5. Gets things done	benefit the community, enterprise team (CET) 2. Individual's behavior threatens CET. Violating safety or security adds risk. Prejudicial behavior threatens the community; not doing one's job means others
3. FULLY performs operational practices as expected		have to do it or it isn't done. (Remember, being a "star"
The individual is: recruited from in- or from outside, as a stand-alone or part of a department		does not threaten a team)

element is not well designed or managed. Poorly or inadequately defined jobs can lead to injury, poor service or even increased turnover when the individual gives up trying to guess or figure out what's expected or what must be done to do a good job. If poor management of the "community" element obscures the vision or mission this can add stress to the organization's environment. The community organization's membership may seek to maintain their orientation to a vision or mission that's becoming harder to see, given the leadership's focus, and so, in turn, may look for other ways to identify with the organization's mission, even if that means leaving the organization.

These observations outline the form and function of each dimension and the sometimes-subtle inter-relationships among them. The discussion is important to understanding the ways events and behaviors affect individual elements and the organization as a whole. As the table illustrates, besides a mix of factors that can put the organization at risk if the individual elements are not well defined or managed, having poorly prepared elements also may mean that the organization is less able to manage the impact of events, whether routine or extreme, when they occur.

ORGANIZATION STRUCTURE SUPPORTS, ADDS CONTROL AND HELPS COMMUNICATE THE ORGANIZATION'S IDENTITY TO OUTSIDERS

An organization's structure also reflects the amount of control the organization seeks to maintain over its membership.[1] Organizations with heavily laden or deep structures tend to be dominated by rules. Religious organizations, cultures and military organizations are examples. In some instances, for example when the organization is closely regulated by an outside organization, it may have its structure imposed upon it. Pharmaceutical, gambling and nuclear power enterprises and some healthcare institutions are examples of closely regulated industries. The organizations that make up these industries have stricter controls, more defined structures and more clearly defined policies and procedures than organizations not so closely regulated.

Table 2.7 illustrates the relationship between types of structure and the amounts of control associated with an organization. Several points

Table 2.7   The Structural Makeup of Different Organizations and the Amount of Control They Exercise over Participants

	ORGANIZATION HAS LOW CONTROL OVER THE INDIVIDUAL (TARGET/CLIENT)	ORGANIZATION HAS MODERATE CONTROL OVER THE INDIVIDUAL	ORGANIZATION HAS HIGH CONTROL OVER THE INDIVIDUAL
HIGH CONTENT • Process- and rule-driven • Membership rules • Rituals and norms	• Medicine/health systems • Fraternities/ sororities • Highway and road systems	• Public schools • Most religions	• Airline security systems • Orthodox religions • Private schools • Cults • Mental institution • SWAT team • Nuclear power plant • Penal system • Police
MODERATE CONTENT • Process-driven	• Universities • Most sports teams	• Car rental • Horse racing	• Insurance companies • Gambling and gaming
LOW CONTENT • Rule-guided • Event- or transaction-driven	• Home improvement (limited control) • Retail stores (limited control) • Hospital volunteer orgs. • Sports arenas (limited control) • Movie theatre (limited control)	• Membership in retail stores (restricts entry) • Post Office • Airlines • Trains	• Terrorist organizations • Organized crime

in this table merit attention. First, since control refers to how closely the organization or its membership has its behavior regulated, the amounts of control can vary within different types of organization. Not all religions, for example, exert the same amounts of control over their membership and the same is true for types of educational institution. The classical concept of *in loco parentis*, a school operating as a guardian of students in place of the parents, ended at the collegiate level during the 1960s but is still evident in lower grade levels. There also appears to be a relationship between the extent to which an organization is liberal or conservative and the amounts of control it exercises.

Levels of control can increase when abuse of an organization's power leads to increased risk exposure for the public. Organizations that handle nuclear material, those in the gaming industry or pharmaceuticals are examples. In these instances, controls are extended over both those inside and outside the organization. Napoleon Bonaparte, the famous French general of the late eighteenth and early nineteenth centuries and who would be classified as an individual contributor, found the extent and amounts of controls placed on him greatly increased following his second attempt to conquer Europe. Many who find themselves at odds with their society can find themselves in a similar position.

While some organizations use security systems to monitor people within their walls, this level of control is typically low to non-existent as a means for managing the overall behavior of people. Retail stores can only hope the presence of these devices will modify behavior so that thefts are avoided. Even highway systems which list rules for participation (e.g., speed limits, information on road conditions) and for behavior while on the road (speed limits, road lining systems and signs) have only a nominal control on driver behavior. Only when the presence of an immediate enforcement system (police or electronic ticketing systems) is evident do the established controls seem to work as intended.

CHAPTER 3

The Enterprise Organization

We begin our detailed review of the four types that make up the organization typology with the "enterprise." The enterprise's underlying theme is best summarized as "direction and order to maximize performance." Figure 3.1 summarizes the enterprise organization's key features both as a freestanding organization and when an element of some other organization. The contribution to the organization's administration, structure and form is the main attribute of the enterprise dimension. Hierarchy, for example, is an obvious element of organization's structure.

From a purely functional perspective hierarchy reflects the number of strata or layers in an organization, how the organization is defined

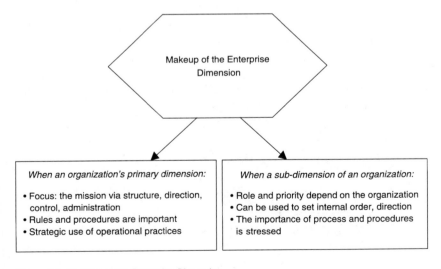

Figure 3.1 Makeup of the Enterprise Dimension.

(e.g., by departments, divisions, etc.) and provides labels associated with positions (e.g., president, manager, squad leader, guru, elder, etc.).

Apart from an organization's formal structure most organizations also have an informal structure. The informal structure is apparent in ways communication is used, ways power and authority are maintained, and how responsibility and accountability are distributed given the vision, mission and day-to-day performance goals and objectives. Structure, then, not only gives an indication of where an individual is likely to be in the organization; it also gives an idea of what the individual might be expected to contribute toward achieving the organization's mission. So one knows the president of the bank is not working at a teller's window, that the leader of the terrorist organization is not the suicide bomber who exploded in a marketplace, or that the coach is not the one skating to a gold medal at the Olympics.

When roles and responsibilities are confused—when, for example, the coach is a player, the terrorist leader is detonating bombs and the bank president is giving you change at the teller's window—those interacting with the organization may be confused and sense that something is not right. Doubling up of roles might indicate, for example, that the organization is under-staffed or is having labor problems, perhaps a strike, and this requires management to do technical, line work. Sometimes it might suggest the staff aren't competent enough to do their work or the leader isn't sufficiently competent to manage the organization. These conditions can occur when management doesn't know how to bring in the right people, to "let go" of jobs once held, or to do one's own work.

Of course, nothing might be wrong in the organization. Some organizations expect a doubling up of responsibilities, even a rotation of key positions like "leadership" throughout the organization. In these instances what one might be seeing are instances where the enterprise dimension seems subordinate to other dimensions. Some organizations might be too small or under-capitalized, so a large workforce with an extensive hierarchy is not warranted or possible. A consultant (individual contributor) can serve as a "bookkeeper," "marketing specialist" and "sales representative." It depends on the organization.

Organizations that require a lot of structure tend to have a larger enterprise dimension; it's the administrative center. It classifies and communicates why the organization exists and how it's to be structured for maximum performance. It is also the point where the organization's image is crafted and maintained. Moreover, since the enterprise dimension is critical for translating an organization's vision and mission into performance, it's also the place where a link is made between the vision and mission and how the organization plans to address the needs, interests or desires of prospective members and stakeholders at large.

As part of an organization's profile, the enterprise dimension contains the blueprint for the organization's purpose and physical makeup or structure. It is the source for the organization's general operational processes and regulation and the entry and exit point for stakeholders. The enterprise's primary functions are to ensure that operating conditions facilitate the organization's growth and that risk, threats or vulnerabilities are managed. When the enterprise is strong and functions well the organization's efforts to grow and manage risk by maintaining order and ensuring operations are facilitated. This is because the focus on organization and control in the enterprise dimension provides a foundation and source for information.

While illustrations of what define and promote growth and risk vary from organization to organization, the need to manage both do not. Business organizations seek to grow their profits while managing risks associated with competitors, the work environment, or employee behaviors. Charitable organizations ("community") manage their own risks and build revenues by ensuring they have enough of the right people and enough well-run, profitable funding events. Teams need to orchestrate their enterprise dimensions to better manage changing demands or challenges. Police SWAT teams or an army platoon may want to ensure their personnel have up-to-date skills and competencies or the best equipment needed to accomplish a mission while not suffering casualties or other losses. A sports team, in contrast, uses its enterprise function to recruit players with the competencies to learn and execute plays.

STRUCTURE PROVIDES THE FRAMEWORK FOR INTERNAL AND EXTERNAL INTERACTIONS

An organization's physical profile typically is described in terms of its hierarchy or levels from the top to the bottom. Hierarchical examinations have limitations but they can tell us something about an organization's capacity to perform. Sometimes management creates an illusion of a structure when, in actuality, structure doesn't contribute much towards the organization's performance. Consider the ways some organizations use titles to create the illusion of a hierarchy.

When hierarchies do have a meaningful role in stipulating direction and control this strengthens the relationship between an organization's vision and mission and performance. When the vision, mission and structure come from a centralized area, like the organization's leadership, there's usually a clearer relationship between the nature and the types of work to be done and how work is to be done, the physical distribution of work and performance expectations. This doesn't mean there are not surprises—just that if those "at the top" provide the right guidance in at least what they mean by performance this should help those actually involved in determining the *who, what, where, when* and *how* of performance.

A second important directional activity used to manage performance is the use of rules and guidelines. Rules, policies and procedures are an especially important stabilizing factor in organizations because they define parameters or benchmarks for behavior. Rules also are useful in establishing operating processes—like a chain of command—that can help define, drive and adjudicate day-to-day activities. While physical structure can reveal a lot of information about the organization's use of hierarchy, the nature and use of rules can provide insights into how the organization operates and what it values, especially in regard to the vision and mission.

All organizations use rules and procedures. Some are obvious and formal, others subtle and still others even personal, for example the use of rules to correct an individual's dysfunctional performance. Rules, guidelines and procedures can cover everything from admission to the organization, how to behave while in the organization and termination from the organization. If the rules, guidelines and the like are used in a restrictive manner, producing a "rule-driven" organization, behavior centers more on "doing what is right" or "not doing the wrong thing."

In contrast, in a "rule-guided" organization participants use rules, policies and procedures as reference points, like signposts. Participants go along with their work, often with greater latitude than in a "rule-driven" environment. Both rule strategies make assumptions about the organization's participants, tasks to be done and the organization's threats, risks and vulnerabilities. Consequently, rules and procedures in rule-guided organizations are important and meaningful, but they typically have less weight or play a very different role from those in a "rule-driven" organization.

Religions and closed societies, like cults or secret societies, often are examples of rule-driven or rule-governed organizations. The role of rules in these organizations can be very significant. The rules are specific and so are the effects of violating the rules. In rule-governed organizations the leadership can use rules to dictate who comes into the organization, and how, requirements for behavior and the extent participation is possible within the organization, especially where special programs or rituals are concerned. The rules may seem extreme to outsiders, but followers see them as in line with, indeed often critical for, realizing the organization's vision and mission.

Table 3.1 illustrates the potential for conflict or stress resulting from the organization's approach and use of rules. In the table there's potential for high stress in three of the four situations, with the potential for protracted or at least stiff competition in one cell, where two rule-guided organizations interact.

There may be a tendency to assume that the situation that's least likely to produce tensions and conflicts is when two rule-guided organizations interact with each other. This isn't necessarily the case. The orientation to rules may be the same, but the nature and types of rules can be quite different. The resulting ambiguity can be just the stimulus needed for emerging tensions and conflicts. For example, the rule-guided retail store may be willing to take returns but what proof does it require of the customer to "prove" the item was purchased at its store? Without the correct documentation (e.g., a receipt), returns within a specific time period (e.g., 30 days) and customer credentials (e.g., the credit card used in the purchase), the routine, open return process may provide just enough ambiguity to become a stressful event for the participants.

It's also important to remember that even a rule-driven organization cannot guarantee performance success if critical operational practices are not in place and used. If participants are poorly disciplined (e.g., no evaluation practices), they don't know the rules (e.g., inadequate information or communication practices), or the rules are ambiguous or unevenly used (e.g., poor direction and control practices) then there's a strong probability problems will develop around the use of rules.

Table 3.1 illustrates how different transactions (events) might turn out (results) given the rule system used to govern behavior, thoughts or activities. For example, in an interaction between individuals or organizations that are from rule-guided systems, the focus is on the interaction or purpose for the interaction. These interactions usually run smoothly. However, since rule-guided systems center more of the control of the interaction with the participants, there is the potential for other factors to surface and thus disrupt the interaction. Personality, for example, is a typical factor latent in all interactions between people. So, if one person's personality is defined by rudeness, self-absorption or generally just being a jerk, activities in the rule-guided-to-rule-guided interaction may not be harmonious. Ask, for example, people who work in or who call into customer service centers.

Table 3.1   Events Arising out of the Interaction of Rule-Guided (R-G) and Rule-Driven (R-D) Organizations and the Potential Impact on the Relationships between Them

	ORGANIZATION A RULE-GUIDED ORGANIZATION	ORGANIZATION B RULE-DRIVEN ORGANIZATION
ORGANIZATION 1 RULE-GUIDED ORGANIZATION	*Event:* customer (R-G) seeks to return an item purchased at a retail store (R-G) *Effects:* the focus is on the exchange not the participant's or organization's "rules" so the interaction should be harmonious.	*Event:* a new recruit (R-G) in the military (R-D) *Effects:* since the transaction takes place in the R-D's arena and centers around the recruit's "learning the rules" stress may be high but interactions more harmonious as the recruit learns (and follows) the rules.
ORGANIZATION 2 RULE-DRIVEN ORGANIZATION	*Event:* a traffic cop (R-D) and a driver (R-G) *Effects:* because the focus can center on "interpretation of the rules" ("I wasn't speeding," "Yes you were …") tensions can arise.	*Event:* the Crusades: Arab (R-D) and Christian (R-D) conflict over the Holy Lands *Effects:* because the participants are guided by potentially equally strong but conflicting rules conflict may arise. Most military conflicts.

When organizations commit themselves (and their membership) to strictly following "the rules" and those rules are strongly linked to the organization's vision and mission, there's always a potential for tensions or conflicts to arise when interacting with organizations that do not share (or worse, are a threat to) their visions or missions. Political parties, competing companies in the same industry, religions and cultures are examples of organizations that can have both deeply set rule systems and clearly defined visions and missions for themselves but are required to operate in societies or in conjunction with organizations that don't share the same rule systems.

Some organizations create stress when they change their approach to rules. For example, when a new administration assumes leadership of a country or organization increased stress and tension can result if it has a different interpretation of what's important or the rules that are needed or not. The effects on tension and stress are not restricted just to those inside the organization.

The relationship among different world cultures or countries is an example. When, for example, countries like the United States change their leadership, other nations might find it difficult to predict or anticipate how the United States will respond to world events, because the way rules are interpreted by one administration may not be interpreted or held in the same regard by a new administration. That's not to imply that organizations should not change leadership over time, it's just something both those inside and outside the organizations need to consider.

Sometimes an organization's ability to control its membership extends beyond the organization's boundaries. This is a basic element of most religions. They believe that good practitioners should continue to "do what is expected" regarding church policies and rules even when they are not within the organization's reach (e.g., in church) or attending programs sponsored by the organization.

Regardless of the situation, an organization's approach to rules helps establish direction for internal and external stakeholders. Rules, policies and procedures also blend naturally with the structure (or hierarchy) that defines the organization. In fact, there tends to be a strong, positive correlation between the amount and type of structure in an organization and the extent to which it is rule-guided or rule-driven.

Rule-driven organizations tend to be more structured than rule-guided organizations. This means they may have a more established hierarchy, more bureaucracy and perhaps even more "office politics." Sometimes this extra structure is warranted, but other times its seems to be just another way to ensure that control and power stay with the status quo (or those at the top.)

Tension also can arise when rule-driven, highly structured organizations come in contact with people who do not embrace being "controlled." Organizations in the 1990s ran headlong into "Generation X," a segment of youth who, as they entered the job market, often brought with them values and behaviors that ran counter to the rule-driven, control-structured organizations many of them joined. All sorts of rule-driven organizations can run into these types of conflict. Imagine what would happen in the terrorist organization that expects a person trained as a suicide bomber to transport the bomb to its destination but won't complete the last act and detonate it.

Rule-driven organizations can seem stuck in the past or out of touch with the cultures or organizations around them. "Casual Fridays," where employees are allowed to dress down from more formal work attire, wasn't embraced by the management of all organizations. "Telecommuting" or time off for either spouse after the birth of a child, and changing dress codes in certain Moslem cultures are other examples.

Sometimes the tensions created can be career- or life-stopping. The Chinese response to a student challenge of government rules at Tiananmen Square resulted in the death of many resistors. In these types of events the organization is not only controlling behavior, it is using rules to justify its actions and to categorize behavior into what is appropriate and what is not. This organizational framework informs everyone, from top to bottom, of where they are, given where the organization's enterprise dimension indicates they should be.

In Table 3.2, potential control over individual behavior—in this case, control over membership or participation in the organization—is illustrated. The information in the columns divides organizations into three "control" categories ranging from those organizations with low control over individuals to those with high control. The rows reflect what "drives" the organization. Content-driven organizations operate in terms of a mission, guiding principles, a charter, values or beliefs. In these organizations, the content binds participants together.

Table 3.2   Organization Motivation vis-à-vis Organization Control

	ORGANIZATION HAS LOW CONTROL OVER THE INDIVIDUAL (*Its motivation:* create conditions that achieve the mission by maximizing exposure to people)	ORGANIZATION HAS MODERATE CONTROL OVER THE INDIVIDUAL (*Its motivation:* create conditions that achieve the mission by regulating people's participation)	ORGANIZATION HAS HIGH CONTROL OVER THE INDIVIDUAL (*Its motivation:* create conditions that achieve the mission by shaping the behavior of people)
Content-driven control of behavior	• Political parties • Medicine/health programs • Recreation parks	• Catholic church • Universities, colleges • Museums	• Conservative religions • Cults • Cultures • Military unit
Process-driven control of behavior	• Car rentals • Sports teams • Retail stores	• Fraternities/ sororities • Public schools	• Manufacturing • Township building permits • Airline security systems
Specific event- or purpose-driven control of behavior	• Department stores • Retail operations	• Costco (restricts entry) • Restaurant dress codes	• FedEx, UPS, Post Office • Terrorist organizations • Hospital admissions

Process-driven organizations seem tied to a particular "way of doing things." Order is most important. First this step, then that step, and so forth. Retail businesses are examples of organizations driven by a "special purpose." They operate to achieve a profit, to accomplish a mission, or to provide a service. Clearly, there is a certain amount of overlap among these categories.

The point to take away from Table 3.2 is that an organization's orientation and makeup can reveal a lot about how the organization can be expected to behave in certain situations and what's important to the organization's leadership and general membership or stakeholders.

Medical and health programs, for example, have little control over participants. Participants decide whether to participate, if they'll take prescribed medicines, or if they'll come back for subsequent visits. Fraternities and sororities are examples of "closed societies." They can grant access to people but, once someone joins, their range of control over participants is limited. Schools and some religions and recreational parks have a similar profile. They can restrict admission but, once admitted, the member can choose to participate as they see fit. (Ever skip a class in school?) There are some controls. For example, students must take certain classes to graduate, but the participants still have a lot of latitude about their choice of a major, who they'll take a class from and, of course, their attendance.

Conservative religions, cults, insurance companies and manufacturing facilities recruit whom they want as participants and then typically have specific expectations about what's necessary for those recruited to maintain their affiliation with the organization. These expectations can cover how confidential information is maintained (e.g., trade secrets and personal confidentialities), ways to follow or adhere to doctrine, or ways to do one's work given set procedures or policies. Failure to participate as expected can lead to penalties or expulsion. Neither recruitment to, nor continued membership in these organizations is a given. Since many of these high-control organizations have learned what is necessary to achieve their missions successfully, participation in these organizations is based on fitting a profile and making sure performance stays within that profile.

The rows in Table 3.2 illustrate another feature of control—the extent to which control is a function of an organization's operational nature. In this instance, three operational orientations, *content-*, *process-* and *event-driven* are illustrated. The content-driven organization controls through a combination of philosophy or ideology, theory and/or program complexity. Healthcare organizations manage individuals via a wealth of material associated with health matters. The complexity of this content prevents most individuals from managing health issues themselves, although the fact they often try means that while the content is complex, control over the individual is low.

Philosophies, theologies and ideologies do not need volumes of material in the form of rules, guidelines or regulations as a control feature; sometimes the organization's designed complexity will suffice. Some community-type organizations have subtle but significant levels of complexity so that interpreters are needed to manage and explain the organization's rules and guidelines to others. Military organizations often maximize control over membership by infusing ideological content into operational practices, policies and procedures. Some might argue that the way the United States Army treated North Vietnamese or Iraqi prisoners is warranted because these people and their cultures are in conflict with the American soldiers' "Military Americanization"—a blend of ideologies (e.g., democracy, the "USA," destiny and "9/11") and practices (e.g., train, drill, execute).

Many Americans were horrified when Iraqis executed American prisoners by cutting off their heads on television, but one could argue that those acts were a product of their own blend of ideology infused into operational practices. In both American military and Iraqi cases, a rational assessment of these organizations and their systems might conclude they are out of control, misguided and dangerous for the well-being of their parent organization—in these instances, the countries from which they come. One side might see these instances as people acting on their own—that the torture, abuse and killing events that occurred are self-organized responses—while others might argue that they are just microcosms or reflections of the parent organization.

Process-driven organizations often seek control through the steps or procedures participants must follow to perform or complete tasks, manage people or events, or participate in activities associated with building or protecting the organization (e.g., planning, development or evaluation processes). Processes and procedures are useful control devices because they stipulate "the way things are done" and sometimes even "how" a process is completed. A manufacturing process may define the steps in the process and also that care be taken to ensure that safety, security, quality and service standards are met.

Sports teams follow certain rules and procedures, and secret societies, fraternities, sororities and religions have rituals, which are used to structure behavior in terms of certain expectations. Highway departments, on behalf of their state or local governments, establish rules for the road, but again, they have little control over the behavior of individuals unless the roads are continuously monitored. Schools and secret societies can institute their process controls through the use of rituals and standards, but they, too, generally have little control over their participants beyond surface levels.

The use of processes to exercise control, however nominal, is obvious. Process controls specify how to work ("put this piece here"), how to deal with people ("salute your superiors") or ways to manage internal events ("use an agenda for all meetings"). Process controls are generally used to regulate how things get done, rather than how people think about the things they do. Specialty, purpose-driven organizations execute control in terms of activity surrounding exchanges between individuals and the organization or its agents.

Retail is a classic illustration of a specialty-driven organization with activity defined in terms of sales transactions or service requests. Terrorist organizations are another example of a specialty-driven organization. This organization's primary "business" activity is the terrorist event: attacks, bombings and intimidation are meant to influence behavior of *all* stakeholders. Those potentially affected by the acts of the terrorist organization exist in states of anticipation. Those doing the bombing concentrate on how to set the stage for the event while those anticipating a terrorist attack devote themselves to preparing for an event without knowing where or when it will occur. Clearly the terrorist organization is extending a measure of control over everyone involved.

ORGANIZATIONAL CONTROL FEATURES

Without proper care and attention, problems related to the use of controls can surface at any time. For example, some have suggested that a lack of oversight led to control issues associated with the abuses that occurred at Abu Ghraib and other sites during the war with Iraq. (See, for example, *Washington Post* 2005a, 2005b)

It's possible that if people are left to construct their own definitions of control they also can determine the scope and scale of their control of power (Milgram 1969). Then, as their personalized control mechanism emerges and matures, natural checks and balances one might use to manage control mechanisms can become dysfunctional. When this happens key design and evaluation features associated with the administration of controls (e.g., legislation; the making of rules and controls; adjudication; the evaluation of rule breakers and even the use of punishments) can be at risk. We've all seen organizations in which control functions were misused. Bias, unofficial or unorthodox evaluation or punishment protocols, attitudes like "it's my way or the highway" are quick indicators.

The use of controls also creates trade-offs for those affected. As Table 3.3 illustrates, as external controls increase there is a decrease in personal control. Loss of personal control can inhibit initiative or the needed urgency an individual might bring to the management of an event, largely because increased controls can prescribe not only what must be done in particular situations, but how the situations are to be approached or managed, if at all. Since there are clearly times when an organization can benefit from individual initiative and drive in planning, problem-solving and decision-making situations, it makes sense to guard against those times when heavy use of controls inhibits needed behaviors that stimulate innovation, creativity and problem-solving.

Table 3.3 summarizes issues associated with an organization's control system, particularly when controls are used to manage individual behavior. The table's contents illustrate the dynamic nature of the use of controls and some of the motivating factors behind their use. Ironically, the use of controls in an organization can be as much a response to the fact that control is necessary for the organization's well-being as a product of poor or sloppy leadership. Consequently, careless or mismanaged use of control can damage the organization, its credibility and, subsequently, its effectiveness, not to mention similar effects on participants and other stakeholders.

Attempts to control people, processes, quality, products and the like are generally restricted to those in the organization, although sometimes an organization will extend its reach to those outside of the organization. Control of those outside of the organization most often is negotiated through the process of "influence."

Influence vs. direct control is a tactical use of power. Limiting controlling efforts to those within the organization is more economical; it's familiar territory so it may not require additional competencies, and it's often safer—control methods and tactics are hidden behind organizational walls. Sometimes it's not legal to extend control efforts beyond the organization's walls. Many organizations may like to control regulators or legislators, but that's not permitted by law. Influencing may be the relied-on alternative.

Finally, although it seems counter-intuitive, having total control, say over an opponent or marketplace, may tend to work against the organization. Competency, innovativeness and "edge" often are strongest when one has to stay on guard or struggle against an opponent. For example, lack of equally strong competitors has caused many in the U.S. military to re-examine the nature and function of its standing military forces.

Table 3.3   Organization Control Profiles vs. Features, Costs and Benefits of Controls

	ORGANIZATION HAS LOW CONTROL OVER THE INDIVIDUAL	**ORGANIZATION HAS MODERATE CONTROL OVER THE INDIVIDUAL**	**ORGANIZATION HAS HIGH CONTROL OVER THE INDIVIDUAL**
Features of the organization's control system	• Participation is voluntary. • There are nominal rules. • Rules can have flexibility. • Controls may exist. • Self-organization is possible; encouraged.	• Most employment situations. • Situations (like stores or clubs) that require membership before entry. • Organizations with entry requirements.	• Participation is voluntary. • Obeying rules required, monitored. • Rules. Little flexibility. • Strong control requirements. • Denial of service adds control. • Self-organization is not OK.
Benefits to participants	• Helps meet ill defined needs (e.g., facilitates browsing). • May meet a variety of needs. • It's something to do with few obligations.	• Key needs met (e.g., status). • There are benefits (e.g., lower prices). • Members pay to belong so they want to be there. • Because people "pay," the org. knows who is coming.	• Order, predictability. • Members meet needs not met some other way. • Members have loyalty. • Members follow rules. • Members seek out this org.
Costs to the participants	• Few, if any, extra costs. • Lose some convenience. • Individuals free to leave. • Can't count on loyalty; little "collegiality."	• May cost more to belong. • May give up personal information (e.g., credit history) to participate. • We/they mentality. • May not be able to count on participants as "loyal."	• May surrender some freedoms. • Punishment may be severe. • Little membership diversity. • Can reduce innovativeness. • Can create dependencies. • "Exclusiveness mentality." • May stimulate resentment in those on the "outside."

New plans being reviewed call for the military to redefine itself and to prepare for a time when its contribution to American and world order might come through police actions rather than warfare per se and to engage in nation-building missions rather than classical "search and destroy" engagement associated with conventional warfare. (See, for example, *Washington Post* 2008: A16.)

THE STRATEGIC VERSUS TACTICAL USE OF CONTROL FOR THE MANAGEMENT OF PERFORMANCE AND EVENTS

Organizations and people are potentially chaotic systems so the need for controls has evolved as a way for adding order and control as a means to reduce risk and vulnerabilities. Indeed, there's a natural tendency when faced with a new or unfamiliar event, situation or interaction to filter, screen or generally view what's occurring through our past experience. This filtering acts as a type of control mechanism to help us simultaneously understand what's going on and/or plan for what might be coming. It's a way of adding a sense of familiarity to something that may be quite unknown. Typically the other(s) involved respond in kind. It's perceived as prudent, even if it increases the potential for stress, tensions and possible conflict.

PLANNING FOR THE USE OF CONTROLS

Regardless of the situation, the use of controls without planning, oversight and evaluation can lead to charges of negligence or carelessness. Planning for controls begins with knowing which controls are needed, the scope and scale of their application and the reason for their use. There are technical and sometimes legal meanings associated with "control words," so getting professional advice from legal resources can be warranted.

Planning for the design and use of rules also should consider the quantity of rules, policies, guidelines, etc. to be used. Too many can create unintentional bureaucracy, bottlenecks or bother for those expected to work with or around them. Controls are meant to help manage the organization's exposures rising from risks, threats or vulnerabilities. If the nature of the organization's activities involves the use of dangerous materials, rules, policies or guidelines for dealing with emergencies are warranted. In this instance, controls operate like a backdrop for managing issues, problem-solving and decision-making. Too many controls can compromise the potential value of having rules, perhaps even leading those expected to work within the rules to develop "work-arounds" as a means for getting the job done despite "what the rule book says." When these types of conditions arise catastrophe may soon follow.

MANAGING CONTROLS

Planning, managing and monitoring are equally important when using controls. Good planning, for example, illustrates the importance of a task. Planning is a valuable tool for gauging where one is today vis-à-vis the past and the future. Its use and potential benefit can't be over-emphasized.

Successful management of controls achieves two objectives. First, management of controls increases the likelihood that tools like rules, policies and guidelines function as designed. This means that they are used as designed and not abused by those with ulterior motives or poor competencies. The second is that controls actually help manage the organization's risk, vulnerabilities and threats. They prove, in practice, to be valid and reliable management tools.

Successfully achieving both objectives implies that organizational practices associated with planning, communication and information management and evaluation be part of the development and monitoring processes. Success depends on those affected by the controls receiving information and training regarding the control system's makeup and use. Fundamental training can include an introduction to the rules, policies, guidelines, etc., an explanation regarding their importance and penalties for violating them.

MONITORING CONTROLS

Oversight may be the most important function related to the use of controls. This process keeps the organization's management engaged in operations and the use of controls. As signs emerge that controls are not working as designed, that new or different controls may be needed or that changes in the control hierarchy (e.g., what was once a guideline could become a rule) are necessary, this information is passed on to those responsible for making any necessary changes.

Monitoring also helps discover the use of controls to hide or cover problems. For example, some use controls to cover weak management, management afraid of losing control or poorly designed systems. Apart from covering up weak management or leadership, controls in this instance can compromise the credibility of the "control system" and possibly the organization's capacity to handle different events, from mundane to extreme. So, if competency is the issue, deal with that and don't attempt to cover up the problem with more rules, policies and procedures.

It's not typically the responsibility of line managers to make or suspend the use of critical controls. Indeed, some organizations, for example communities, often interpret the need for and use of controls quite conservatively. These organizations have such a different relationship with their membership that controls can be used like those one would see in a family. Leadership in these organizations may assume that the organization operates *in loco parentis* (in place of the parents) because of a belief the participants are not capable of managing themselves. Attempting to reduce or eliminate the use of controls in these organizations can meet significant resistance.

Emergencies or extreme events also impact the role of controls. A fire event in a building can change rules governing "access," "chains of command" or general operating procedures in the building as restricted areas or exits are opened and protocols regarding the relationships among people are suspended so people can avoid danger. During an emergency it's important to know which controls can be suspended and, of course, how soon after the emergency they can be reinstated.

Finally, monitoring helps to update or eliminate some controls. This is particularly true when the controls one might have used are obsolete, simply not needed or when they just cause more trouble than they are worth. Letting an organization's "rule structure" get encumbered by obsolete, petty or otherwise useless controls can weaken the credibility of the entire system. Not only may people not take controls seriously, inconsistent use of controls or the enforcement of otherwise obsolete controls can lead to serious problems and even accusations of bias, hostility or mismanagement.

DISRUPTING THE ENTERPRISE ORGANIZATION:
THE SELF-ORGANIZATION OF CONTROL AND OWNERSHIP

Since an underlying focal point of this book is why and when people in organizations take it upon themselves to construct their own standards, goals and objectives for performance regardless of what the organization desires, it makes sense to review how, where, why and when the enterprise can be vulnerable to attack or disruptions. Rigidity, for example, is a frequent weak point for the enterprise. The desire to maintain controls through rules, processes and procedures can lead to problems if the reliance is too rigorous. A lack of flexibility can make the smallest disruption a critical threshold or breaking point.

The enterprise's linear nature extends to its use of benchmarks and timelines so that if sufficient flexibility isn't built into a process then missing a few dates can lead to turmoil. In some instances the nature of these approaches to control, planning and related practices also leads to internal turf or boundary issues and frequently to a "we/they" attitude toward those outside the organization. So the enterprise, like each of the organizational types for that matter, has its own profile and characteristics. Collectively, this profile or these characteristics define the organization and are much like a person's personality; all organizations may share common characteristics but a given organization, through its structure, culture, rules, people and other factors, develops a "personality" unto itself.

Rigidity and lack of flexibility in the approach to goals, timelines and processes are most susceptible to attack if they are unreasonable given the enterprise's vision/mission. Fruit and vegetables have to be picked before they rot in the field or on the vine but that doesn't mean there is no time for workers to rest, to eat or to relieve themselves. Supervisors have a right to administer rules and procedures, to assign work and to evaluate and reward performance but these are not tools to be used to abuse people and their dignity.

When the elements of control (e.g., policies and procedures) and the administrators of control (e.g., supervisors and managers) become abusive, the opportunity for the enterprise's membership to self-organize a response becomes possible. When this occurs, the emerging form of self-organization may be passive, such as the whistle-blower's anonymous letters or phone calls, or active, such as work stoppages, demonstrations or physical attacks on people or property. It's important to note that none of these self-organized responses have anything to do with leaving the organization; it may not be a viable alternative or even an option (e.g., "I can't quit, I need this job" or "There's nowhere else to go").

Of course the potential for self-organization in these instances can be diffused or managed, largely through the meaningful use of organizational practices. Effective use of communication and information practices can open doors for the membership to express their issues as well as let the membership know the leadership's position on the issues. Knowledge management practices can improve membership and supervisory competencies and skills while evaluation practices are used in a variety of ways to provide information and also demonstrate a commitment to change. Evaluations can isolate the nature and causes of problems, the effectiveness of change programs or improvements in the overall environment.

SUMMARY OF THE ENTERPRISE PROFILE

The enterprise organizational type has its own profile and, importantly, is a component of the other three members of the typology (just as they are of the enterprise organization). The enterprise organization focuses on achieving its mission through tight control of the organization's key elements, for example, its people, processes and operations. Policies and procedures are critical for the enterprise again because of the value these bring to the organization's management. The enterprise is an organization where retrospection is vitally important both to understand emerging problems and to proactively respond to process, product and service needs before they arise.

These features of the enterprise are apparent whether the organization is a stand-alone entity or a dimension of some other organizational type. When it is a component part of the other three organizational types (i.e., the community, team or individual contributor) the enterprise's function materializes through management, planning, organizing and controlling activities aimed at maximizing the performance of those organizations.

When operating as an element of the other three organizational types, the enterprise contributes to performance management activities that shape how the organization behaves in its efforts to achieve its mission or to meet stakeholder needs. In this capacity, the enterprise function serves as the organization's control and operations center. It is from here that rules and structure, including the vision, mission, goals and objectives, are identified and communicated for the organization, its membership and key outsiders. Since the enterprise is an organization's "business center," it is the point where the organization's image, its brand, is positioned for those outside the system.[1]

Inside the organization the enterprise dimension is the organization's executive, legislative and judicial components. It provides order and direction through policies, procedures, guidelines and/or regulations so that performance is managed against these, and that any infractions or violations are addressed. This is an important role, for it connects the vision and mission (what is expected) with performance (what is observed), and finally evaluation of the effort extended. Therefore, if the enterprise organization or the enterprise function within an organization operates as expected, five objectives are achieved. First, there is order within the organization and in ways the organization works with other organizations. Elements of the organization like structure, hierarchy, rules and regulations communicate this control. Order isn't a given, however. Changing circumstances, critical events or crises, or even new programs, can disrupt established order.

A second objective is control. Oversight of rules, rituals, practices, procedures and processes are the typical ways control is defined within organizations. Control can be a significant feature of some organizations. Control defines who can and cannot be part of the organization, if a person can advance within the organization and, of course, if someone's relationship with the organization is terminated. Control is a powerful function within all four organizational types: the enterprise, community, team or individual component.

Two very important objectives for the enterprise to achieve and manage are the synchronization and homogeneity of acts and behavior, especially around the vision and mission. This can translate into unique behaviors. Integration of operational practices ensures key practices are not only in place and used but that their use vis-à-vis all others is understood and monitored. Another objective of control at the enterprise level is the standardization of an organization's brand so that it's possible to feel as though you are, in fact, in or interacting with the same organization wherever you are.

Military organizations have mastered the ability to synchronize and dissolve differences among their units, posts and camps around the world. Ranks, processes and procedures, titles, even the "look" of different camps or military posts are standardized so that wherever the soldier is, it is the "same" army, navy or air force. This not only increases the likelihood that control and order can be maintained, but it reduces the need to "relearn" control and order requirements as one moves from base to base. This benefit alone can result in more time spent on performing tasks or activities at hand than learning where you go to eat your meals. Synchronization and homogeneity create a synergy that can keep down costs and improve productivity, whether you are an employee of a global company transferred to a different part of the world or a member of a terrorist organization attempting to detonate a bomb 3,000 miles from your home.

Finally, all of this emphasis on control by the enterprise helps ensure a sense of continuity, smoothness or permanence for the organization's stakeholders, especially its members. There is a sense of history whether one has been part of the organization for 20 years or just one month. This is significant. Continuity is a critical ingredient in establishing and maintaining culture and an enabling feature for those seeking to use their talents to perform their tasks, come up with new, innovative ways for thinking about things, or for simply understanding "why we do things the way we do."

In the chapters that follow the remaining three organizations, the community, team and individual contributor, are presented and defined. This is an important point. Organizations are classified as one of four possible types; however, all organizations are also a composite of these four types—with the type that is dominant the way to label the organization. An organization classified as an enterprise has more of the features associated with that type of organization than it does features associated with the community, individual contributor, or team organizational types. What adds to an organization's distinctive nature is the way the other organizational types define the organization. An organization defined as an enterprise with strong community then team then individual contributor features is different from an enterprise defined by strong individual contributor then team then community dimensions. Moreover, these different combinations also can vary in strength or amount. A community organization, like a group of monks with a vow of poverty, may have small amounts of team characteristics and very tiny amounts of individual contributor or enterprise characteristics. All four categories are present, just in varying degrees.

CHAPTER 4

The Community
Continuity over Time through Operational Practices

Figure 4.1 outlines the second organization type, the community. The figure highlights key features of the community organization as a stand-alone organization and when part of another organization. Organizations dominated by the community dimension can be the most difficult for someone to join or enter but, once in, you're there. Entry barriers can include detailed screening, ritualistic admission processes and even pledge or novitiate periods—complete with hazing and gauntlets designed to test one's physical, mental or emotional makeup to see if they "qualify" to be part of the organization.

In addition to stiff entry requirements, once in the community, failure to follow or adhere to prescriptions, rules, moral principles or practices may result in dismissal. The community organization can be quick to demonstrate that it can be far less forgiving of transgressions than the other three organizational types. These tough entry and performance expectations are true for most community organizations largely because they have deep-seated values or principles that are tied to the organization's vision and mission.

Community organizations exist in both secular and non-secular arenas. Each is organized around a vision and mission but their approaches can vary dramatically. The non-secular community, like a religion or cult, can be passionate about its vision, mission, values, culture and ethics. In fact, these provide the stimulus for the organization's growth, development and survival. Likewise, the non-secular community's features are primary attractors for participants and the means for setting standards and regulating participant behavior and performance. Moreover, communities like religious organizations, cults and secret societies are especially likely to use entry criteria linked to its vision- and mission-driven values to

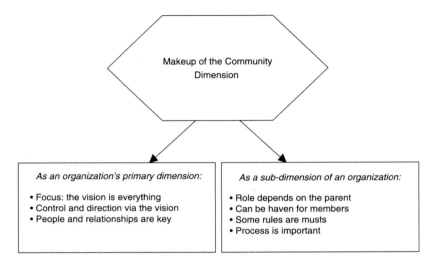

Figure 4.1 Makeup of the Community Dimension.

restrict membership to those who embrace the most fundamental of community standards or principles. These organizations can and often do expect total commitment to the organization and its mission.

Secular community organizations also perform in terms of a vision and mission, but participants may approach the mission with a level of indifference, making other features of the secular community organization their reason for being part of it. Public schools, military organizations and government regulatory agencies are examples of secular organizations that people affiliate with for reasons other than the organization's mission.

A postal worker might work for the post office because it's a job. Likewise a soldier might have joined the army because of a sense of duty, because it's a job, or because it provides an opportunity for college tuition reimbursement. Another person might become a high-school teacher because of a vocational decision and not because of strong alignment to a particular school system's philosophy. These community organizations may even be marked by a noticeable division between those leading the organization or responsible for its formation and those working for the organization. Participants who do not necessarily support or share in the organization's mission still can help it fulfill its charter or mandate— the two groups simply may not put the same value in the organization's vision and mission.

Non-secular communities typically will not tolerate such latitude. In non-secular organizations there's typically strong agreement among the membership at all levels regarding the organization's vision, mission and values generally. Members of these organizations affiliate with the organization for a reason; they know where they want to belong and where they do not want to be. Jews are not Lutherans nor are terrorists likely to embrace the appeals of the U.S. government to stop their attacks. In non-secular communities, one not only embraces the organization's mission but members also can be expected to pledge some level of allegiance to the community and, conversely, sometimes against opposing organizations. The extent to which participants are expected to and do pledge faithfulness, loyalty, devotion and fidelity to a vision or mission is an important feature distinguishing secular from non-secular communities and community organizations generally from the enterprise, teams/groups, or individual contributor organizations.

Some small, local community organizations form as a response to the actions of other organizations. These communities, sometimes classified as unions, social movements or special interest groups, often embrace and promote specific issues or positions. Communities of people affiliated with the civil rights movement, abortion or anti-abortion or non-smoking movements formed because of sentiments for or against these issues. Regardless of the stimulus leading to the emergence of a community dimension, however, the focus for potential members quickly becomes clear: "We welcome anyone interested in our beliefs, mission or 'reason for existing.' If you have specific skills, we'll try to use them. What we need is energy and effort. We are looking for workers."

Community performance is linked to the relationships members of the community have with each other. The "community" gets things done because the membership acts, thinks and works as a unit united around a cause, vision or mission. Consequently, successes *and* disappointments are measured as a community. Enterprises (and, as we'll see, teams and individual contributors) do not share this sense of collective action to the same degree. Turf battles, office politics and budget fights can cause people, groups and departments to seem so disruptive that one often hears expressions like, "they succeed despite themselves."

This isn't meant to imply that there is not dissent or division within the community organization, because there is. Divisions within religions are an example. Martin Luther's dissent against the Catholic Church is a classic illustration that contributed to the emergence of the Lutheran Church and Protestant Reformation. Division within religious communities is evident today. Current conflicts in the Episcopal and Catholic Churches have caused splits and dissent among the membership of those organizations (Griffiths 2008; Jasper 2009a, 2009b; Tokasz 2009).

Government agencies fit the criteria for being classified as community organizations, and divisions within their ranks because of turf issues, leadership and conflicting missions are typical. Some research on the tragedies associated with two NASA space shuttles, Columbia and Challenger, searched for conflicts within this community-type organization as a contributor to the accidents. At issue were questions regarding instances where pursuit of "the mission" may have lead to shortcuts in the design or use of the shuttles (Adema 2004; Cabbage 2003; Dimitroff et al. 2005).

What actually separates and sometimes magnifies the difference between secular and non-secular communities, especially in their management of internal conflicts, is the role of the organization's vision and mission as potential unifying devices. Both secular and non-secular community organizations rely on rules, structure, practices, processes and procedures to guide or direct organizational activities, sometimes even becoming part of the culture.

"Culture," in its most ubiquitous form, is information. According to Ehrlich (2000), information embodied in "stories, songs, tools, customs, morals, art objects, oral histories, books, television shows, computer databases, satellite images, electron micrographs" are the grist for an organization's culture (Ehrlich 2000: 62–63). However, what makes culture unique from organization to organization are the processes that provide "the capacity to invent, modify, store and transmit" it from one generation to another (Ehrlich 2000: 63).

Unlike the "hard" structural elements like hierarchy, rules and processes, culture is a soft organizational element; it adds dimension, perspective and interpretation to other structural features (Schein 1985). Moreover, the relationship between a community organization and its culture is clear: a community's culture is at the organization's center acting like a repository for values, ethics and mores. For both Ehrlich and Schein culture is learned and part of becoming a member of the community is learning and accepting its culture. Moreover, once learned, the community's culture becomes a tool for use in understanding and working in the culture—something like a template for interpreting and developing acceptable ways to manage events as they arise—for knowing how to behave.

Because a community organization's existence is tied to its mission, its culture can become an extension of that mission. This happens for several reasons and with noticeable effects on the organization's membership. For example, in a community organization, more so than in the other three types, the organization's culture is stable and tends to remain consistent and constant across the various groups, departments or divisions making up the organization. This occurs in part because of the culture's link to the organization's mission and policies, procedures and practices, but also because groups within the organization reinforce the culture and its role by defining themselves in terms of the culture.

The culture/mission bonding also is reinforced because of the nature of the community organization to be close-knit and embedded in a belief system that transcends the culture and mission. People who join the community do not separate themselves from the mission or culture; for the membership they're one and the same. This not only strengthens the bonds between participant and mission/organization, it's an economical way to utilize or conserve emotional, cognitive or physical resources. Everything about becoming a functioning and contributing part of the organization can be enhanced because like-minded people join like-minded people.

This makes the community organization, particularly the non-secular community, systemically modular: it's the plug and play of organizational types. People are not hiring on for pay as one finds in an enterprise nor are they getting their egos stroked like those in the individual contributor organizations or by being the potential star of a team. People in these organizations can see themselves as tools, existing for the benefit of the organization. They'll "do anything" for the organization because they see themselves as doing it for the vision or mission.

The farther the organization is from the public's eye, the easier it is to disguise the actions or behaviors when rushing toward achieving its mission. Indeed, people or policies that resist the "single view" often promoted in closed societies or organizations may be eliminated or made dysfunctional somewhere along the way so that resistance to what the community organization wants or the direction in which it's headed is reduced. Jim Jones' cult, the Peoples Temple, or Hitler's Nazi party are historic examples of community organizations that gained strength, purpose and momentum by blending the organization's mission, culture and participants into one single, motivated force while simultaneously closing their community organizations to the eyes and scrutiny of outsiders.

There are potential drawbacks to the extended mission/culture, however. A certain amount of inwardness can develop when the culture, mission and participant become too closely tied to one another. This can blind the organization's participants to the need for change. It can lead to distrust or disrespect of outsiders, and it can lead to extremism, a sense of "all or nothing" for those involved. It's possible for the member of a community to become so bound to the organization's tenets that anything else is rejected.

Perhaps this is what motivated Reverend Joseph Illo, pastor of St Joseph's church in Modesto, California, to send letters to his parishioners saying they "might need to go to confession before receiving communion if they vote for a candidate who promotes abortion rights, such as Barack Obama" (Nowicki 2008). In covering the story, reporter Sue Nowicki wrote:

> In the new letter [sent in response to the reaction his first letter received] to the 5,600 households in the parish, Illo does some confessing of his own. "I realize that (my previous letter) goes beyond what the Church has actually stated," he said in the letter dated Dec. 19. "The Church does not state that voting for a candidate who promotes the practice of abortion is always a mortal sin."
>
> (Nowicki 2008)

An all-or-nothing interpretation of one's mission/culture may make it easier to focus the energies, effort and thoughts of participants in an organization but this can put unique parameters around judgment and perspective. When organizations require their membership to interpret their lives in terms of such extremes, the potential for abuses "in the name of the organization" can occur. Obviously this condition can occur in any organizational type. For example, the leadership or participants of team or enterprise organizations can be so focused on their mission that they may neglect rules and procedures. A team's athletes may take performance-enhancing drugs to increase the likelihood of winning the big game, or a factory's manager may look the other way when the organization violates OSHA or EPA regulations covering worker safety or chemical spills. But the "closed" community may be particularly susceptible. Lack of perspective can put the organization at risk, or it can be so rigid in its approach to change that small disruptions can lead to large crises.

BECOMING A MEMBER OF THE COMMUNITY:
PHASE I—PRE-COMMUNITY

Every organization has some type of joining process but the community's is particularly unique. Awareness of this process is important because the parameters a community might put on an individual who is a member actually begin well before membership is a reality. As a result, a member's opportunity to initiate non-community responses to situations, to construct self-organized responses, is reduced.

Three stages typically define a community's membership process and each contributes to shaping the candidate and his/her role for the community. The first stage, the pre-community membership period, is defined by a subtle give and take between the applicant and community. The objective of this stage is to ensure there's a fit between the applicant and the community. The focus is information exchange. The applicant may be tested or examined against key criteria. This can require interviews, testing, examinations and/or a general screening before an offer of "temporary" admittance is made. Clearly other organizational types may screen or test their candidates for "fitness" but the orientation of the community organization's screening may have a stronger emphasis on ensuring the candidate thinks, believes or adheres to a certain creed or philosophy rather than merely ensuring the candidate can do the job or is not a risk.

MEMBERSHIP PHASE II: FULL PARTICIPATION

The second phase associated with community participation is a period marked by full participation. During this period involvement increases and, typically, levels of mutual affinity, fondness, closeness, trust and congruence between the member and the organization increase. As importantly, levels of tolerance, responsibility and compatibility increase with all bonded by a general sense of harmony.

Throughout this period members can develop levels of friendship that approach a type of kinship, and this in turn opens channels of communication, information and knowledge management that serve to facilitate growth, movement and contribution in the community. At its peak during this phase the member may take on higher levels of involvement and responsibility, perhaps even engaging in efforts to recruit new members to the organization.

MEMBERSHIP PHASE III: IMMERSION AND INTEGRATION

The third period, immersion and integration, reflects levels of heightened maturity within the organization and marked increases in range and diversity of contribution and involvement. For the organization this is marked by an ever-evolving order, standardization and uniformity among its membership. For the participant the period is marked by increased participation in community events as a member but also as a planner and designer of those events. Friendships increase and an overall sense of closeness can develop which, when necessary, can solidify in "them-not-us" or "we/they" sentiments toward those outside the community.

This is a critical point for the community organization. Trust is a dominant theme in this organization, and the role of trust is more than a label. As Yim et al. review in their research, it is a dynamic reflection of the roles and bonds that exist between the member and organization (Yim et al. 2008). For example, at this level of membership the participant is extended the care, custody and control of the organization as a whole, not just some part of the organization or some job or assignment (Johnson et al. 2008). In some communities the participant learns the organization's inner operations and often its inner secrets, too. It's on a parallel with the storeowner letting the "kid" close up the building at the end of the day. It's a rite of passage, so when a member achieves this point, the phenomenon of trust is unquestioned and, conversely, violations of trust have powerful negative outcomes.

Violations of trust, in effect violation of any of the organization's fundamental "conditions for participation," challenge the ability to believe in or depend on the transgressor. And it's a two-way street. Just as the participant can be guilty of violating levels of trust so can those in the organization's leadership positions. The news is full of examples of the effects of such a breakdown in this critical performance standard. In his article, "The Customer Strikes Back," Mike Beirne (2007) reports on a new tool dissatisfied customers have for demonstrating their anger at organizations that violate spoken or unspoken understandings regarding their relationship: embarrass the brand on the Internet, to an audience of millions. According to Beirne, in the "Old Empire," angry customers could call or write, often to no avail but now they are capturing mistakes, violations of trust, poor service and the like on video cameras and posting their findings on the Web.

Most organizations assume people bring an understanding of what trust is/means and how it is used into the organization. The organization wants to "recruit" trustworthy people, not "train" people to be trustworthy. The organization's role in this instance is one of supporting what one has learned or illustrating how something one has learned elsewhere applies to situations or events in this organization. So the vague notion that "trust is important" becomes translated into a performance standard like "here is how trust, as we see it, helps develop strong relationships with our customers."

Table 4.1 provides common examples of trust violations at leadership levels in different community organizations (e.g., religions, political parties, towns and townships organizations). These examples seem to be an all too common feature of the news but what's most notable about

Table 4.1 Undermining Levels of Trust: Performance Failures at the Leadership Level in Four Different Community Organizations

COMMUNITY ORGANIZATION	EXAMPLES
Religious communities	• Charges of sexual misconduct • Abandoning core principles • Using the religion's resources for personal benefit
Law enforcement communities	• Profiling • Physical abuse • Abuse of the system (e.g., using databases for personal use) • Internal crime within the police
Local government	• Abuse of position of power • Use of position for personal gain (Eminent Domain) or retaliation • Partisanship; unwarranted criticism; "metaphoric slandering" of an opponent
Political organizations	• Abandoning core principles • Using a political position for personal gain • Creating division within the organization or country • Nepotism

them is their potential for destabilizing not just particular community organizations, but also efforts to establish these types of organization.

For example, a political organization's "no we didn't/yes we did" approach to charges of misconduct can damage its credibility and contribute to uncertainties about other institutions. Successfully challenging one institution can lead to widespread examination of other organizations in the same class (e.g., religions) or for the same types of "trust violation" across all organizations regardless of their type.

Perhaps the most distressing observation about Table 4.1 is that while it's easier to document individual examples of sexual misconduct within a religion or abuse of power by the police or within local government, it's difficult to determine if the behaviors are widely distributed across these community organizations or restricted to the behavior of a few. Abuse of power, bending the rules, looking the other way when faced with ethics violations, can happen in any of these community organizations—the very type of organization society often wants to believe sets an example for how life or performance should occur.

The effects of trust violations by an organization's leadership can have peculiar effects on an organization's members. If you have a religious community that tells children not to lie and to respect people and life, how should the membership feel after its leadership violates these tenets? Violations of principles within religions, cults and secret societies in general can be especially enlightening about the membership's and organization's needs. In the face of poor, completely objectionable performance, the membership often clings to the organization's basic tenets. In short, they rise above the actions of their leadership and re-establish their personal bond with the organization and its vision and mission.

BUILDING RELATIONSHIPS TO MAXIMIZE THE COMMUNITY'S ORGANIZATIONAL PERFORMANCE

While relationships in some form or other are important to all organizations, the emphasis on relationships inside or outside the organization may be quite different across different organizational types, as Table 4.2 illustrates.

Some organizations focus on internal relationships, others focus more on external relationships and some attend to both. The real significance of relationships to organizations and, in turn, the practices used to develop these relationships, centers on the contribution of relationships to the organization's future.

SELF-ORGANIZATION OF THE COMMUNITY DIMENSION AS A MEANS FOR DRIVING AND SHAPING CHANGE

Often an individual bases primary attraction to an organization on the assumption that the organization has the capacity to fill some personal need, want or desire. The start and growth of social movements, for example, often is related to the shared belief among a collection of people, for example to redress a wrong or a desire to resist perceived oppression or hardships. In many instances, the formation of these organizations is a classic example of self-organization. People come together without being told or directed and find a way to demonstrate against abortion, smoking, unfair labor practices or war.

These micro-communities (micro-comms) reflect the makeup of their membership. They may be defined by race or sex, by job types or skills (e.g., clerical and administrative staff may form their own internal community), or by employment level within the organization (manager vs. hourly). When they appear within a larger organization the members of micro-comms can see them as a safe haven where people with similar interests and backgrounds gather. The micro-comm can be a place to

Table 4.2   Relationship Type by Organizational Type

ORGANIZATION FOCUS	PRIMARY RELATIONSHIP ORIENTATION	RATIONALE
Community-based	Focus on internal relationships	C-based organizations can be insular, isolated and sometimes even provincial in nature. There's a strong need for support from within regarding the organization's direction, individual confirmation, recognition and advancement. "Externals" are to be coped with.
Enterprise-based	Focus on external relationships	Often E-based organizations define their mission in terms of external stakeholders (e.g., customers). Products and services are developed for these "externals." Success, then, often depends on the sentiments of these groups.
Team-based	Dual focus: internal and external	Clearly internal relationships are most important for critical T-based practices (e.g., cooperation, collaboration). The team's mission is often defined in terms of the needs, wants, desires of external stakeholders.
Individual contributor	Focus on external relationships	Internal relationships are a means to an end, and the "end" in this instance is satisfaction of external stakeholders. Success depends on the extent to which "externals" are satisfied.

escape to, away from the watchful eye of administrators or managers. These places, even within the parent organization's property lines, are places where one can, given the "rules" of the community, talk openly about things, people or events inside or outside the organization. These communities belong to these participants.

As the self-organization process unfolds so do other processes important for the community's operation and success. Communication and information management functions, for example, can be significant. For newcomers this is a place to get the messages, ideas or impressions as they are exposed to the community and larger, parent organization. Here those with a deeper history in the parent organization serve as mentors. New members are "shown the ropes" as jargon or organization-specific language is translated. The "grapevine" as an information source often is centered and formalized here. This grapevine, enhanced with the parent organization's existing technologies like email and voice-mail, expands the sub-community's reach throughout the parent organization and to other micro-comms within this or other, different organizations.

In large organizations people can use micro-communities to be with "someone like me." They are a naturally forming haven away from the formal "outside environment" and a place where second languages are spoken, prayers are said or the needs of special interests are met. They help release frustrations, are a place where anger or hostilities may be diffused before they rupture into larger problems. This is a valuable service for members of the micro-community and of potential benefit to the parent organization. While the parent organization may make rules to manage problem behavior and use people skilled in executing those rules, it is the micro-comm that can create "neutral territory" where people can negotiate on behalf of a segment of the organization or the organization as a whole.

Some organizations encourage the development of micro-communities so that their membership can be incorporated into knowledge management efforts designed to improve the skills and competencies of people in similar positions or with the same duties and responsibilities. When organizations launch system-wide safety or security programs, for example, it's often best if these programs are tailored to meet the specific needs of specific micro-comms. So the manufacturing community's safety program may look different from the program for the administrative community and theirs may look different from the program for the management community. Tactical use of naturally occurring micro-communities not only saves time and money but increases the likelihood that training, in these instances, will be better designed to meet the particular needs of particular people.

Still other organizations allow micro-comms to form as a way of promoting their efforts to achieve diversity. Care must be taken, however, to ensure diversity programs do not become little more than attempts to use statistics to glaze over systemic problems like racism or sexism.

STABILITY IN COMMUNITIES IS NOT ALWAYS A GIVEN

Because people are typically drawn to community organizations because the organization fits needs or expectations that closely match the membership's values, attitudes, opinions or beliefs, trying to introduce change in these organizations can be very difficult. Communities, unlike the other three organizational types, not only are characteristically hard to change, resistance to change may seem like a "way of life" in some communities. Resistance to change in certain communities is one way the community prevents or manages threats that potentially might emerge from within the organization. Moreover, a general resistance to change combined with the fact that people are drawn to, or have a personal, deep-seated attraction to the community's mission allows everyone in the organization to see resistance to change as a personal way of being. People in communities can find it almost impossible for them to behave in any manner that might harm or cause the organization to be different, to change. As a result, members not only invest in the organization, they can also take a strong stance to protect the organization from attack or internal turmoil.

Despite conditions that reduce the likelihood of change occurring within communities there are times when change is needed. For example, sometimes the significance of an organization's vision/mission may not have the same attractiveness or "draw power" it once had. Cults, social clubs, political parties and religions, for example, often pursue a vision or an idea of personal interest to its members. If the bond accounting for the members' attraction is disrupted for enough people (e.g., the vision is no longer viewed as important) the organization will falter.

Other times, the organization is no longer viewed as a tool for meeting important needs that can't otherwise be met. Community organizations like schools, police, fire departments and government agencies exist because they provide services individuals typically cannot meet on their own. If these services are no longer needed (for example, the student graduates) or the need is met in some other way the organization can lose its appeal.

Finally, some communities fail because the organization's leadership loses its capacity to manage the organization. Perhaps the leadership has lost its credibility with the membership and there's a feeling the leadership no longer represents the organization's vision/mission. Or perhaps indiscretions or poor choices result in disapproval of the leadership's behaviors—the membership may not see a leader's behavior as matching or consistent with what they expect from someone in that role for "this" community and a change must be made.

But if change is needed it is important that before changes are introduced special care is taken to manage the overall change effort vis-à-vis the organization's special characteristics or features (e.g., history, tradition or close-knit membership). In other words, deciding to organize a change effort has its risks in any organization but it can be particularly risky in communities. So if someone within the organization seeks to introduce any form of independent, self-organized change usually several things must be considered.

First, those leading the self-organization effort need to have access to some accurate and, ideally, verifiable information. Only good, solid information can unseat a fixed, perhaps value-laden, position or belief in a community. This information should identify the typical important matters one associates with a change effort, such as the costs and benefits to the organization and its stakeholders, but it is very important to identify how the proposed change links to the community's mission.

Second, it's always best if those engaged in the self-organizing effort are trained in techniques and processes related to the change process. This seems obvious but because roles in communities can be well defined and limiting few people in the organization may have the range of skills or competencies needed to launch and manage a change effort. Communication, information and knowledge management are key skills for "change agents" but they may be foreign to the membership in some communities where only a few lead and most are followers. For example, improving the evaluation skills of everyone in the change effort has a tendency also to make them "seekers" for more information in support of the self-organization effort, but when the membership is taught to follow and not question, or to do and not evaluate, these skills may be hard to learn and develop. The benefit of making everyone involved in the change effort an evaluator has its merit because this demonstrates that it's OK to challenge or evaluate what may otherwise be topics closed to discussion, investigation or change, but adding evaluation and judgment where it may not have been encouraged or allowed can be threatening for some.

It's also important to create or to demonstrate that a viable alternative exists or is feasible. Just criticizing the status quo isn't sufficient in the community organization, it's important to show that there is a viable alternative to whatever is creating stress and tension. Potential recruits to the change effort want to know something different exists, particularly if they are going to take a risk and jump ship too.

Once others have decided to go along with the change effort switching from what was to the new state should be made as easy as possible, particularly if the proposed change will have a large or significant effect on the community. Ensuring changes are introduced without unneeded stress or strain is important because communities, more so than any of the other three types of organization, typically don't see a lot of change. Imagine what it would be like to introduce change in communities you know. The schools, religions, government agencies, political parties, fraternities and sororities you know seldom experience wide-scale change, especially in core areas like the organization's vision, mission, processes and procedures. Communities tend to have a deep-seated history of thinking about or doing things in a particular way and that makes them very resistant to change so any proposals to "do things differently" must take that into consideration.

Finally, it's important that the proposed change really is an alternative to what exists. If the proposal effects a change in the organization's leadership then the new candidates must be different when compared with the current leadership. The same is true for changes to processes or ways of doing things, programs or what the organization values as important. If potential followers of the change effort do not see any difference between what was and what is proposed then do not expect them to stay around.

SUMMARY OF THE COMMUNITY ORGANIZATION

The community organization is the second of four organizational types to be discussed. What makes the community dimension different from the other three is the nature and role of the mission to the membership. Members are attracted, join and remain with the community organization as long as its mission meets their needs.

In this chapter we reviewed the role of community organization as a stand-alone organization and as a facet of other organizational types. The community dimension helps maintain focus on the organization's vision and mission and it helps build levels of cohesiveness among the membership that can transcend other, more formal structural elements of an organization. When done right cohesiveness and cooperation grow; however, when not well managed the community dimension can cause internal, private networks (e.g., grapevines) to develop and operate.

Organizations may use the features of the community dimension as a diversion from the drudgeries associated with the tasks at hand. Social activities or events are a product of an organization's community dimension and can serve as diversions from the mundane, tedious nature of the daily work environment. An organization might use its community dimension to draw upon its membership's behaviors, attitudes, opinions and beliefs to stimulate action not possible through other dimensions. Socialization factors that stipulate how people are expected to behave aren't easily and meaningfully added to a mission statement and do not usually belong in a job description, but they can be linked to part of an organization or its culture via the community dimension. Peer pressure, rituals and mentoring are socializing activities that fit nicely into the community organization.

In times of crisis, enterprise-driven organizations often rely on the community dimension to help others in the organization in a fire, a downsizing, or other extraordinary events. On the other side of the coin when the emerging environment presents the membership with increasing stress or pressures and a nurturing community is not available, those affected sometimes turn to outside communities or build separate communities to deal with these conditions. Companies that use Employee Assistance Programs (EAPs) have made a link between their organization and outside organizations that supply the needed community features they may not have as part of their operating makeup. Unions, too, are examples of community organizations emerging to fill a need by employees who believe they are not receiving the levels and types of care and support from within the larger parent organization.

The community dimension can be a primary driver for change within any organization because it facilitates the coming together of people who share similar ideas and feelings. Moreover, those who do share common ideas and values also are likely to have a strong affinity for the organization's vision and mission. Sub-groups within organizations often develop because of a need for something different from what the organization has to offer. They are an alternative which allows people seeking change (e.g., from practices perceived as unfair, people who may be biased or disruptive, or processes perceived as dangerous, unsafe or ineffective) to find relief from what's distasteful, potentially harmful or generally out of their control.

Finally, the community dimension can be a source for the development of unplanned, and sometimes undesired, competing new organizations to develop. These unplanned or informal sub-organizations can lead to stressful conditions for the existing organization (conflicts and related behaviors), periodic disruptions or social movements or, perhaps, the formation of new organizations.

CHAPTER 5

Teams
Missions Accomplished through Collective Action

Organizations consolidate human activity in three ways. First, people can work alone, by themselves. This might be in a particular job or a one-time assignment. Receptionists, people in human resources, sales or accounting fall into this category. People in these areas may be part of a larger department for logistical reasons but they often do the bulk of their work alone.

Then there are people who do their work as part of larger groups, sometimes called departments, office pools or "work areas" (e.g., "you'll work in the 'typing area'"). These individuals are part of a mass production process where much of the work is standardized, flows in an orderly, somewhat predictable fashion and is expected to do so, all things considered, over time. Finally, there are people whose work is designed around accomplishing a particular task and, because of the task or organization's overall mission, there are specific jobs that must be done in a particular way and often against a deadline. These are teams and small groups, the focus of this chapter (see Figure 5.1).

Two team organizations familiar to most people are sports teams and project teams. These teams usually have a fixed number of people who can "play the game" or work on accomplishing a mission. This doesn't mean that there are not sometimes large numbers of people working in support of these teams. There are coaches, trainers and ground crews for sports teams and clerics, financial analysts or sales personnel supporting project teams. They "support" the team, they do not "play the game," "score a point," "negotiate with the client" or "verify client needs." In fact, some of those in support areas may never be in a position to actually see the game when it is being played (e.g., ticket-takers or parking attendants) or ever meet the client they've grown to "know" through reports, emails or the like. Consider the auditors,

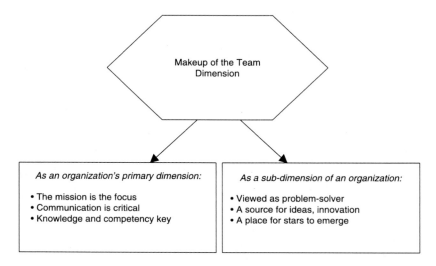

Figure 5.1 Makeup of the Team Dimension.

people in accounting or receptionists in many organizations who may have ongoing contact with clients but are not members of the project team designed to meet the clients' needs.

We've come to talk about those in support roles as "part of the team," but, in the truest sense, they are not. Their compensation is typically not *directly* based on team performance (if the center of a basketball team plays poorly and is traded, that doesn't mean we also remove the ticket-taker at Gate 2, Level 2, or the receptionist. Sometimes we even talk about the fans of sports teams as "part of the team" but try and fire one of them!).

People in support roles are part of the larger organization's many groups (e.g., the security department or the fan club) or they occupy the individual positions the organization needs to handle general, daily affairs. The team's coach or the announcer in a sports enterprise are examples. They are part of the enterprise organization.

People are recruited for teams because they have certain skills or qualifications. They are hired to do certain jobs or to fill roles that can require specific and often advanced skills. These jobs or roles are necessary to achieve a goal or accomplish a mission, like winning a game, freeing a hostage, or solving a problem affecting "the breakage of goods as they move from the loading dock to the production area." Often activity or work done in teams requires a need for ongoing, close collective action.

Functional groups that work in support of other groups or departments aren't set up that way. "If you've typed one report you've typed them all" is the type of mantra associated with functional groups. Sure, there may be different charts and graphs, but the underlying process or format doesn't often differ. Work is more routine in support groups from the entry level to top administrators.

Functional groups also can accommodate a wider range of skill sets. This isn't to demean the work done in the organization's support groups. There are many professional roles and responsibilities (in finance, human resources, sales, technical writing or research) that are important for the organization's success, but these positions and the people who fill them do not, and frankly cannot, function as teams function. Their jobs are designed around organizational processes (e.g., taking orders, typing reports, preparing balance sheets, rotating the tires on a car) and not to solve a particular problem or work in a close-knit fashion to solve a particular problem.

The information needs of teams are different than those of others. There are three types of information *all* people need. First, they need information that tells them how to do their job and what's expected of them. Accounting is an example. Even though accounting is a general practice and a profession with specific standards it can be done "differently" at different organizations. Job descriptions, along with the directions a supervisor provides, help fill this information need.

People also need information that tells them how to handle different processes. Processes like communication, safety, quality or information management are not the same from one organization to another. Every organization has different needs and requirements, and these must be communicated.

Finally, people need information about the organization's policies and procedures. These are often the "rules" that apply to day-to-day behavior and activity. This information can cover a variety of topics (attendance, security, safety and health) and is often provided to new members in orientation programs or through printed materials like brochures. In some organizations this type of information is provided on the first days at work, for example, in one-on-one communications or under the guidance of a mentor through a "buddy system." But communication, not training, is the vehicle.

Teams, because they tend to be more independent than, say, a functional group or department in the same organization, may disregard or use all of these information formats, depending on the assignment at hand. That's because the team's orientation locks on to the mission, whereas a functional group's orientation locks on to pre-established processes or procedures. So, since events, as described earlier, can range from routine to extreme a team managing a routine event has very different information needs from when dealing with an extreme or rare event. It's just like the sports team that changes its "game plan" or the SWAT team that changes its "response plan" to the event or situation at hand. Functional groups, like the accounting department or a factory's product line, do not have the same flexibility. The established processes functional groups follow to accomplish their goals and objectives define how they approach their work.

TEAMS AND PROBLEM MANAGEMENT: THE PRODUCTS, OUTCOMES AND IMPACTS OF A PROBLEM'S EFFECTS

When organizations encounter a problem, particularly serious problems, processes or practices used to manage day-to-day events may not be useful for managing them. In fact, they may even contribute or be related to the problem's inception. One recourse used in organizations when this happens is to form special teams to address the problems. These can be labeled project teams, problem-solving teams or established as an ongoing part of the organization. SWAT teams or bomb squads used by the military or police are examples.

The organization's functional areas involved in production or processes may not have the time to handle a problem. They have their own work to do, and may not have the skills to address or manage the problem. Consider the range of problems illustrated in Table 5.1. Problems can emerge anywhere in an organization and from any or, worse, many of these areas. Those engaged in driving organizational processes, products or services often do not have the bandwidth to handle their own work let along problems of the type described.

Some may not even see that a problem exists. Again, those in production or service delivery areas can be so immersed in their activities that problems can surface without them having the time or interest to see them. Other times a lack of training, fear of reprisal or a sense that any cure may be worse than the disease may contribute to people simply "looking the other way" when problems occur. Special teams can be separated from constraints posed by existing workloads, inexperience, time requirements or other inhibitors.

Special interest or project teams work differently from functional groups. Functional groups, for example, are "process bound" so there is often little extra time available to devote to non-process matters. Consider how difficult it can be to collect staff for needed training on new processes or technologies or on special topics like safety. Time

Table 5.1 Problem Identification Worksheet: Illustrations of Problems Organizations Often Face

PEOPLE-RELATED PROBLEMS	PROCESS-RELATED PROBLEMS
• Fatigue, so errors occur, accidents happen • Illness; time away from work • Injuries. Increased insurance costs • Poor training or education for assignments • Confused about the job or what is expected • Uncertain of mission, goals, objectives • Arguments and infighting • Turf issues • Anger, mistrust • Home issues cause stress, distractions	• Poor support for mission, goals, objectives • Insufficient time to do work • Highly technical work • Burdensome processes (e.g., too much security) • Boring work • Mentally demanding • Unskilled teammates • Dangerous
MATERIAL- /EQUIPMENT-RELATED PROBLEMS	**MANAGEMENT-RELATED PROBLEMS**
• Dangerous • Not in good working condition • Training manuals are missing • Training doesn't keep up with changes • Equipment doesn't match what's needed • Inventory is not in time or insufficient	• Poor supervisors: unskilled, biased, lazy • Avoidance management practices • Little performance management practices • Poor attitudes: "My way or the highway" • Poor perceptions, treatment of people
CULTURE- AND ENVIRONMENT-RELATED PROBLEMS	**PROBLEMS RELATED TO EXTERNAL SOURCES**
• Bias, confused, afraid/fear, stressed • Unorganized, high pressure • Tension between supervision and workers • Dangerous	• Burdensome rules and regulations • Litigation • Challenges and competition • Attacks • Audits and reviews isolate discrepancies

constraints for project teams can be more severe because their work is often dedicated to deadlines. Since project teams only have "time for the problem," there can't be distractions—the "problem" is why they exist. Indeed, the only time issue the team has is the deadline or "time to resolution."

Teams and problem-solving also cost money. Teams such as these, that is problem-solving teams, do not contribute to making a product or providing services. It is true that solving a problem may improve quality, reduce risks and improve service, but added costs or potential expenses associated with the use of these teams may not have existed if processes and practices were in place from the beginning. Moreover there is always the risk that after investing days, weeks, months and hundreds, millions or, especially in instances of conflict or war, billions of dollars, many old problems still exist and, often, newer problems seem to arise to accompany them. It is no wonder people want to walk away from the problems they face by saying things like "It's just the cost of doing business," "What do you expect? People will never change" or "That's just the way life is!"

DESTABILIZING THE TEAM

There are three ways to destabilize a team or team's efforts: deny them the resources needed to function, confuse the issue (make believe "everyone's on the team") and prevent "stars" from rising. Consider the under-resourced team.

A team without resources is just a group of people sitting around a table. They may want to act but they may not have the talent, skills or other resources needed to act, particularly in a meaningful way. Organizations also rely on teams because the problems that arise can be complex or require special skills to resolve. All problems are unique. There may be similarities across different types of problem and their risk to the organization not immediately apparent, but each problem is unique unto itself. Consider the exercise that follows as an illustration.

Completing this exercise should make it clear that producing a list of possible causes for a problem may be fairly quick and easy. However, the exercise also illustrates the nature of the challenge for an organization when attempting to solve a problem and, ideally, prevent it from re-occurring. First, a problem's cause(s) can be very complex. The list you generated, for example, may only contain "possible" causes. They

---

Exercise

Illustrating the Complexity of Problem Identification

Pick one of the problems listed below and, without regard for the "quality" of your answer, generate a list of ten reasons why the problem exists—in other words, list what might have "caused" the problem.

Consider the following three problems:

1. People here seem to resist change whenever it's introduced.

2. People behave rudely toward one another.

3. Those in leadership positions tend to avoid difficult problems.

List possible causes for the problem you picked.

may only be a manifestation of some core or root problem yet to be uncovered! Your list also reflects the thoughts of one person. Having two or three others speculating on a problem's cause, particularly if they have some familiarity with it, can uncover ideas you might not have considered. Last, consider the information presented earlier in Table 4.1. That worksheet illustrates sources of problems in an organization, so unless the problem-solver has a broad view of the organization some key problem sources may go unnoticed. Again, one value of teams is that they can be comprised of people from throughout the organization.

With a complicated organization and limited resources, problem-solving teams have a hard time chasing problems as they emerge from sources, of varying levels of intensity, and requiring different skills or tools to manage them or bring them to resolution. Add to this the fact that sometimes addressing one problem can result in more complications as problem-solving efforts stimulate the emergence of more problems and the impact on a team without sufficient resources only increases.

A second way to destabilize team efforts in an organization is to confuse the relationship between teams and team behavior and the behavior and activities associated with functional groups. Problems here arise from two issues. First, functional areas can sometimes suffer from an organizational inferiority complex. Functional areas are where the "work gets done" so they can be viewed as the "place *not* to be" when compared with teams who seem to have all the perks, fun and freedom. Second, while teams often are self-starting and driven by a sense of urgency to "get the problem solved" or the game won, functional groups do not have those innate motivational drivers. The work in functional areas seems to go on and on, the same old thing, day in and day out. As a result, managers often rely on rallying cries associated with teams to motivate those in work areas or functional groups.

We hear the use of words and phrases like "teamwork," "Let's show them we're a team," "Where's your team spirit?" or "There's no 'I' in the word 'team.'" It's an interesting strategy but it usually doesn't help those in the functional group because the very nature of the work they do, or the processes necessary to do their work, do not fit a "team" model.[1] Calling a group of people a team is something like calling a station wagon a sports car because someone has added oversized tires, pin stripes and lowered the body. It's not a sports car. It can't behave like a sports car; it's a station wagon that looks different.

In fact, one of the reasons training and instruction designed to help groups "become" teams fail is because people in various non-team jobs can see through these words designed to motivate people to perform in a particular way. The instruction a group gets telling them how to be a team just doesn't apply to the jobs they do, the organizational lives they lead, the way they are expected to process the work they do or, sometimes, even the pay they get. Of course, we have learned to call this on-the-job resistance to "team concepts" "resistance to change" or "not willing to play the game" but in reality team concepts *do not fit* most work groups.

How or when are people who do not talk to others in the course of doing their jobs or who do not do work with a clearly defined relationship to someone else, going to have opportunities to practice the interactions, collegiality or cooperation one may see in a team? If a company wants *everyone* to have and practice these values, calling them a "team" is not the way to do this. These values often appear as characteristics of teams but they're really characteristics of the cultures in organizations.

They are cultural, not team-specific, values. If these types of values appear in a team, it's not because these are characteristics inherent to teams but rather because certain teams (for too many reasons to go into here) can create sub-cultures within the general organization, that use/need these characteristics to function. If the organization's senior management wants everyone in the company to espouse and practice the types of values one sees in teams then changes must be made at the source: the organization's culture.

Finally, and not to belabor the point, calling a group of people a team and providing training around this concept does not produce teamwork or team-like behaviors. Not only do the mission and type of work differ between an organization's teams and functional groups but so do the way teams and groups process the work they do. Communication, quality, service, information and evaluation processes are relatively similar among teams (regardless of the industry) but they can vary widely among departments of groups, *even in the same organization*. These processes have to vary. They have to be different. The jobs to do, the tasks/assignments to be done and the end results vary, so the processes which connect different jobs, task/assignments and processes tend to differ; they have to differ to support the different requirements of each job, task or assignment.

Except in those situations where people function as a team to complete an assignment that only a team can complete (as in sports or for a project), the concept "team" is an illusion. We in the United States have come to use the word "team" as a convention; a means for describing a "better way of doing things generally." This is a misnomer at best but the potential for confusion and dissonance can be significant. So what is it people (in teams and groups) are asking for when they say they need "to change things" around here or when they ask for some training to improve their "teamwork"? What are they looking for?

It appears these requests for change surface in organizations to improve two things: operational processes that cover the way things are done and/or the fundamental instruction people need to do their job or get by in the organization as a whole. One thing people seem to be asking for when they say they want to be more like a team or to improve their teamwork is to improve *the way* they do their work. That is, the way(s) things or processes "happen" in their job or groups. Employees seem to match their impression of what they see happening in teams to what they do not see or want to see happening in their own groups or jobs. Employees in a group may see players "pass the ball" and they'd like someone to "pass information" they need to them. They do not care if they are a team or not. They just want the processes to change so they get the information (or whatever) needed to do their job.

Employees may see a team member acknowledge another's good shot and they'd like a little recognition for the work that they've done, too. ("How about a 'high five' for the way I typed that paper or for the way I handled that angry customer?") Or, perhaps they want to take a break and get into a "huddle" before the start of a workday that they believe is going to be tough. They may want this huddle for "support," for a little "collegiality," to make sure everyone is "on the same page" or just so they know they're not going to be alone that day!

In short, employees can feel the tensions and sometimes even the pain caused by poor processes and sometimes the call "to be more like a team" is just another way of asking for help to improve the processes which define their work. From another point of view, expressing sentiments like those just described also may be signals that if change doesn't come from above those seeing a need for change may seek a solution of their own—perhaps through self-organizing activities.

When change is needed in a team, for example if a team member isn't performing as expected, that poor performance is evident and can easily be quantified. Poor performance by one team member can stop the team. Team and team members do not need training in how to do their jobs. They have been (or should have been) selected for the team because they possess the required skills. What they often need is training and instruction on how *to process within the team*. This might include training on how to listen, to communicate, to plan or organize. But, in reality, even these process skills may not be as critical or nearly as important as doing the job one is expected to do, on time and as it needs to be done. Getting things done in teams is, in fact, fairly routine and the reason why the team exists.

This is one reason why teams can have "stars." Stars are often individual performers and sometimes they do everything right in the job but sometimes few things right with others on the team. Is the team going to get rid of this person because of poor planning, listening or general "social" skills? It's not likely. Or, would they?

A third way to destabilize a team is to negate the role of stars in the team. Tensions can surround a team's "stars," "high achievers" or "outperformers." Their performance brings them to the attention of others and makes them special to the team and its stakeholders. They are in the team and are recognized for who they are and what they contribute— both the good and the unpleasant. Those with a stake in the team's performance tend to like stars or high-achievers. They "set an example," "raise the bar," are "go-getters," are "producers." Others, most often within the organization, may not like them for the same reasons.

And it's not as though people can't work with or "work around" this person. The star does what he/she *is expected to do and more*—and sometimes that's the issue. Consider this scenario:

> A student, in an advanced and difficult statistics course, got the highest grade on the mid-term. When the student found out the instructor intended to post those grades—with names—the student protested. Not out of humility but because of the negative peer pressure from others in the class. "The group" would have avoided, perhaps even ostracized the star because she set an example, a level of performance, they did not achieve. She weakened their case that the test was unreasonable, too hard.

The issue here is not with the star student or the instructor but with their department's management. Here the managers were trying to build a culture with values such as "Let's not be competitive," "Let's everyone get along and be happy" and "Let's everyone be 'the same'." Anything else created confrontations, conflict or dissonance and, of course, had to be addressed—they make for more work.

The only caveat for the star is that it is critically important that the star always performs as a star in order to get and keep getting the perks of a star. Stars are tolerated on teams because the true star genuinely helps the team accomplish its mission. In a well-managed team stars are admired for their accomplishments and game performances while shortcomings are tolerated or endured—with management. The contribution of the star in functional groups, however, is a little different. There is a level of anonymity in groups and departments that can hide from view both the star and the poor performer. This doesn't mean the impact of good or poor performance isn't felt in groups and departments. The impacts are there, too. It's just that it is often easier to see good and bad things in smaller units, like a team, or to "work around" the same in a large group or department. The question of interest, however, is what's lost when one loses or restrains a star because of socio-political, personal resentments or fears?

SUMMARY OF THE TEAM ORGANIZATION

Simply functioning as a team (e.g., doing things in conjunction with others) does not mean the team or its members know how to behave as a team, are functioning well as a team or, if necessary, could teach others to be good team members. Problem-solving is a good example. Most teams that seem to function well as a team do so without being familiar with or knowing how to work as a team. That's often because they are collectives of individuals brought together around a common goal or assignment with the skills and competencies needed to achieve those goals. Individual pursuit of the assignment organized within a collective unit is what brings them success, not a team effort. Once the goal is achieved or the assignment has ended, they can just as easily take on another assignment with the same "team members" or simply disperse back to where they came from or move on to other teams.

Initially, the label used to classify people as a group or team seems of little importance. Indeed, except in certain arenas, for example sports, the use of the word "team" seems more of a value judgment about how people should behave than a description of the general function or role. Sometimes, saying someone is part of a team or is "joining a team" implies that he should behave in a particular way. In fact, there is an extensive vocabulary for use in describing the values of teams over groups. Expressions like "team work," "team spirit" and, of course, being a "team player" are examples. These terms do more than merely describe preferred behavior; they also are used to set parameters for controlling behavior.

Usually, however, use of the word team is reserved for collectives that are expected to perform with some goal or product in mind. Athletic teams that function for competitive reasons are considered different from those that form for recreational pursuits, and project teams are (or should be) considered distinctly different from the department to which the team's membership is attached. Project teams are formed to complete some special function (e.g., to plan a party), to do research or to centralize a program activity (e.g., safety or quality teams).

Organizations have solved problems using this labeling strategy for generations. "We are being attacked by our neighbors so let's form a (big) team (we'll called it an 'army') to fight them off." Or, "We need to have an annual awards party so let's ..." Or, "There seems to be a problem with the quality of service we are providing so let's form a 'SWAT team' to investigate the problem to tell us what to do to improve our service." Or, "We have ten new projects coming which will mean we will have to hire 100 new people over the next three months. Form a 'hiring team' to do the basic selection while the rest of us keep involved with our ongoing work."

In each of these instances two things are generally understood to be associated with putting these teams together. First, teams are formed for a particular reason: to solve a problem, to represent a sports organization, to conduct a study. Organizations form "quality teams," "SWAT teams," "hiring teams" or "disciplinary teams" to augment the work of others. These teams become a form of "collective competency" or collected energy but in actuality they are little more than employees, members of the organization, reconfigured into various teams-of-people-that-work-together-on-special-assignments.

Second, in the ideal situation, people selected to be part of these teams have certain skills or experience one can associate with the problem or needs at hand—not necessarily because of their "team skills." For example, "We need to know why our customers think our service is poor and can be improved, she has good interviewing skills so put her on the team." Or, "He knows the work to be done and always seems to ask good questions. Put him on the hiring team."

Once the assignment is over, the team members return to other things like doing their regular jobs. Now it's evident that organizations have used this "We have a problem ... Let's form a team" strategy with success but it is also clear that this can be an expensive way to solve or address problems. Pulling together a group of people to solve a problem can be a quick remedy but it has its limitations. First, it means they are not doing the work they were initially recruited to do. More importantly, however, "problem-solving" teams tend to address surface issues and seldom do away with the "root cause" or "real" problem *because they literally do not have the power or are not in a position to do that.* All of the work of teams in this instance rests, in the end, with the organization's leadership. If they haven't the desire or skills to manage the problem the team's time and work are wasted.

CHAPTER 6

The Individual Contributor and Urgency

Every organization has characteristics of the four organizational types (enterprise, community, team and individual contributor) with one dimension dominant. So a community organization has more features of that dimension than the other three, an enterprise more features of that dimension than of the community, team or individual contributor and so on with all of the different types of organizations. As Figure 6.1 illustrates, the same is true for the individual contributor organization.

Three factors increase the opportunities for self-organized behavior to emerge in any of the four types. First, if an organization's structural or process features (e.g., key practices, policies, processes or procedures) are incomplete or missing this leaves the door open for individuals or groups to create their own processes or practices that they need to manage a particular event. Second, sometimes members of the organization establish rules, policies, procedures or the like that are in place to manage an event or situation and create (self-organize) their own response without permission or direction. Finally, some organizations encourage or are inclined to the emergence of self-organized responses to manage situations or events. The conditions are set up to stimulate innovation, creativity or because the organization or its members are likely to find themselves in situations where few things seem routine and when inventiveness or "work-arounds" are a matter of course. These types of condition are especially evident in the individual contributor organization, this chapter's focus.

The individual contributor organization is unique in one primary way. Unlike the other organizational types, the individual contributor organization may comprise, or be primarily defined in terms of, one person and not a collective of people, the way we think of most organizations. This doesn't mean that the individual contributor organization

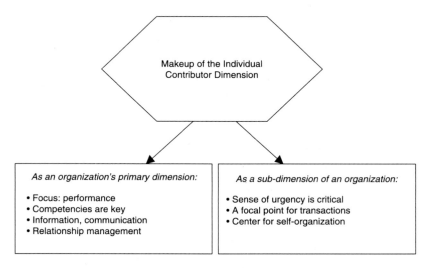

Figure 6.1 Makeup of the Individual Contributor Dimension.

doesn't have affiliations or relationships with other people—that's its inherent organizational nature: there are times when only one or two others define an individual contributor's relationship.

In most cases identifying an individual contributor organization seems like naming an occupation, but it's much more. As Table 6.1 illustrates, many individual contributor organizations seem like jobs that almost anyone with the right competency might have. Indeed, what seems to separate those titles on the left from those jobs on the right is their level of independence of choice. The individual contributor organization has more freedom to choose, or at least to a greater extent, and most jobs listed on the right do not.

All of this raises a question: is there really a need to classify or define such a small entity as an organization and, if so, is there value in making such a classification? The answer to both parts of this question is yes. The need to classify small entities as organizations comes from the characteristics and role of these organizations. Consider the extremes like the sniper, terrorist, professional golfer, evangelist or archeologist. It's not uncommon for these individuals to have the structural elements of a large organization: a vision, mission, policies, procedures and practices. They are just often limited to only one person. To ignore these singular, small organizations is to potentially ignore the beginnings or manifestations of a larger movement, sources of risk, threat or vulnerability for a larger organization, or the contributions of potential

Table 6.1   When is Someone an Individual Contributor or Working in a Role or Job Classification?

YES AN INDIVIDUAL CONTRIBUTOR	WHY	NOT AN INDIVIDUAL CONTRIBUTOR	WHY
Doctor	Can set fees or not charge, decides how to treat patient.	Cashier at a restaurant	Cannot choose to charge a patron or set a price.
Lawyer	Can set fees or not charge, decides how to pursue a case.	Politician	Must follow party line, bosses or lose support.
Consultant	Can bill, set fees. Choose work or not, prepares own plan.	Factory line worker	Has to do the job as defined, no shortcuts.
Internal consultant	Targets issues, decides on a course of action.	Department manager	Follows a plan, meets a goal or budget.
Cab driver	Selects riders. Determines length of ride.	Bus driver	Follows the route. Stays on schedule.
Real-estate agent	Can adjust commission. Has control over who's a client.	Department store clerk/associate	Can't refuse to offer service, can't set price.
Serial killer	Decides when to act, whom to attack.	Police officer	Works an area, assignment. Follows polices, procedures.
Golfer	Decides on whether to play or not, how to hit shots, clubs to play.	Baseball 2nd base player	Plays all balls hit to the 2nd base area, when hitting does as told, etc.
SPECIAL CASES			
Sniper (independent)	Can decide to fire or not. Can accept a contract or not. Can determine when to act.	SWAT team sniper	Has to take the shot if there's an opportunity. Competent. Trained to follow procedures.
Terrorist (independent)	Picks target, selects terrorist device.	Terrorist (in an organization)	Does what is told. Follows procedures, plans.
Researcher	Picks focus, plan of action, hypotheses and tests.	Team researcher	Is a contributor, has an assignment, follows protocols.
Racist	Decides when to act, whom to attack.	Gang violence	Follows the crowd (gang), expected to "go along."
Activist	Picks a target, self-starter, identifies activities. A "personal" mission.	Activist as part of a movement	Does what is told and when. Is told the mission.
Electrician (independent contractor)	Can set fees or not charge, decides how to pursue a job.	Electrician (as part of a company)	Does what is told. Follows procedures, plans.

partners, stakeholders or other fruitful relationships that can meet the needs of a larger organization without having to build or otherwise secure the resources these entities possess. Classification, in short, is important.

Treating singular entities as organizations helps define their relationship to their own or another's stakeholders or supporters. If the assassin is merely treated as an individual, one only targets the event and the performance. However, if one treats the assassin as an extension of the organization that secured his/her services, then one may uncover deeper issues associated with the performance of the event. To treat an assassin as an individual instead of an individual contributor organization can be the difference between a murder and a conspiracy.

Looking at individual contributor organizations helps define their relationship with adversaries. When a competitor decides to subcontract work to individual contributor organizations, it's making a statement about its own organization. Perhaps it doesn't have the management talent or the capital to invest in staffing these resources as its own. Other times subcontractors are a means for improving the credibility of a function, service quality, responsiveness or commitments among key stakeholders (Beverland et al. 2007; Reilly 2008).

Subcontracting work makes one dependent on the work performed by the subcontractor—an outsider. Clothing and shoe companies in the United States had their reputations attacked because of the behavior of their manufacturing subcontractors (Kortelainen 2008; Lim and Phillips 2008; Meyer 2008). Garrett Brown's (2008) research uncovered creative ways some companies comply with corporate social responsibility programs. They can hire "fabrication engineers" who program computers to generate multiple billing hours and sets of wage records, or they can create "shadow factories" that produce an order under terrible working conditions while buyers or their corporate responsibility staffs are shown the clean, well-lit factory around the corner.

Looking at individual contributor organizations is a unique way to understand the motivations, strengths, risks and vulnerabilities behind this special type of organization. Kever (2008), for example, reviewed a change in the ways students choose activism versus protest to demonstrate their personal sentiments. "'It's not really as much protesting as students taking charge,' said Murray Myers, senior at the University of St. Thomas." Kever concludes that activism isn't dead on college campuses, an example of a "community organization"; it's just surfacing in different ways.

The same is true in enterprise organizations. Whistle-blowing is a popular channel for individual contributor roles to emerge.

Whistle-blowing can be used in any type of organization but, perhaps because of the often rigid nature of the enterprise's mission, structure, policies or practices this type of organization is likely to create a foundation for the individual contributor role to emerge. Any hole in a policy or procedure or rule that is unjust or, perhaps, dangerous creates an opportunity for self-organization in the form of the rise of the individual contributor.

Part of the value of looking at the role of individual contributors is the role they play in illustrating how often those in positions of authority aren't successful in managing a situation because they focus on people or personalities and not the problem or issue at hand. The *Industrial Worker*, a magazine published by the Industrial Workers of the World, described a situation in which an employee filed a complaint regarding conditions in the textile plant where he worked. The employee, also an organizer for the Industrial Workers of the World Union, complained that there was no heat in work area. The organization's response to this opportunity to address the issue and provide heat was to attack the individual. "Tom K.," writes the *Industrial Worker*, "filed the complaint in May 2008 over a one-day suspension in December 2007 and threats to 'write him up' (discipline) and fire him" (*Industrial Worker* 2008: 3). The complaint resulted in a National Labor Relations Board ruling in favor of the individual contributor and negative press for the organization.

Unionization, the development of a particular type of community organization, often occurs so that individuals can safely signal dissatisfaction with an organization or its policies, procedures or practices. Unionization efforts typically start with one person, the individual contributor, who independently organizes a network, a team organization that can turn into a union, a community organization. For example, Rafael Irrizarry, in a recent issue of *Science Letter* (October 2008: 3848), accounted for the need of labor union when he said: "We're organizing to improve our working conditions. Right now many of us can't get by on the salaries we make, we don't get any paid sick days and many of us can't afford the health insurance." When individual contributors are subcontractors or adversaries, understanding their operational profile, behaviors, needs, frustrations or desires helps in building plans for their management. Rosenbloom's (2008) review of Wal-Mart, Lim and Phillips' (2008) examination of Nike and Kortelainen's (2008) review of labor condition auditing in the People's Republic of China illustrate how criticisms can make even very large organizations or countries change in response to pressure.

Finally, individual contributors within an organization or as stand-alone organizations fill voids by providing unique skills and talents not already available. Realtors help facilitate the finding and buying of houses, whilst doctors, electricians and lawyers provide specific assistance in technical areas beyond the reach of most people. When inside a larger organization, the individual contributor serves a similar purpose but this dimension can vary significantly depending on the type of organization.

Some organizations, like the enterprises discussed earlier, use internal individual contributors to manage safety and health programs, and organizational development or change programs. Size is one factor determining if and how individual contributors are used, but other times it's the nature of the organization that determines the need. Technical enterprises may need individuals with very specific skills, such as chemists, software engineers or efficiency experts. In these instances the individual contributor fills a specific role and may be the only one devoted to that task in the entire organization. It's a department, an internal organization of one. Other types of organization, such as closed, secret community organizations, seldom use external individual contributors. They either do without or simply isolate their need(s) and grow their own internal talent. Cults, religions and terrorist organizations are examples.

Table 6.1 illustrates the differences between an internal individual contributor and a job type that may be similar. In these examples, the "same" job or assignment differs in the extent to which the activity is defined by the individual (the extent to which the individual can make personal choices), and the extent to which the individual operates in a chiefly "stand-alone" capacity but under the direction and control of others. That doesn't mean the individual contributor doesn't have support or can't collaborate with others. It means that he can and does function as an independent agent.

SO HOW DOES THE INDIVIDUAL CONTRIBUTOR ORGANIZATION WORK?

To individual contributors performance is everything. If they can't perform as expected, they can be out of a job, lose a contract, hurt their reputation or image, in short, possibly lose their capacity to operate as an individual contributor. Certainly performance is important for the other three organizational types, too, but the difference is that because of the focus on one person in the individual contributor organization, if that person fails, the system is under serious threat of failure. And if there is that level of failure in any organization, the consequences can be dire.

Failure or lack of performance can translate into loss of independence, and that can result in a dissolving of the individual contributor organization. If an electrician fails to perform well as an individual contributor, the only choice available is to join an enterprise if he/she wants to continue working in that profession. (Note: in contrast to the fate potentially facing the individual contributor, an electrician who is part of a community, enterprise or team organization may receive a poor review but be allowed to continue, could be transferred or join another organization in a similar job.)

Knowledge and competencies must be high to exceptional. A person in this role has something to contribute that may have value and is capable of fulfilling often very specific needs. Doctors and lawyers have fulfilled educational requirements and often have some level of specialization. The same is true for most professional occupations. While not all individual contributor organizations need a type of certification to document their knowledge levels, they do need to be recognized as competent by those wishing to use their services. A group seeking to hire an assassin needs some indication that the person can carry out the task at hand—that the candidate for "this position" has achieved a level of marksmanship or, perhaps, has trained and been "certified" in a "terrorist training camp." These credentials signify the likelihood this individual contributor can successfully perform as expected.

Any individual contributor, from the drug-runner, politician, baseball pitcher or hitter, racecar driver, must be able to demonstrate the competencies, "potentially" to perform as expected. Independent consultants are dependent on excellent communication practices to perform successfully. This implies a capacity to use information and communication to keep clients informed, as well as to collect the data, intelligence or advice needed to enhance the knowledge required to perform as expected.

Individual contributors maintain some link to a larger organization but have their own vision for themselves. They have formal or informal procedures that guide their work and, most importantly, they measure their performance against generally accepted standards. They may be monitored but not directed in the strictest sense. While a manager shares the responsibility for the work of a subordinate, individual contributors are responsible for what they do. They may even set up their own schedules for projects, and they may prepare their own plans. The issue for the individual contributor is performance, and this performance is always associated with someone else in some capacity or other.

While the individual contribution organization may have greater latitude in what tasks get done and how, the role of others in defining the level of acceptability of performance is significant. Dancers, artists, doctors, electricians, judges, cab drivers, even the terrorist who detonates the bomb, are examples of individual contributors whose work is always gauged against the expectations of another: did the performance observed match what was expected?

A weak link for the individual contributor organization is its dependence on others for a successful evaluation or as sources of the information needed to accomplish an assignment. It's through people that the tasks needed to achieve an organization's goals are evaluated. But effective transactions between people are not simply "done." They are constructed in terms of the nature of the situation, to meet the needs of the people involved and reflect the competencies and character of those constructing them.

Individual contributors' roles are unique but they do not have to be. People sometimes occupy the role of individual contributor because they have key competencies or skills that others in an existing group or team do not have. A small organization may have a need for a lawyer on its staff but not a department of lawyers. Another organization might have a need for a computer programmer with technical expertise in the field but doesn't need a department of programmers.

In other instances, some people find themselves labeled as individual contributors because they are hard to fit into existing groups and departments. They might be a poor fit because of the organization's incapacity to handle special positions or because of the need to have certain positions for a brief period, such as during a crisis. Other times people are separated out as individual contributors because while they offer valuable benefits to the organization, they do not "fit in" with the rest of the organization, and the organization "can't afford to let this person go." We've seen these people. They are the stars, the ones with the ideas, the ones who can sell anything, the ones with tenure and the ones whose fathers own the company. Whatever the reason, they don't fit in with others but they're kept on in the organization—as individual contributors.

Some organizations find it easier to achieve their mission if they are made up of a majority of individual contributors rather than groups or teams of people. Terrorist organizations, for example, often operate more effectively if organized around a collection of individual contributors, each with skills and competencies to perform and complete several tasks or activities. It's hard to control or stamp out these organizations because the organization as a collective doesn't exist; it only exists in the minds of individuals and their attempts to achieve a mission.

THE ABILITY TO INFLUENCE OTHERS IS OFTEN WHAT BEING AN INDIVIDUAL CONTRIBUTOR IS ALL ABOUT

The relationship between an individual contributor's generic or value-added participation is a significant feature of this role in an organization. Value-added participation can be defined as that contribution that doesn't just *meet* expectations, it *exceeds expectations.* Contributions of these levels benefit people or an organization in such a way so that the people, organization, or both, are clearly better off because of the individual contributor's effort. Value-added contributors do not just "get the job done"; they make people and places *significantly* better than they were before the contribution was made, as Figure 6.2 illustrates.

So if a for-profit organization, like a retail store, increased in value, and the change in value could be definitively traced back to the contribution of a specific individual, then we can say that that person's contribution was the difference between "doing the job" and making a "value-added contribution." But value-added contributions aren't restricted to translating into increases in an organization's financial worth. A teacher whose work can be directly attributable to increased competencies in students may be the source of a value-added contribution. The students "benefit" because of the instructor's interventions. An individual contributor's interventions led to the acquisition of new knowledge and information.

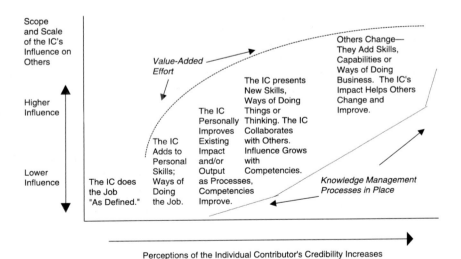

Figure 6.2 Value-Added Participation: Maximizing Change as a Function of One's Credibility and Influence.

An athlete whose participation helps the team win or draws large crowds to the stadium makes a value-added contribution to the team or sports organization. If, too, the fans feel they enjoyed the game more because of the player's skills, competencies or contribution then they are also receiving value-added benefits. They may be happier when they leave than when they came. They may have spent a lot of money on tickets, food and sports paraphernalia but "it was worth it!"

So what makes some individual contributors value-added contributors to an organization or its stakeholders? How can an individual contributor, or anyone for that matter, make value-added contributions in the course of doing his/her work? Just thinking about people or organizations we have known who can be classified as value-adders points to three important factors. They are motivated with a prudent sense of urgency, they are competent, and they are highly credible; they are trustworthy, believable people with whom we interact.

Urgency is marked by a balance. The manner in which one approaches issues also influences one's credibility. "Urgency" reflects both the vision one has of the difference between what a situation is and what it should/could be and a state of readiness for action to achieve a desired changed state. This process of managing one's urgency shapes the formation of individual behavior and/or an entire organization's approach to both planned and unplanned events.

Urgency is not a headlong rush to action. The urgency we're looking for is prudent, grounded in a component of an organization's operational steady state. In this instance, urgency reflects the mental, emotional and physical approach one takes to thoughts and actions. "Providing good customer service" is an example of "urgency" in many good retail environments. Secret or closed organizations might have a sense of urgency built around maintaining the secrecy or security of their operations. Likewise, a student with a vision of attending a top university might have a high sense of urgency to do well in classes so as to maintain a high grade point. Urgency means knowing what *is* important.

Competence is the great enabler for the individual contributor. Competency needs to be mastered on two levels. The first level is reflected by five categories. These are the skills and abilities needed to do a job, work in a company, be in a relationship, engage in cultural interactions, or do any of the other things that happen to us daily. The first four categories are outlined in Table 6.2. The fifth competency, cultural competency, is a constant across all situations.

Four core competencies include the "basic skills" associated with the job to be done or situation to be managed and a category labeled "interpersonal/group." This category reflects the skills and competencies useful when interacting with others in the situation. "Administrative competencies" reflect the managerial, administrative, sometimes even bureaucratic detail work associated with the job or situation. A fourth category, "occupational" competencies, defines those skills that may be specifically associated with the work to be done or the situation. An accountant needs occupational competencies in the field of accounting, but an accountant who happens to be trying to save a person from drowning needs a totally different set of "occupational/situational" competencies. (The fifth competency, cultural competency, helps people to interact successfully with members of different races, religions, sexes and cultural groups, to name a few.)

The illustrations presented in Table 6.2 are for four different situations. A quick review of this table illustrates some of the unique

Table 6.2   Competency Requirements across Different Settings and Events

SITUATION: PLAYING BASEBALL		SITUATION: ARGUING WITH BEST FRIEND	
Occupational/ situational competencies	Administrative competencies	Occupational/ situational competencies	Administrative competencies
Hitting	Coaching	Problem-solving	Fact-finding
Running	Field direction	Debating	Note-taking
Catching	Position management	Solution building	Relationship mgmt
Basic skills competencies	Interpersonal/group competencies	Basic skills competencies	Interpersonal/group competencies
Logic	Listening	Planning	Listening
Problem-solving	Cooperating	Logic	Verbal communication
Decision-making	Communicating	Organization	Discussion
SITUATION: BUYING A CAR		SITUATION: GETTING A JOB	
Occupational/ situational competencies	Administrative competencies	Occupational/ situational competencies	Administrative competencies
Shopping	Meeting management	Research/job search	Note-taking
Decision-making	Negotiation	Interviewing skills	Meeting scheduling
		Resumé writing	
Basic skills competencies	Interpersonal/group competencies	Basic skills competencies	Interpersonal/group competencies
Basic math	Listening	Telephone	Listening
	Questioning	Writing (letters)	Speaking

challenges people and organizations face as they try to develop and use the competencies needed to do a job or handle a situation. For example, the importance of a competency varies from situation to situation. "Problem-solving" can be considered an "occupational or situational" competency in an argument between two people and a "basic skill" for a baseball player.

The need or potential value of a competency also can change as conditions change. The ability to speak clearly becomes a more important competency for an adult than it is for a child. This is an important point for a second reason and that is that competencies are learned and developed skills. People aren't born with competencies; they learn them. And, if competencies are learned, that means they have levels of achievement that can be marked and measured over time.

People lose their effectiveness when they stop consistently maintaining or developing new competencies over time. This is especially true about critical, life-long competencies like communication, relationship management, listening, or the like, that are needed throughout one's life and across a variety of situations. Competencies also can reveal something about the performance one might expect from people, whether in our organization or as participants in a competing organization. This, in turn, adds to perceptions of the other's credibility as a co-worker or adversary.

Credibility is a by-product of competency; it is reflected in a person's behavioral style, the way they do their work. But credibility is not just tied up in the ways one maintains personal or specialized competencies. Rather credibility is often directly tied to the ways competencies, in conjunction with urgency, are translated into behavior. We not only can do things differently with age, education or experience but others *expect* us to behave differently as we achieve these benchmarks.

Unfortunately, some people may not believe they need to maintain or develop competencies with time. Consider Figure 6.3. The two lines on the left side reflect the level of performance the company needs at a given point in time (the double line) and the level of competency the Chief Operating Officer (CEO) currently possesses (the dotted line). In the figure we see that the CEO's competency is a little below what is needed (perhaps new accounting or technologies have been introduced that the CEO is not familiar with yet) but the difference is not critical.

However, on the right side of the chart, the moments after the "X" event has occurred, things are quite different. The company might have gone public (which can demand new finance and business development skills the CEO does not have) or it might represent a crisis the company is facing (perhaps a hostile takeover or bankruptcy) that demands

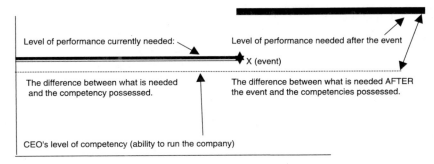

Figure 6.3 Performance, Competency and Time (time may be linear but performance and competency must be dynamic).

skills the CEO does not have. In this case the level of performance needed (the heavy, dark line) is much further away from the dotted line that represents the competencies possessed. In this case, the CEO has not done anything to develop the skills or competencies needed to manage events like the one that occurred at "X" so it's conceivable the CEO's credibility will suffer as a result.

Impressions of the person who has not maintained needed competencies are seldom positive, particularly if the person is in a leadership position. Table 6.2 illustrates a key fact regarding this point: an individual typically needs more than a few competencies to be successful. For example, the skills that contributed to a baseball player's success may not transfer to different situations or settings. Team managers or a job as a sports announcer are certainly related to the athlete's work but they require new and different competencies. The settings are different, have different performance requirements and, subsequently, different competency requirements.

Finally, as Figure 6.2 illustrated, the potential value of maintaining one's competencies, particularly for individual contributors, can help an individual increase credibility and thereby potentially increase one's capacity to help and/or influence others. This, in turn, can impact the level of change experienced by those the individual contributor is influencing and this, in turn, can have positive impact on the organization.

Credibility for the individual contributor can have one significant dimension associated with it that transcends competency and that is professional ethics. Since this person, sometimes more so than most others in an organization, has the potential not only to influence and conceivably benefit others, but also the organization as a whole, the position often requires it be managed with the highest ethical standards.

Financial advisors, lawyers, police officers, politicians, teachers and doctors are examples of positions with significant spans of influence. These positions impact people's lives. Consequently, successful performance requires that everything associated with the position reflect standards associated with it.

The list of expectations is long but not impossible to achieve. It includes behaviors like honesty, fairness and integrity. It is assumed people in these positions will not steal from their clients, will not participant in efforts to entrap their clients, will not falsify data or information, will not take bribes, will evaluate students fairly and will not violate patient confidentialities. Perhaps what makes "ethical behavior" so unique for the individual contributor is that what looks so much like a learned competency is merely just another human trait.

DESTABILIZING THE INDIVIDUAL CONTRIBUTOR

Individual contributor organizations can be destabilized in several ways. One important device used focuses on undermining or challenging the individual contributor's credibility. This can be done in a variety of ways, from the legitimate to those methods that are clearly underhanded. For example, challenging the decisions, processes or results achieved, particularly those relying on the individual contributor's services, is one way to impact their credibility.

The goal here is to cause those relying on the individual contributor to question whether or not using this resource is the most effective way to manage a situation. For example, if the individual contributor is an independent consultant one might ask if a team of people might better manage the issue at hand, perhaps implying that the individual contributor does not have the resources needed. This tactic often is associated with people jealous of, or threatened by, the presence of an individual contributor.

Additionally, since ethics is such a critical requirement for many individual contributors anything that can compromise or bring the individual's ethics into question can potentially impact the individual contributor's credibility. Recent history contains examples of very competent politicians, religious leaders, financial and business professionals whose actions challenged their ethical character and, in turn, their capacity to hold their positions. What makes ethical challenges most significant is that while they may be made by another, it is the individual's personal behavior that ultimately undermines his/her credibility.

A second way to compromise an individual contributor is to create distractions that keep the individual contributor from tracking on the problem or task assigned. Distractions can come in many forms. Mental or emotional distractions, for example, created by an ethical dilemma, can chip away at the time the individual contributor has to complete an assignment. Sometimes these are in the form of personal attacks, other times the distractions surface in the form of issues designed to look as though they are related to the matter at hand but, in fact, are not.

For example, an individual contributor brought in to "improve operations" or organizational processes might be sidetracked in a number of ways. The use of rumors or false allegations meant to suggest that processes are not broken, that the problem is poor management, is a potential way to distract the individual contributor. These types of device can make a seemingly straightforward project look more like a quagmire and well beyond the individual contributor's scope of interest or expertise.

Burying the individual contributor in minutia, bureaucracy or detail, as opposed to strategic issues, can lead to physical, mental or emotional burnout, which are effective ways to undermine an individual contributor's effectiveness or range of work. In this instance the focus isn't on diverting the individual contributor's attention from the prescribed mission but rather to make processes, sometimes very natural processes associated with accomplishing the mission, a drag on the individual contributor's energy or activity.

This can result in anything from physical fatigue or emotional frustration as the individual contributor simply tries to do what is expected. This is an especially effective device because is demands few resources on the part of those attempting to destabilize the individual contributor and, in many instances, those used are often readily available.

Finally, a truly effective way to hamstring individual contributors is to have them report to people without vision—bureaucrats, low-level supervisors or people easily threatened by those with a sense of urgency, strong competencies or particular capabilities associated with a task or mission. Most organizations have people like these who have managed to survive purges or who dodge responsibility by being in the right place at the right time, having friends in the right place, or simply being part of an organization afraid to tackle key tough personnel issues. They simply rise to power and ineffectiveness.

SUMMARY OF THE INDIVIDUAL CONTRIBUTOR ORGANIZATION

There's nothing contrived or hypothetical about these illustrations; in fact, there are often many opportunities to see these and other tactics used by any number of organizations. Political organizations, cults and religions, educational centers and businesses with weak operational practices ultimately find they are unable to support efforts to achieve the organization's mission. Indeed, this is another illustration of ways aspects of complexity theory can be mapped in organizations.

Each of the illustrations discussed is an example of self-organized behavior; individuals taking it upon themselves to organize and use these and other tactics to disrupt a targeted person, program or activity. Sometimes organizational theorists use labels like "resistance to change," "turf wars," "personality conflicts" or the like to describe the use of these types of tactic but they are, in fact, just other examples of inappropriate, self-organized behavior.

PART II

Challenges to Individual and Organizational Performance and Effectiveness

The formula seems so simple. Build your organization so that participants can manage life's conflicts, opportunities and challenges and add the right mix of properly constructed activities that focus on achieving the organization's vision and success will follow. It's a theme reflected in business, religions, self-help books, advice columns and even efforts used to manage world affairs: invade Iraq and the United States, with better equipment, experience and skills, will control Iraqi behavior. Well, the logic is, at least, simple.

One soon finds, however, that dealing with life and life events is not that simple. Life, it seems, is full of events and people that can produce hassles and situations that are difficult, sometimes seemingly impossible to control or manage regardless of one's available resources. Indeed, life's "little complexities" can so shape the behavior, activities, even destinies of organizations and individuals that few things seem to turn out exactly as planned or expected.

If this were a perfect world, one would not expect to see the number of complaints and business failures, rules, regulations and government agencies established to protect people and organizations one does. However, negligent, sometimes even malicious, actions seem to pose ongoing threats to the health and well-being of people wherever they are. There are reports of lawyers and doctors who behave unethically, of religious and political leaders who are morally corrupt and terrorists willing to launch fear campaigns at anyone, any time and anywhere. Even driving one's car can pose serious threats to one's health and well-being. Roadways may be in need of repair and the role of the aggressive driver can make even the shortest trip a nerve-racking experience.

This book's underlying theme addresses two issues. First, the material presented seeks to explain how behaviors, actions, events and performances like those described emerge and, second, how organizations or people in organizations can prepare for and, if needed, respond to undesirable circumstances when they do emerge. The early chapters laid a foundation for answering these questions by outlining some fundamental features of organizations. They presented elements that simultaneously define an organization's capacity for performance and illustrate ways poor design can contribute to poor or unsatisfactory operation. In addition, the early chapters introduced examples of ways factors outside an organization also may affect an organization and its participants.

In this section, the inherent nature of events and the role of risks, threats and vulnerabilities are explored in detail. Risks, threats and vulnerabilities are performance challenges that may emerge because of an organization's design, the ways the organization developed, or the nature of the organization's purpose or pursuit. They often accompany the construction of events an organization is expected to manage.

However, risks, threats and vulnerabilities also are unique because they can emerge after engagement in an event. History contains examples of organizations exposed to great risks, because of exposure to natural events, like a tornado or hurricane, or an adversary's sudden attack. The attacks on the United States on 9/11 continue to shape the lives and lifestyles of people in the United States and, in some cases, countries around the world.

What makes events so important to an organization is the pivotal role they have as links between the organization's vision/mission and its performance. Events are that place where the organization seeks to achieve its mission through performance while struggling to keep risk, vulnerabilities and threats in check. Complexity theory is used as a tool for both describing and explaining the ramifications associated with poor event management in organizations. The theory makes certain assumptions about the relationship between the ways and manner in which events unfold and its application illustrates why approaching events in a straightforward, linear fashion may be of only limited strategic usefulness, regardless of the resources, amount of planning and preparation used in anticipation of the event.

Change and events are, for the most part, naturally occurring phenomena in organizations. The emergence of events marks a point where two dynamic phenomena, the organization and the event, come into contact. The question framed in the following chapters is how or to what extent can organizations maximize the likelihood they'll get the results they want from events that constantly change and foment change in the organization(s) and people they affect.

CHAPTER 7

Performance Effectiveness and Threats, Risks and Vulnerabilities

A number of factors influence the successful management of an event. The model in Figure 7.1 summarizes key components of the event-management process and introduces the wide-scale potential of threats, risk and vulnerabilities to the organization. As Figure 7.1 illustrates, threats, risk and vulnerabilities present potential challenges to an event's successful management.

An organization's overall strength is a measure of both the resources and the quality of those resources available to deliver ongoing operational activity. Strength is a composite measure. It is a combination of the typical core resources one associates with organizations (e.g., financial funds and human competencies) and the process resources available, such as the capacity of the organization to meet internal and external stakeholder needs. Finally, as a composite measure strength is widely distributed in the organization, so an organization needs more than just people, financial reserves or the best technology. It needs depth across all critical areas.

Readiness is a measure of the organization's capacity to respond, its capability to manage events as they arise, whether in anticipated or unanticipated ways. In many ways readiness is both a key operating organizational dimension and a "fail-safe" should a crisis emerge. In either case readiness is a measure of the membership's (leadership's or the general population's) vision and proactive nature. Individuals demonstrate readiness through the capacity to adapt to changing situations—the capacity to invent a response to events, situations or circumstances as they arise. At the organizational level readiness is most apparent in programs, practices and procedures. A "succession plan," for example, is a prudent way to prepare for the loss of key personnel just as an evacuation plan is a prudent way to prepare for potentially life-threatening emergencies that may arise.

Organization Type and Format	Effectiveness Profile	Hazard Profile	Event Phases and Performance Expectations			Effects	Consequences: Evoking Future Challenges		
			Pre-Event	Event	Post-Event		Risk	Threat	Vulnerability
Community Enterprise Team Individual Contributor	Participant Performance Makeup • Competencies • Urgency • Experience	Risk, Threat, Vulnerability				Results and Residuals			
	Organization Makeup • Culture • Practices • Structure					Product			
						Outcome			
						Impact			

Figure 7.1 Event Flow Associated with Event Management: Full Stream View, From Organization Type to Consequences.

RISKS, THREATS AND VULNERABILITIES REFER TO THE EXPOSURES FACING THE ORGANIZATION

Failure to build and maintain a strong "effectiveness profile" can make the organization susceptible to three potentially debilitating phenomena: risks, threats and vulnerabilities, the latter perhaps the most insidious of the three. The active challenges to an organization's effectiveness stems from the ways these three can become part of, enmeshed in, the organization's daily operation, because they can influence, overshadow or aggravate without necessarily materializing. As Table 7.1 illustrates, what makes risks, threats and vulnerabilities interesting, unpredictable and dangerous is that they are not simply negative products of unsuccessful organizations; they may be associated with any organization.

A weak effectiveness profile can become interpreted as an "exposure profile" as risks, threats and vulnerabilities unfold. Risks are among

Table 7.1 Opening the Door to Risk, Threats, Vulnerabilities: Possible Negative Products, Outcomes and Impacts Associated with Problem Events

REPRESENTATIVE PROBLEM EVENTS	REPRESENTATIVE NEGATIVE PRODUCTS	REPRESENTATIVE NEGATIVE OUTCOMES	REPRESENTATIVE NEGATIVE IMPACTS
"Airport security is 'uneven'" (vulnerability in a controlled setting)	• Travelers feel hassled • Terrorists see gaps as opportunities	Airline travel drops off, finger-pointing in Washington	Potential knee-jerk reaction, more bureaucracy, more restrictions, confusion
"Competitor releases better product" (potential threat from outside)	• Our sales are down • Lots of talk • Increased quality emphasis	• Customer confidence drops • Credibility as a innovator is challenged	Lower profits, loss of market share, customer loyalty erodes
"Employees don't know what's expected of them" (risk employees may not do what needs to be done)	• Work is incomplete • Missed goals	• Poor productivity • Employee frustration • Faulty performance reviews	Angry employees, other departments and/or customers confused
"Customers slow to pay bills" (risk cash-flow issues)	• Cash flow problems • Credit problems building	Credit rating suffers, cannot purchase goods for production	Lose customers, image is tarnished, some slow payers default, profits hurt

(Continued)

Table 7.1 (Continued) Opening the Door to Risk, Threats, Vulnerabilities: Possible Negative Products, Outcomes and Impacts Associated with Problem Events

REPRESENTATIVE PROBLEM EVENTS	REPRESENTATIVE NEGATIVE PRODUCTS	REPRESENTATIVE NEGATIVE OUTCOMES	REPRESENTATIVE NEGATIVE IMPACTS
Difficulty quitting smoking (risk of health problems)	• Doctor forecasts health problems • Pressure and arguments at home	• Missed time from work • Physical damage to the body • Cannot smoke indoors • Increased costs	Some ridicule, lower self-esteem, reduced stamina makes it difficult to play with kids
Biased managers (vulnerable to litigation)	• Biased hiring decisions • Biased performance reviews • Favoritism	• Disgruntled employees • Employee conflict	Poor morale, talk of unionization and/or potential legal action
Poor cross-cultural communication interactions (risk of conflict)	• Avoid international travel • Tendency to stay "with one's own" • Learning foreign languages	Stereotypes or prejudices develop	• Biased view of the world • Little tolerance for other groups • Tendency to see attributes as racially based
Poor customer service (risk customer dissatisfaction)	• Customer dissatisfaction • Loss of sale	• No desire to shop there again. • Customers "spread the word"	• Business suffers • Consumer protection agency is asked to investigate
Terrorist detonates bomb (threat of injury, loss of life)	• Injuries • Destruction • Notoriety	• Fear • Confusion • Anger	• Diversion of funds to troops • Reduced freedoms • Finger pointing

the most familiar of the three components of a hazard profile. *Risks* often occur naturally—for example, as associated with the "cost of doing business." Risks are phenomena often associated with an organization's inherent nature or the conditions under which the organization functions. There are risks for a law-enforcement organization just as there are risks associated with their adversary, the criminal organization.

Risks are important for several reasons. They can result in loss, they can be indicators of inherent vulnerabilities, they may result in the emergence of a threat, or they may create the potential for vulnerabilities to arise (e.g., when a risk weakens the organization so that it is vulnerable to attack, loss of market share, defeat, etc.).

An organization's risk exposures can shift attention from positive activities to speculations regarding the organization as a "gamble." This is because "risk" tends to imply "uncertainty" and uncertainty can create a sense of doubt regarding the organization's capability to perform as expected, a sense of suspicion or perhaps that one is not getting the full picture. On another level, risk can lead to skepticism about the organization's true potential or general concern about the organization's capabilities. Risk is a potential liability and not an asset.

Threats are meaningful, existing or potential phenomena that can negatively influence the organization. Threats are most significant when made by aggressors or strong opponents. Threats also are significant when they can result in loss, when they are imminent, or most likely to occur. Finally, what makes threats particularly distracting is that, because they are beyond the scope of the organization to control, they can only be prepared for or anticipated.

Threats can result from poor planning or preparation, for example, a threat of action brought on by the mismanagement of an assignment for a key customer. Threats from the outside can come from adversaries, monitoring organizations (e.g., regulatory bodies) or natural phenomena (e.g., tornadoes). The potential for the threat to effect the organization directly links with the organization's vulnerabilities and general exposure profile. The potential for loss increases as the right match between threat and vulnerability emerges, and the greater the vulnerability and likelihood the threat will materialize, the higher the risk levels. So, threats can emerge from inside or outside the organization and they may be real or potential but they are a liability because they always have an effect; they cause those in the organization to shift attention to the threat.

Vulnerabilities are exposures that reflect a potential for the organization to suffer from or succumb to some or all of the negative effects of threats and risks. Vulnerabilities are most significant when threats (e.g., from aggressors or competitors) are present, when they can result in losses that aggravate already bad conditions or when the right conditions are present for them to emerge (such as when an organization is vulnerable to a hurricane or flood).

Vulnerabilities are best viewed as liabilities—not assets. Since vulnerabilities are real and not imagined, they have an added effect on the organization's readiness profile. Resources that might otherwise be used to advance the organization are held "for an emergency" or diverted to fund activities designed to address or contain the vulnerability. Time management issues, for example, can signal that potential vulnerabilities exist or that actual vulnerabilities are creating problems, additional workloads, or process breakdowns, slow-downs or stoppages.

Vulnerabilities and risks are within the control of the organization to prevent and manage. Threats, which reflect intent and capability of someone else, are often beyond the control of the organization to prevent. Usually the organization's best defense against threats is the preparation of responses in advance and sufficient readiness should the threat materialize. Finally, it is easier to predict potential vulnerabilities and risks than threats because of the organization's role in creating them. Good operational practices, proficiencies in key competencies and fundamentals (e.g., performance management and communication and information management) can help manage them and their effects.

MAPPING THE RELATIONSHIP BETWEEN BEHAVIOR (PERFORMANCE) AND THE EMERGENCE OF RISKS, THREATS AND VULNERABILITIES

Figure 7.2 describes the relationship between thresholds and behavior. It's presented here to illustrate ways behavior can contribute to the emergence of risks, threats and vulnerabilities. The levels presented in the figure can be interpreted as rating scales. On the upper path, the ascent of positive behavior begins at that point where the organization establishes norms for behavior. For example, as in a retail store when an employee is instructed, "When dealing with a customer ...", or as a parent educates a child on roadway safety, "Before crossing the street be sure to look to your left and then to your right."

Behavior that exceeds expectations defines the first significant level on the ascent. Here the capacity to manage the event(s) is an important characteristic. Conversely, the risk is that performance can regress, but if that regression is to the norm, then that's still acceptable. If the regression continues farther that's another issue.

Evaluations performed at this level tend to focus on acknowledging over-ordinary performance, with hopes that the performance will continue. Communication tends to be friendly, as one might expect. Knowledge acquisition may be nominal but, interestingly, it's sufficient for innovation to occur, as the individual strives to meet or exceed the norm. Additionally, this is also a point where the emergence of positive, self-directed behavior occurs.

The second level reflects behavior that may be distinctly different from the norm. The behavior remains acceptable but it is clearly different

The Norm	Extend the Norm	Exceed the Norm	Forsake the Old for New
At this point the norm is established with a good deal of activity around expected behavior.	This threshold marks a real but still related relationship between the norm and the emerging behavior.	This threshold marks the new organization's birth. Its relationship to the norms is evident but distinct. The norm must catch up or be lost!	The new behavior has emerged and must be maintained. A new organization may emerge. Its lineage to the former can be established.

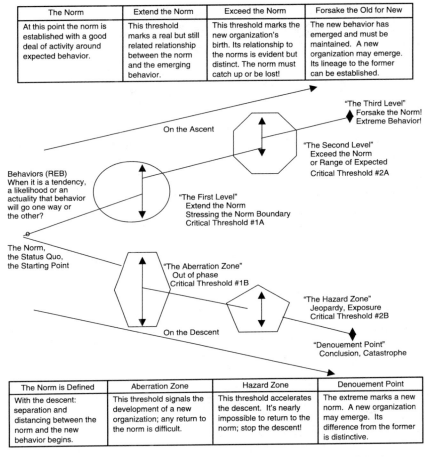

The Norm is Defined	Aberration Zone	Hazard Zone	Denouement Point
With the descent: separation and distancing between the norm and the new behavior begins.	This threshold signals the development of a new organization; any return to the norm is difficult.	This threshold accelerates the descent. It's nearly impossible to return to the norm; stop the descent!	The extreme marks a new norm. A new organization may emerge. Its difference from the former is distinctive.

Figure 7.2   The Genealogy of Behavior: The Manufacture of Positive and Negative Behaviors (a major shortcoming of most performance measures is that they deal only with the positive or "ascent score").

from what was expected. The behavioral process is organized, focused and evaluated through ongoing, self-monitoring efforts. Risk exposures at this level are personal but they can leave the individual vulnerable to undesirable conditions, as when individuals "burn out" or become disillusioned because of lack of support.

Level three is notable for two distinct reasons. First, it reflects the highest level of "good" behavior. Behavior at this level reflects an exceptional display of the core, normative behavior. However, this behavior is so extreme it carries with it higher than average risk for failure because the behavior displayed greatly exceeds what is planned or expected. It's the type of behavior that can result in awards for bravery, or death. It's like the person who extends the normative expectation for "emptying a building during a fire emergency," to behavior that has the individual emerge as a hero for rushing back into the burning building several times to rescue trapped co-workers. It is behavior that results in potentially extreme benefits for the organization … or risks disaster. It is the basketball player who, rather than play it safe and "go for a tie," takes it upon himself to risk taking a shot, loses the ball to the other team, and they score and win.

Behavior at this level is self-monitoring, systematic and within a narrow range; it's behavior with a very personal purpose. Most behavioral practices reflect the strained nature of the situation. Knowledge, information and communication practices are restricted and focused on factors associated with the situation. As misunderstandings or communication gaps surface, relationship practices may be abandoned, as those on the "outside" extend peer pressure to rein in individuals perceived as "having lost focus."

Emergent, self-organized behavior can pose a threat to the organization if it leads to fragmenting or dissent. Martin Luther's complaints, for example, may have been valid and warranted but the emergence of an entirely new sect within the Church was the extreme outcome. Behavior can stimulate cultural change at this level. The behavior associated with emerging change may be within the "spirit," within the culture's rules, policies and procedures, but far enough outside the boundaries that are perceived as acceptable that the change risks trends and directions contrary to those supported by the culture. Change of this sort is seldom acceptable in any organizations.

Movement up or down, self-organized behavior, in the model is marked by crossing key thresholds. The construction of rational decisions marks the move from, and in some instances a break with, established norms, practices and/or expectations. The already reviewed hero's positive, proactive behavior is a case in point. On the other hand, the behavior of those who violate laws, codes of ethics or generally accepted social conventions (like "we don't bring weapons into a school room and shoot classmates") are examples of behaviors on the descent. Clearly the potential threat of tragedy can occur on either the ascent or descent from the norm but it's most likely when behavior is on the descent.

The descent begins with a negative departure from the norm. Unlike the first ascent stage where the norms boundaries may be tested or "pushed," when the descent begins the norm is simply ignored. If the norm is, "Answer the phone by stating your name and asking how to be of service," then the alternative at this level may be merely answering the phone with a "hello." If the norm is a "speed limit of 35 mph," then drive "at a speed of 45 mph."

Even as one moves in a self-organized, ascending relationship to the norm, the ascending move continues to be in accord with the spirit of the fundamental norm. This is not the case in a self-organized descent from the norm. With the descent the individual is making a statement about both the salience of the norm, one's regard for principles upon which the norm is based and a certain willingness to accept growing levels of risk, threat and vulnerabilities because of one's acts. The latter is especially likely as one gets further from the norm.

A move, either ascent or descent, requires that a threshold must be crossed. The most notable feature of thresholds is that they mark a point where rational decision-making occurs in this behavioral change process. The individual recognizes trade-offs or risks associated with following and deviating from the norm and then acts. It's what Tim Harford refers to as people behaving rationally. "Rational people," he writes,

> respond to trade-offs and to incentives. When the costs or benefits of something change, people change their behavior. Rational people think—not always consciously—about the future as well as the present as they try to anticipate likely consequences of their actions in an uncertain world.
>
> (Harford 2008: 4, 9–10)

Our approach extends Harford's notion to include their actions in a "*certain*" world, a world where the publication of rules, norms and laws are designed and published to reduce or eliminate ambiguity, and expectations regarding how one should behave are clear and violated.

The descent from the norm signals a distancing between the individual and the organization. It's distancing that can be observed in the ways dissenting individuals or groups regard operational practices. Communication may be measured, unfriendly, even hostile or threatening. Information and evaluation practices may be limited and sometimes only nurtured for the dissenting individual(s). Finally, relational practices are self-centered to reduce risk (e.g., of discovery) and perhaps abusive or threatening toward others. For example, if the descent from the norm is "aggressive driving" at the first level, this can advance into "hostile driving" at higher levels where the driver attempts to harm the other driver or that driver's property.

From level one the descending process can advance from threatening to dangerous or frightening. The critical nature of this threshold is that when the deviation is on the part of an organization (e.g., the United States' departure from a peaceful position toward a hostile relationship with Iran), it signals the transformation toward a different organizational profile, in this case an organization at war. When an individual creates the deviation the change can reflect emergence of a new persona, different moods or a behavioral style in response to the emerging situation(s) at hand.

It's not within the scope of this work to explore all of the possible conditions associated with these divergent moves from the norm, but it is interesting to note that when divergence results in conflicts, interpersonal dynamics can change in a variety of ways as the nature of risks, threats and vulnerability emerge. In contrast to a positive ascent where the individual may manage much of the ascent at a very personal level, the opposite can be true when observing a descent from the norm. Many who study conflict resolution see acts associated with conflict as forcing the organization to add to its capacity to perform in what may be emerging as an increasingly hostile environment. In other words, it's as though those moving toward anti-social conditions have to begin to behave in more anti-social ways in order to perform successfully in events associated with the changing conditions. The same isn't true for those on the ascent; they don't necessarily "act happier" as they engage in over-the-top positive behaviors.

Both organizations and individuals can seek collaborators, associates or sympathizers who "understand why the downward divergence was necessary." These may be allies who can share the view or rationalizations that the shift from the norm was necessary, or compatriots who can join in the revolt against the norm, against the organization (Bueno de Mesquita 2002; Harrison 2006; Schellenberg 1982). The need for the development of new relationships with people of a similar mind stems largely from the fact that the "descending organization/individual" is not only diverging from an established norm, but also from the organization/individual who posted the norm. In other words, one doesn't usually need a lawyer for doing the right thing better, but one might need one because of increased risks or vulnerabilities resulting from choosing not to do the right thing from the beginning.

The third level, the hazard zone, marks a point of near-no-return. At this point the issue isn't poor customer service, it's rudeness bordering on hostility. Behavior and associated risks here are at the extreme. The behavior is not ridicule; it is blatant discrimination and the risk is not reprimand, it's punishment that can lead to dismissal. Within organizations, this level marks a point where decisions that led to this level consolidate into new policies, procedures and practices that reflect the organization's new position. A revolutionary organization (community) at this level moves from objecting, to demonstrations, to acts of resistance, to recognition that one risks arrest and detainment. Each conclusion marks a further step in the process and deeper solidification of the new persona for itself, the opposition and those in between or "on the fence."

Communication practices can evolve into rancorous threats or malicious displays bounded by guarded, secretive intra-organizational communications to reduce risk. Knowledge and information practices may become reactive activities designed to serve the new organization's need to preserve itself and to address vulnerabilities. In short, the organization's overall processes tend to reflect a position that is defensive, combative, hostile and potentially pathological. The same can be true for individuals at this level.

The last level of descent, denouement, marks a distinct break between the norm and the current state. If there is an emotional link between the two, it is usually negative. If separation hasn't already occurred, it does now. The time for remediation or ultimatums is passed; it's "termination for cause," "declarations of war" or "divorce." Relational behavior is self-serving, communication may become hostile and in some instances threatening, vicious or warlike. Physical behavior, too, can become excessive as threats materialize into extremes and terms like "going postal," "suicidal" or "threats to national security" are labels to describe potential conditions or the basis for reactions from others.

This brief synopsis of the genealogy of behavior as it unfolds over time or circumstances sets the stage for in-depth illustrations of complexity theory in organizations. The genealogy model is particularly useful as a means for gaining insights into two key elements of complexity theory: emergence and the self-organization of behavior. Of particular interest are three issues. First, what is the critical point signaling the move from one stage to a threshold in the emergence process? Second, what defines the threshold for each stage and, third, what types of condition trigger the move from a threshold to the next stage?

The sum total of an organization's effort to design, build and maintain itself and its operations becomes its "effectiveness profile," its "brand" or image to uphold among stakeholders. This profile is a composite of three factors: past performance, readiness and overall strength or capacity to perform. Additionally, performance also reflects an organization's attractiveness as a function of three key features: its accomplishments (for example, its success in building effective structures, systems and environments); second, the organization's progress in achieving its mission; and third, its fulfillment of stakeholder needs. Ideally, performance is measured against a priori defined indicators rather than some *post hoc*, "feel good" convenience scores.

THE EMERGENCE OF RISKS, THREATS AND VULNERABILITIES

An organization's generic strengths, use of operational practices and procedures and overall competency to perform are among the resources potentially available to manage risks, threats and vulnerabilities. If we think of organizations ranked on a performance scale (like that introduced earlier) from strongest to weakest or poorest, it's logical to conclude that the stronger the organization, the more likely it will be able to control the maturation of risks, threats or vulnerabilities.

Table 7.2 provides illustrations of signs that critical states may be emerging for the organization. In the table, the information presented reflects the organization as a whole, the department or group level and the individual's perspective. The table's contents illustrate physical, cognitive, emotional and psychological factors that define critical states associated with risks, threats and vulnerabilities and these, in turn, are mediated by prior experiences (history of direct *and* indirect experience) and existing conditions.

Maturation of a Risk

Risk may also go unnoticed when key practices and programs are weak or missing. The American car industry offers another example. Quality and service programs so common today were not as prevalent in the 1980s, so when American buyers looked to the Japanese for fuel-efficient cars during the oil and gas shortages, they often found better service and quality as well. This accelerated the risk of competition for the American manufacturers.

Proactive organizations try to anticipate emerging risk. They conduct audits or evaluations, at least in key areas known to carry certain potential risks. If there are known risks, efforts often focus on identifying and ranking them in terms of their importance. Exposures are communicated to stakeholders and programs launched to manage the risk.

It's a straightforward process. The organization's leadership knows the risk challenges facing the organization, sees them as part of the "cost of doing business" and deploys appropriate management strategies to address them. The "right" people are in place, doing the right job at the

Table 7.2 Roots of Self-Organization—Signs Possibly Indicating a Critical State is Emerging: Representative Organizational and Individual Examples

	ORGANIZATIONAL LEVEL	GROUP OR DEPARTMENT LEVEL	INDIVIDUAL LEVEL
Mild or early signs of problems	• Give backs, gifts, rebates • Media/web reports of problems • Inventory shrinkages appear	• Unwanted turnover in key areas • Missed milestones • Poor quality/service • Problem management is the focus	• Good performance • Routine matters slip • Missed deadlines; lost time • People stop talking to each other • Skipped processes or routines
More severe signs of problems	• Miss launch dates • Turnover of key staff • Lost time due to injury, illness • Complaints re: products, service • Launch special programs • Investigations • Cultural entrenchment	• Bickering • Appeals to the outside for help • Special teams manage problems • Finger-pointing	• Can't keep pace with company needs • Problems are mishandled • Customer complaints • Errors, broken processes • Cover-ups • Anger, mistrust, fighting
Critical signs of problems	• Competitive advantage slips • Loss of key stakeholders • Rise in litigation; risk profile • Overt attacks	• Process failures • Internal rebellion or dissent • Division • Sabotage	• Problems backlogged, avoided • Poor performance patterns evident • Members seek outside help

right time. You get a sense that if the worst happened, the organization would survive despite the pain, costs, damages, etc.

Dangers to the organization grow as risks are unaddressed or mature. A risk may mature as a natural part of its lifecycle, but sometimes behavioral factors associated with an organization, like negligence, facilitate risk growth. Programs or processes may be in place, but their design may be outdated, inappropriate or suffering from misuse. Similar issues exist for participants. The competencies of those responsible for managing risks may not have kept pace with changing risk exposures.

Sometimes key practices are missing. Relational, informational and communication practices are especially important for managing risk but if "open-door policies," "enablement programs," "suggestion boxes" or even extremes like "internal audits" used to monitor programs or behaviors are poorly designed or underutilized this can compromise their potential effectiveness as operational practices. At the other extreme, some organizations, like closed cultures or communities, build extensive and systematic internal spy-on-your-neighbor programs to inform leadership of perceived or potential risks in the organization. This approach can have benefits but it reflects a use of operational practices that are so extreme or restrictive that an organization's full functionality strains under a preoccupation with practices or "doing it right" versus achieving the mission.

Sometimes risks mature because they are viewed as the responsibility of the organization's leadership, an orientation that can lead to the development of significant problems. In these organizations, "risk" may be a topic of conversation for "people at the top," limiting perspective of the organization's performance and/or future to a few key people who may, in fact, be too far removed from day-to-day performance to understand the full nature and characteristics of the risk at hand.

Other times an organization's local culture may keep discussions and preparations for risk at the local level, even though emerging risks pose systemic impact. Just because a fire might occur in the machine shop at the plant's far end, that doesn't mean that the *entire building* shouldn't be involved in an evacuation plan.

Finally, an emerging risk's potential magnifies when those in the organization want to believe they have attended to potential risks but they haven't. If bureaucracy interferes with the real nature of potential risks urgency can be compromised and the risk can go unattended. Some use the post-9/11 terror alert system in the United States as a case in point. First, there was confusion about what the different colors or danger levels meant, then about who was expected to act when levels changed and, finally, if there was a real need for this system at all. So now, the once prominently displayed rating system has all but disappeared from government web pages and television channels.

One potential contribution of the use of complexity theory in this instance is as a tool for understanding how risky situations emerge and, as importantly, how interventions or tactics used to counter them also emerge. The theory's key components, emergence and self-organization, for example, are immediately applicable to examinations of responses constructed to manage a risk, threat or vulnerability. When faced with an emerging risk most people will take some level or type of action, whether it's prescribed or not. So when they take risk avoidance action on their own, without direction from others, they are acting in a "self-organized manner."

Maturation of a Threat

Many of the observations made regarding the emergence and maturation of risks apply to discussions of threats to an organization. However, while threats may have some level of risk associated with them, threats are particularly unique phenomena for an organization.

Threats mature on two planes: as an impending menace in their own right and as a metaphor or psychological construct, in the mind of those expected to manage the threat. In the first instance, threats follow a lifecycle that may have no apparent origin. The threat's "causes" may be vague, non-rational or seemingly non-existent. Consider recent acts of violence on U.S. school campuses, like Columbine or Virginia Tech. While it may be possible to isolate the rational nature of the act from the attacker's profile (e.g., Harford 2008) the link between an attacker and the victim may be harder to discern. Attacks like these are "extraordinary events beyond the scope of the organization." They may be anticipated and planned for, but why should an organization concern itself with something that *may* be or become a threat? Which is the more proactive response: setting out to discover as many possible threats as possible, then designing practices to address them or building and operating a well-functioning organization so that it has the capacity to respond appropriately to whatever materializes? The question is rhetorical.

A threat is salient when it is perceived as existing—in either a real or a potential state. A threat's lifecycle is straightforward. The lifecycle begins before its actual emergence when preconditions for its existence are established. Once recognized as potential or real, the threat begins to affect behavior in the organization. People respond to it, they think about it, can worry about it, they dismiss it. Left unaddressed the threat continues to develop into maturity. If the threat can harm the organization, a final stage unfolds where, if left unchecked, effects associated with the threat emerge.

Threats also need to mature in the "minds" of the organization's participants. This begins with the capability to perceive the threat, which may not be easy. Advisors may have convinced the organization's leadership there are no threats, or poor data or information management practices can contribute a "no threat" message. At other times, even behaviors like arrogance may rule over reason: "We're the strongest." "Who could wage a meaningful threat on us?"

The perception process becomes a series of assessments and judgments aimed at gauging the threat's consequences. There are two requirements when assessments and judgments are the center of one's focus: there should be little or no bias in one's thinking and the quality of information received must increase over time; information must be defined by higher levels of accuracy. It's not enough to say of an opponent, "They've got a good team." As game day approaches it's important to know the team's shooting percentages or the number of "stars" on the team, perhaps the team's health or general capability to play at their best. Information blends with evaluation and knowledge management practices, and all combine with existing communication practices to make information useful.

Finally, responses to a threat are constructed, realizing, of course, that *choosing to ignore the threat* is, in fact, a response. Responding to a threat means more than implementing a plan; it means ensuring that the organization has the resources necessary to complete the plan and that those involved in the plan are prepared to implement it. Many organizations fail at this point because their participants and operational practices can't quickly adjust to the changing circumstances a threat may present. What would happen if a fire started in the basement of a church, during the Girl Scout meeting, or in the fourth-grade classroom of the elementary school? These are everyday settings but do those potentially affected know how to shift safely from a non-emergency to an emergency situation?

It seems impossible to believe that some threats are simply ignored, but they are. There are threats of employee action for discrimination or harassment, but they're ignored. Religious organizations have known about behavioral issues of their membership, but did nothing. Communities may ignore threats of accident or injury because of poor building construction, unsafe roads, or the actions of authority figures. The administrators may know there are impending threats, but choose not to act perhaps because the events are not life-threatening but this doesn't mean they won't have a negative impact on the organization.

A threat's potential to increase in magnitude is a function of several factors, but three are significant. First, there's the threat's makeup. Threats that appear to be meaningful are more significant than idle threats or "bluffs." In these instances, the threat is strongest if linked with some potential loss but, as illustrated in Table 7.2, threats that are multidimensional seem more effective; they are sufficiently complex to require the expenditure of a variety of resources throughout the organization.

A second criterion necessary for threats to mature is the nature of the threat. Is the threat easy or difficult to carry out? Threats that are easy to deliver are more meaningful than those hard to deliver. Threats begin as communicated events and are immediately evaluated. If the threat's target doesn't believe the threat can be delivered, it is less meaningful and those making the threat perceived as less credible, at least as far as delivering on the threat is concerned.

Finally, a threat's saliency directly relates to the organization's level of preparedness for this type of threat. Referring to Figure 7.3, threats, like risks, achieve a critical point beyond which the threat moves from being merely possible to likely. Stronger organizations often have plans and practices in place that anticipate the potential for emerging threats. Identified or "known" threats are ranked given the risk they pose the organization. When possible the threat's source is identified and the threat is monitored with organizational processes and practices modified as needed. In strong organizations, proactive, visionary self-regulation and attention to detail become the foundation of strategies and tactics used to manage the impending threat. It's not just that these organizations have effective programs in place to help identify and manage threats, but that these organizations regularly use the programs and keep them updated.

Sometimes organizations surrender their "protection" from threats to other organizations. Security organizations, enterprises that recruit or screen candidates, individual contributors that handle legal or healthcare issues emerge because there is a need for the services they offer that organizations can't provide themselves. There's always a trade-off when

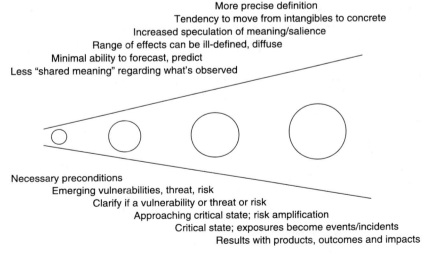

Figure 7.3 Emergence of a Critical State.

relationships are built out of positions of weakness and one that surfaces when protection or safeguards are farmed out to others surrounds issues of "ownership." It's not uncommon, for example, for disputes to arise regarding the responsibility for managing an emerging threat or the consequences associated with action taken.

The risk here is that those providing the service do not need loyalty to the organization to help protect it. They are simply "doing a job." Why should they care about an organization's operating culture or mission; it's not theirs. This was a criticism often heard regarding some of the contractors used during the war in Iraq: they were simply providing a service.

Related to this trade-off is the fact that when an organization subcontracts services, the organization runs the risk of not learning how to think about threat-prevention/protection for itself. Obviously, many organizations do not have the resources to handle everything for themselves but this doesn't mean they should surrender thinking about threat management simply because someone else is assuming the responsibility. It is characteristic of threats that emerge to be disruptive, so those responsible for managing threats (and/or risks and vulnerabilities) must understand their role and responsibility even when the bulk of the management effort may be subcontracted. Failure to maintain this level of engagement makes the organization potentially vulnerable to even more performance pitfalls.

Sometimes, particularly in retrospect, it hard to believe an emerging threat wasn't recognized or taken seriously as it emerged and developed. But there can be some rational, logical reasons why this occurs. Table 7.3 illustrates that while deciding on a strategy to manage a threat is critical, any action taken in response to a threat hinges on the ability to see the threat and, in turn, believing that it is, in fact, meaningful.

A quick review of the list illustrates a point made earlier and summarized by Tim Harford in his book *The Logic of Life* (2008). Simply stated, decisions not to take a threat (or risk or vulnerability) seriously are the product of rational, conscious deliberation. People gauge the threat's salience to them or their organization and they construct a response: to act or not.

When an organization's "threat management performance" falls below minimally acceptable levels, the organization's risk exposure can increase in scope and scale. Routine protective measures may not be in place or, if they are, they may be under the direction of people not fully skilled in their administration. Consequently, regard for a threat's potential may be missed even as it achieves a critical state. Then, when the threat emerges, the capacity to organize an effective response is compromised and, as often as not, it can be up to others to quickly organize a response.

Table 7.3 Why Threats May Not be Taken Seriously

The threats aren't real.

The threat seems out of reach; those threatening are not nearby.

Those making the threat don't have credibility; they are not perceived as capable of delivering on the threat.

Previous threats did not or have not materialized.

Those threatened don't know about the threat (until it appears).

The threat seems unwarranted and unjustified.

It's not a "big threat"; this organization only deals with big (not small) threats.

No one told those in the organization to take the threat seriously.

We have enough other things to worry about that are more pressing.

The threat does not have "high costs" or penalties associated with it; it's not high risk.

The threat is or is perceived to be someone else's responsibility.

There's been a lot of "crying wolf" in the past: why is this different?

There seems to be a lot of political "fear mongering." Does someone want us to be afraid?

Those claiming a threat is imminent have low credibility and are ignored.

There's a false sense of security because "we're the biggest on the block."

There's an over-reliance on technology. "We're beyond reach."

The threat seems too far away. "I don't live near a 'hot zone.'"

Having the capacity to manage threats throughout their lifecycle is the ideal but it comes with costs or demands for the organization and its participants. The range and scope of these costs, however, may be best defined in terms of how capable the organization and its personnel are at marginalizing *any* threat's potential rather than in how well prepared they are at anticipating and responding to every different and particular threat that may arise. The differences between these two strategies may seem subtle but they are, in fact, quite significant.

Maturation of a Vulnerability

It should be apparent that an individual's choice to prepare a personal, self-organized response to a situation is a function of more than a few factors. When an individual is faced with a situation demanding action but no action is prescribed, it's up to the individual to decide what to do. In this case the individual is free to construct a response. A second situation occurs when there *is* a prescribed response, but the individual rejects it (or, perhaps, forgets it) and constructs another. At issue here, and one that exposes an organization to potential harm, is the opportunity for individual self-organization of a response that may make the organization vulnerable to increased threats or risk.

Vulnerabilities are treated separately from risks and threats because vulnerability is a sign of inherent problems in the organization; they are most often caused by the things those in the organization did or should have done, but didn't. Vulnerabilities can be linked to programs or the capabilities of people or teams—to virtually any element of the organization. Regardless of the cause, vulnerabilities create unwanted exposures for an organization that can lead to additional performance management issues.

It is possible to rate an organization's weaknesses that are attributable to its vulnerabilities, just as one might rate its capacity to perform or the quality of its products or services. In well-prepared organizations, vulnerabilities are managed on an ongoing basis. These organizations have a mature sense of urgency regarding potential exposures and their consequences. Since vulnerabilities may be naturally occurring or "caused," well-prepared organizations often have practices and programs in place that are adaptable to changing situations or conditions. Known vulnerabilities are ranked in terms of their priority with programs and activities tailored to meet them.

Less prepared organizations may have some practices in place but key programs may be missing or their use uneven or inconsistent. Needed competencies, for example, may be identified, but follow-through may be missing (e.g., hiring people without key competencies just because "we need *someone* to do the job" or not having succession plans in place because they take "time, money, expertise and energy to produce which we don't have").

Organizations in the middle of a "vulnerability spectrum" generally have structures in place to support change efforts but, again, inconsistencies can rule. Programs may be in place but not participants or vice versa. Alternatively, participants may be willing to participate in programs that can reduce vulnerabilities but management can't or isn't prepared to support them. Sometimes vulnerabilities are part of the fabric of the organization and thus seemingly invisible or, worse, untouchable.

The irony is that these are good organizations, the type that are often described as succeeding despite themselves, and their success seems to make them blind to their vulnerabilities. They do a lot of things right but bad habits, friends over function, or "my culture, right or wrong" type attitudes only aggravate already borderline conditions. Poor decisions, poor choices and poor actions can lead to in-breeding, limited scope and over-reliance on a few key people. In the end, this can serve to enable vulnerabilities to turn into real problems.

Organizations classified as "below average" regarding their preparedness to manage vulnerabilities probably already know they have a problem. Management may find itself spending a lot of time and resources dealing with issues that seem to be surfacing everywhere. In these organizations, a lot of time can be spent in meetings devoted to handling a seemingly endless array of problems. This wouldn't be bad if the problems were life-threatening and warranted the attention they receive but many may be minor, perhaps not resolved when and where they occurred.

Another clue that these organizations are in trouble is the ongoing need to use consultants to repair fundamental operations. In these instances, resources that could be used to develop the organization are diverted to handle everyday matters. Vulnerabilities in these organizations have achieved a critical state, and risk levels associated with them increase so that stakeholders, like regulatory agencies, creditors or key customers, demand that issues be addressed.

Sometimes it's hard to imagine that organizations with significant vulnerabilities even manage to exist. They do, often because they are one-of-a-kind operations or an organization an entire stakeholder segment is dependent upon. The media and consumer groups regularly report on organizations with dangerous vulnerabilities. They come in all types: they may be school systems, religions or cults, government agencies or manufacturers. The commonality they share is that vulnerabilities attributable to poorly produced products, dangerous working conditions or practices, or performance that generally fails to meet the basic standards set for them, can put the organizations in harm's way. Indeed, sometimes the leadership of these organizations only recognize the scope of their vulnerabilities when a competitor, regulator or alternative organization appears on the scene.

Organizations that receive poor vulnerability ratings often have deficiencies in key programs and practices as well. Consequently, the scope of their vulnerability is not limited to one or two matters. These organizations may find themselves in ongoing reactive modes as vulnerabilities materialize into events and incidents. When this happens the organization may appear off-balance or out of sync with competitors or stakeholder needs and this threatens the organization's attractiveness to stakeholders.

Red flags are raised when organizations become at risk because they have vulnerabilities linked to another's carelessness. Banking, the stock market, the nuclear industry and airlines are examples; their capacity to function is dependent on the capacity or performance of others. A partner's vulnerabilities can wreak havoc on whole industries. A plant with poor working conditions and angry employees may be vulnerable to a strike or job action that can negatively affect the production, distribution and sales of other plants.

CONCLUSION

This chapter illustrates two fundamental themes regarding the role of risks, threats and vulnerabilities. The first is the role each can play in affecting an organization's capacity to operate, perhaps even jeopardizing it, and the second is their role as catalysts for self-organization in organizations. The first of these is obvious. Consider Table 7.4.

Table 7.4 lists different risks, threats and vulnerabilities for the four organization types. Each is so diverse that some may not seem to warrant classification as potentially harmful to an organization, but organizations and their resources also differ widely. So what may not be of concern to one organization may be a real issue in other organizations.

Second, it's also important to recall that all risks, threats and vulnerabilities always have an impact; they cause people to react, to shift attention to them and to draw on the organization's resources. To illustrate this consider the "Community" row in Table 7.4. "Exposure to new ways or ideas" is a possible risk, but the way that risk materializes and affects the organization is somewhat dependent on the type of community organization. A secret, closed community that feels the need to exercise significant control over its membership may be reluctant to tolerate new ideas or ways of doing things. The organization may feel that to do so can challenge its mission or values. There may be little tolerance for ambiguity in these organizations and those seeking to explore new ideas may find themselves doing so on the outside, after being expelled from the organization.

An organization's inherent nature, however subtle, contributes to the ways risks, threats and vulnerabilities emerge and affect the organization and its stakeholders. Some organizations may find it hard to reduce risk, threat and vulnerabilities—they seem to be "one of the costs of doing business." Terrorist organizations may find themselves under constant threat of attack because of the relationship they have with their adversaries. Indeed, only if they surrender or are defeated may their threats be abated, and then sometimes only with the agreement to

Table 7.4 Representative Risks, Threats, Vulnerabilities by Organization Type: Opening the Door for Self-Organizations

ORGANIZATION TYPE	REPRESENTATIVE RISKS	REPRESENTATIVE THREATS	REPRESENTATIVE VULNERABILITIES
Community	• Exposure to new ways, ideas • Lose its leader • Cultural change from within	• Lose sight of mission • External attacks; sanctions • Lose membership	• Changing times, interests • Defectors, loss of unity or focus • Restricted, limited resources
Enterprise	• Loss due to accident/injury • Loss of stakeholder base • Loss from internal exposures • Loss from external exposure	• Doesn't achieve mission • No resources to perform • Poor leadership • Poor management	• Excessive regulation • Brand dilution • Insufficient staffing
Team	• Rising star(s) move on • Exposing strategies/tactics	• Injury/loss of key people • Defectors; loss of unity • Loss of focus	• Lose key player(s) • Poor readiness (e.g., planning) • Poor skills; lack of depth
Individual Contributor	• Accepting too "big" a project • Partnering with others • Too widely diversified	• Insufficient competencies • Poor networks • Poor relationships • Lost time to productivity	• Limited resources • Lack of depth • Large-scale change

surrender their entire organization—in short, complete capitulation. Organizations under the guidance of a regulatory body also may find it difficult to dodge or remove the threats of action. In these cases, only when certain conditions are met and demonstrated are risks or threats removed.

RISKS, THREATS AND VULNERABILITIES AS CATALYSTS FOR SELF-ORGANIZATION

Risks, threats and vulnerabilities add complexity and uncertainty to organizations. If a military unit is anticipating an attack and is fully prepared, for example, it has plans, processes, procedures, practices, materials and people resources ready, then the only unknown is when the attack will occur. The unit has reduced levels of uncertainty associated with the impending conflict and it can have a better sense regarding how it will perform.

Insufficient preparation compromises the capacity to know how the organization or its resources might perform given risks, threats or vulnerabilities. In the face of events that demand action, lack of appropriate practices often requires those potentially affected to construct their own response. In terms of complexity theory, this creates an opportunity for the construction of a self-organized response.

Under the right circumstances, constructing a self-organized response can mean the difference between success and failure, gain or loss, or having a satisfied or unhappy customer. Self-organization is not without risks, however. At the moment a self-organized response is constructed the individual, not the organization, is defining how best to meet the vision, mission or needs of the moment. Self-organization is not an accident; it reflects a conscious choice to act or behave in a particular way. Moreover, as Sole and Bascompte (2006) point out there are a minimum of five criteria that must be established for behavior to be labeled as self-organized. These criteria include:

1. Localized interactions. An organization's participants involved in self-organization activity tend to focus their interactions among themselves. They rely on each other partially because they have a history of performance with each other, partially because of geography since no other resource may be available and partially because time constraints don't allow for the sourcing of other resources.

2. There is an absence of well-defined top-down control. "Although top-down control appears to be present in ecosystem organization, it is seldom a strict one, often counterbalanced by bottom-up forces" (Sole and Bascompte 2006: 13). In this instance, the state of emergency defined by the impeding risks, threats or vulnerabilities fills a void created by an absence of control from above.

3. There is variability in the organization. This is a key point given the above discussion. Poor, inadequate or inappropriate structure, content and operations increase variability in organizations and, if pervasive, can stimulate the likelihood that self-organization occurs. Without even the subtle contribution of guidelines, procedures or local conventions individuals can either ignore situations not covered by the organization or its leadership or can initiate action on their own.

4. There must be an opportunity for those in organizations to be exposed to change and, most importantly, to be able to adapt to that change. Restrictive, high-control organizations attempt to limit change and, if it occurs, to manage how the organization and its participants adapt to the change. This level of control limits opportunities for self-organization to occur and this, in turn, can lead to trouble when the organization is faced with threats or unfolding risks with no one available to interpret the event and define a course of action. "Followers" are designed to be followers, not leaders.

A manufacturing facility can manage participant action and change by having very defined procedures in place, by having machines that operate only in certain ways or, if these fail to bring desired controls, by doing away with the intervention of people and using robots wherever possible.

Other organizations may not be able to exercise these levels of control. A retail store or restaurant cannot easily manage the behavior of all of its employees. These organizations have to trust that the selection processes they use, combined with the training and evaluation processes they introduce, get people to perform the way they want. In the end, this limited control means there are elements of behavior over which the organization has little control, and this variability opens up opportunities for self-organized, self-directed behavior to emerge.

5. Finally, there is the capacity for change. Sole and Bascompte refer to this as "evolvability" and describe it as the presence of mechanisms allowing new features to emerge within an organization. "This is an intrinsic feature of many complex systems," they write, "from cellular to economic webs. The capacity to respond to changing conditions on an evolutionary time scale is obvious from micro-evaluation to macro-evolution" (Sole and Bascompte 2006: 14).

In the face of risks, threats and vulnerabilities, and assuming these five criteria are present, there are opportunities for self-organized responses to risks, threats and vulnerabilities. Ironically, too, when one does witness self-organization processes the behaviors demonstrated can mimic those seen in a well-structured, controlled organization and environment. It's just that an individual or small group is defining the response to take and not some anonymous, amorphous organizational entity.

Planning, for example, can be a reactive, self-organized response by a thoughtful, disciplined individual. Planning that is part of a self-organized response does not have to be elaborate or even complete, just sufficient to manage the situation at hand. Operational practices also can be quickly defined and implemented as self-organized responses to reduce levels of susceptibility to risks, threats or vulnerabilities. "Quick" audits are conducted. "Known" dimensions of risks, threats and vulnerabilities are identified and ranked and programs implemented. This quick process-change effort ends with exposures and tentative responses communicated to stakeholders.

Being proactive in these instances can place great demands on available resources as they are shifted from a designed activity to activities constructed to deal with emerging events. Self-organization may not result in an ideal use of resources but it may be their best use when risks, threats or vulnerabilities are emerging for a poorly prepared organization.

CHAPTER 8

Spectrum of Events
Self-Organization from the Ground Up

Everything in organizations centers on events. An event can be small and local in scope, like a sales transaction, a ritual or an awards ceremony, or grand in scale like a sales campaign, or a battle or a war. Organizations are expected to successfully manage a variety of events, but performance doesn't always materialize as expected and sometimes events expected to carve a path toward success and achievement can end in disaster.

Most events seem relatively straightforward, some even routine. Everyday events like the transaction between a clerk and customer at retail store, the orientation of a new member into a club, a performance evaluation, or a sports team's handling of the loss of an injured key player are the types of routine events managed on an ongoing basis. They may not always be pleasant or desirable, but they are features of organizational performance, and most of these events are usually not surprises.

Other events are more dramatic with some even coming as a shock. A fire in a factory, a student showing up in school carrying a gun, or a terrorist flying an airplane into a building are events that few have prepared for but may become part of people's personal and professional worlds. A spectrum reflecting the range of events those in organizations might be expected to manage is sketched in Table 8.1. These events range from routine ones that are regular, expected and often planned for to those that may come as a "complete surprise" to the organization's membership.

THE SPECTRUM OF EVENTS
It's obvious that understanding how events materialize and potentially affect organizations is important. But, given the range of potential events

Table 8.1 The Spectrum of Events

1. ROUTINE, ANTICIPATED, EVEN PLANNED-FOR EVENTS WHICH UNFOLD WITHIN THE FRAMEWORK OF GENERAL ACTIVITY	2. UNANTICIPATED EVENTS WHICH EMERGE BUT ARE WITHIN THE FRAMEWORK OF ORGANIZATIONAL OR GENERAL ACTIVITY	3. EXTRAORDINARY EVENTS THAT ARE WITHIN THE ORGANIZATION'S HORIZON BUT MAY BE ANTICIPATED, PLANNED FOR	4. EXTRAORDINARY EVENTS THAT ARE WITHIN THE ORGANIZATION'S HORIZON BUT TYPICALLY MAY NOT BE ANTICIPATED OR PLANNED FOR	5. EXTRAORDINARY EVENTS BEYOND THE SCOPE OF THE ORGANIZATION THAT MAY BE ANTICIPATED OR PLANNED FOR	6. EXTRAORDINARY EVENTS BEYOND THE SCOPE OF THE ORGANIZATION THAT ARE NOT TYPICALLY ANTICIPATED OR PLANNED FOR
FOCUS: maximum control to shape the event so it meets the organization's needs.	FOCUS: bring into control. Manage the event and effects. Possibly add to repertoire.	FOCUS: instill some control. Manage the effects. Search for a cause?	FOCUS: manage the effects and recovery. Consider possible future plans.	FOCUS: since these can't be controlled, emphasis is on preparation and managing the effects.	FOCUS: since these can't be controlled emphasis is on managing effects and recovery.
EXAMPLE: sales or recruiting events, assembly activities, personnel reviews, sales transactions, rituals.	EXAMPLE: customer complaints, employee theft, celebrations, disciplinary actions, loss of key personnel.	EXAMPLE: loss of key person, fire in a manufacturing facility, lay-offs, on-site injury.	EXAMPLE: new technology, loss of key stakeholder, discrimination claims, aggressive driving, defections, sabotage.	EXAMPLE: terrorist attack, regional natural disasters, employee theft.	EXAMPLE: natural disaster (e.g. hurricane), unethical behavior of external stakeholders (lawyers, doctors), stakeholder injuries, terrorist attack.

that those in organizations might encounter, several questions come to mind. For example, is it possible to prepare for the range of events mapped out on the spectrum? Or, to what extent, if at all, should organizations prepare for those events that *may* occur and, if they decide to prepare for "possible events," which ones should they target and how thorough should their preparation be?

Ensuring events are successfully managed is primarily a performance issue, and approaching event management from that perspective seems logical because why should organizations exist if they're ineffective in managing the events that define each day? Retail stores are expected to have staff who can effectively manage sales transactions, fire departments are expected to have people who can effectively manage fires, and religions are expected to have people who can manage the spiritual needs of their communities. However, even seemingly routine events can be mishandled. In fact, it's somewhat commonplace to observe examples of breakdowns in an organization's management of key, but routine, events.

We've become familiar with incidents of poor performance. Performance breakdowns can surface as "poor customer service" by a sales clerk, a violation of client confidences by a lawyer or a project team's failure to meet a promised deadline for a client. The inability to manage routine events successfully frustrates us for two reasons. First, there's a sense that failure just shouldn't happen. After all, these are "routine," often everyday, events and transactions. Second, those who manage the systems that drive these organizations are frustrated because theoretically they have often designed systems and processes to prevent such breakdowns from occurring. They have constructed what they believe is an effective organization so it is frustrating to see people who have been trained, and who know what is expected, fail to deliver.

Indeed, we not only expect people to do the right thing after being given guidelines, but we sometimes expect them to extend themselves and their capabilities by "self-organizing" responses or solutions as they "think on the run" or "take ownership" of their assignments. In other words, there may be some latitude in deciding how to manage an emerging event but not to the extent that an expected routine becomes out of line with the organization's vision or mission. To paraphrase Krugman again, "self-organization is something we observe and try to understand, not necessarily something we want" (Krugman 1996: 6).

A quick examination of the spectrum of events illustrates potential challenges facing organizations. For example, despite the fact that on average 80 percent of an organization's activity is devoted to managing daily events it is easy to see how the emergence of events in categories 2–6 can emerge within a given day. It's also easy to speculate on the range of effects that might be associated with the different event categories, effects not restricted to those near the event. A fire can affect an entire community, not just the firefighters and those in the building where the fire occurs.

Physical and psychological stresses can result from managing even day-to-day events while those events further down the spectrum can be totally debilitating. A sales transaction may be a routine event for a clerk at a fast food restaurant, but it only takes one unruly customer to disrupt the flow for both employees and customers. For other professions, even routine events can be stressful. Law enforcement and military personnel regularly face routine events that are dangerous, even life-threatening. The pervasive nature of danger associated with the routine events in these professions can translate into lost time due to emotional stress and fatigue—and then a category 6 event occurs!

Finally, what may be routine for one party to the event doesn't mean the event is routine for everyone involved. A medical procedure may be routine for the surgery team that has handled hundreds of these events but it isn't routine for the patient experiencing her first time in a hospital. The same can be said for something as "everyday" as a sales transaction. The sales person may handle hundreds of customers a day but it might be an entirely new experience for the customer to be at that store buying this type of gift. Different levels of experience and competencies can make an event routine for some players, or extreme or dramatic for others.

The spectrum presented in Table 8.1 is a useful tool for outlining potential factors associated with the management of events. For example, it is intuitive to believe that the nature and requirements of an event change as one moves up the spectrum from routine to extraordinary events. There may be few in an organization with the experience needed to manage events in categories 5 and 6 when they emerge. These events can require an extraordinary response by participants, sometimes just to "get by."

Worse, there may be little or no time to prepare for these events and this only adds to their complexity. Activities around the 2001 attack on the World Trade Center in New York illustrate this. Some of those on the scene, people with no medical training or apparent supervisory experience, attempted to treat or console the injured or to coordinate communications or traffic flows. In short, patterns of behavior emerged to fit a situation few had experienced or even dreamed possible.

The spectrum also facilitates speculation about types of behavior needed to manage different events. Listing representative events that might occur along the spectrum is a useful first step by itself. Once done, knowing the kinds of events one might expect to see helps identify competencies needed to manage each and it illustrates the potential workload of those expected to handle the different events. For example, handling an angry customer might require problem-solving, communication, evaluation and information management skills while responding to a fire might only require a few skills by comparison (e.g., call the fire department and get out of the building!). Most importantly, however, laying out the types of event that a given organization might conceivably experience helps identify potential risks, threats and vulnerabilities associated with the organization and these events. It can be an eye-opening experience.

People are the obvious wildcard when thinking about events, and their management can spawn an array of questions. For example, why after being trained do some people fail to act as expected? Or, why after performing well in the classroom does that person fumble and fail to perform even the most routine task well? Why does someone who performed well yesterday not perform well today? Finally, why, how and to what extent do people "self-organize" their behavior to construct a response that is completely out of line with what might be expected and certainly might be required?

Complexity theory and other tools help get at answers to all of these questions. Watts, for example, noted that while

> knowing the rules that govern the behavior of individuals does not necessarily
> help us to predict the behavior of the mob, [however] we *may* be able to
> predict the very same mob behavior without knowing very much at all about
> the unique personalities and characteristics of the individuals that make it up.
>
> (Watts 2003: 26)

Getting baseline information like that just described is a good place to start but so is the development of a general understanding of the role certain key variables play in event management.

Competency is an important ingredient in performance but sometimes it's how events shape the ways competencies are demonstrated and utilized that's really meaningful. If one's competency style is too rigid, too linear, it may not be able to adapt to the changing situations brought on by emerging events or an organization's structure that is too narrowly defined. Athletic performance is a case in point.

It always seems striking to see organizations whose memberships have what seem to be similar competencies perform so differently. The evolution of sports teams is a good illustration. Historically, raw sports skills have always been an important part of the equation for the team's success. The team whose competencies centered on maximizing strength and ability usually had the upper hand in competition. However, changes in the way modern sports teams are built changes current approaches to competency.

Now teams without player strength, weight or height advantages can improve their competitiveness by augmenting traditional performance indicators with enhancements to the whole team's physical, cognitive and psychological dimensions. For example, many teams adapt training programs to include the collected knowledge of an opponent's history, playing conditions or even sophisticated formulae mapping physiological and psychological features of different teams and players.

One hears of the smart coach who strategically uses a pool of resources during a game, a clever jockey who knows how to "read" changes in field or track, or the fast-thinking "pit crew" that was the key to victory because they thought systemically about the race process rather than just a series of routine pit stops. A strong (competent) owner, manager, coach or player knows the bigger, stronger or better paid team doesn't always have the right equation for success against the team using a fuller array of support services and operational practices aimed at extending and complementing existing competencies.

THE ROLE OF COMPETENCY IN HUMAN PERFORMANCE

Competency is a dynamic, human construct defined by five dimensions: the first of these are *specialized competencies*, those directly related to one's primary job or assignment. Specialized competencies are the fundamental reason why individuals are typically recruited for the work they are expected to do. Accountants are expected to have specialized accounting skills, nurses to have medical knowledge and nursing skills, and lawyers, legal skills and knowledge. So important and refined are some specialized competencies that some professions require that the professionals in those roles must be licensed (e.g., plumbers and electricians) and, in some instances, maintain their skills through periodic training and development (e.g., lawyers).

Rather, all jobs, tasks, assignments, even chores, have core "specialized" competencies needed to do them well. It may seem a bit extreme, for example, to claim that lawn mowing has certain core specialized competencies associated with the job but, if you're the client, or if you're an 11-year-old about to take on this new summer job, you know there are key things one does to mow a lawn safely and according to the requirements of the customer hiring this young entrepreneur.

Managerial and/or administrative capabilities, a second category of competencies, are supportive activities associated with all tasks. Even our young lawn-mowing entrepreneur has to account for time spent mowing, collect fees and pay bills associated with this endeavor. After all, what kid wants to mow lawns and earn less than it takes to pay for the gas, blade sharpening or mower repairs associated with the business?

Mathematics, speaking, writing and computer skills are representative of a third class of competencies, *basic skills*. Some form of basic skills is part of every position within all organizations. At the high end these can include the ability to work with computers or software like computer databases and some also may be linked to certain positions. One expects executives to have basic skills in finance and accounting competencies, for example. These are not professional competencies for the CEO; these are basic skills for this position.

Social and interpersonal skills and competencies are associated with all jobs, tasks or assignments in both formal and informal organizations. One expects religious advisors to be excellent listeners, people in organizations to work well together, to cooperate if they are part of a department or team or, conversely, not to be rude or generally harass others. Key words associated with social and interpersonal competencies include cooperation, collaboration and teamwork and extend to concepts like empathy, credibility, character, patience and *esprit de corps*. Finally, *cultural competency*, a fifth category, is not restricted to interactions between or among different races, sex or age groups but includes appreciation for the types of thing that mark the differences among these people; their religions, politics, education, types of job or work done and appreciation for the arts. Cultural competencies reflect and promote ideals and mores as well as the idiosyncrasies that define mundane features of the organization and its culture.

Collectively these five competencies both define the manner in which people fit into and function within an organization and illustrate how people in their social systems differ from the members of physical and biological systems, like the ant colony, beehive, or even grains of sand contributing to the formation of a dune or hill. Since the focus of self-organization studies in organizations is the individual, whether alone or in groups, the distinctions regarding competency help establish important baseline information for studies of self-organization in organizations.

PRACTICES AND PROCEDURES SHAPE BEHAVIORS NEEDED TO MANAGE THE EVENT SPECTRUM

Competencies unfold within the parameters of an organization's structure. The spectrum of events draws our attention to the fact that what's appropriate for routine events may be inappropriate for an extreme event. The point seems obvious but one wonders how many bank tellers are coached on what to do during a robbery or if waiters are trained to respond to a guest having an allergic reaction to, or choking on, a piece of food? These are extreme events but not out of the ordinary for those settings.

Some organizations stumble not only because they concentrate on expected events, events "within" their control, but also because they tend to over-emphasize matching people to certain tasks without regard for the organization-as-a-vision or the organization-as-a-mission. So, the pizza shop concentrates on making sure the delivery person has enough money to make change or that the pizza arrives at the customer's house (the transaction or event point) in a timely fashion. But what if the pizza shop doesn't ensure that the delivery person is a safe driver? If the driver has an accident on the way to the delivery should the potential for an accident have been included in the pizza organization's plans for the "range of events" associated with the pizza delivery process and ultimate sales transaction? If a plane carrying the top three leaders of an organization crashes, is the crash the important fact or is the fact that the organization has no successors, succession plans or succession processes in place to ensure organizational continuity? Clearly both the crash and its after-effects are important but not in the same ways.

Other organizations make the mistake of basing assessments of their success in managing events in terms of the simple termination of the event: "It's over. We accomplished our objective. We must be successful." Consider, for example, these events: a sale is made, a sermon is given, a class is taught, a prisoner confesses and a meeting ends. In each case, the event described may have been, in its completion, defined as the objective achieved; something to be checked off as having occurred "as planned." But what about that period (regardless of its length) after the event is concluded? Was it a sale or a "quality transaction"? Was the sermon helpful to the congregation or something "everyone endured"? Did learning occur in the class and how will you know? Was it a confession or simply one person giving up because of punishing torture? Was useful information exchanged at the meeting or did it just kill time?

Figure 8.1 outlines the relationship between behavior (performance) and effects in terms of three paths. The first of these paths, "actual

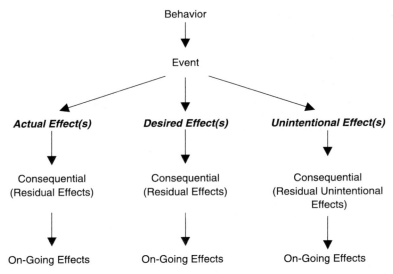

Figure 8.1   The Relationship between Behavior, Events and Effects.

effects," reflects what happened—the facts. The second channel reflects the "desired effects," which may or may not be the same as those in the first path. These are what the organization, group or individual planned or hoped would happen.

If we were thinking about performance and effects as a mere linear process we could end our analysis here. But, as you recall, we prefer to think about this dynamic relationship as a process so, in addition to the desired and actual effects, a third path emerges, unintentional effects. Unintentional effects also have a range of goodness associated with them; they're often things those in the organization didn't consider, perhaps even wouldn't have considered as part of the event.

Organizational training that focuses solely on either events or their effects misses the point. Disasters, whether natural (e.g., earthquakes or tornadoes) or events that are products of human activity (e.g., airplane crashes, terrorist attacks or automobile accidents) have long-lasting effects. Indeed, events can be secondary to the effects associated with them. Hurricane Katrina was the event but it was how the hurricane, in its aftermath, was handled that lingers in the minds and lives of people. Likewise, a terrorist bombing is the event, but it is the bombing's effects that can mark the bodies and lives of those impacted—whether injured or not—long after the event has ended.

EVENTS ALWAYS PRODUCE RESULTS

One important characteristic of events the spectrum brings to our attention is that all events produce results. Two things stand out about results: first, the range and types of possible results associated with events can be extensive and, second, with careful planning and design it's often possible to anticipate, even predict, the results that should be associated with a particular event.

Consider the following multiple-choice question:

The sales transaction ends with the customer buying the product, but the customer is so dissatisfied with the nature of the transaction that the customer:

     a. decides never to shop at that store (organization) again;
     b. finds a way to do without the product in the future;
     c. tells others of the event as the customer experienced it; or
     d. all of the above?

This little example illustrates that the post-event thoughts, actions and activities may be more significant than the event per se. Table 8.2 contains other examples of events and an area where you can speculate on the range of possible after-effects associated with the events listed.

In each of these examples, the after-effects may be more important than an immediate end result. Is the CEO's salary excessive? What should shareholders expect as a return for this investment? Big or little, the bomb went off. What does this say about security, the terrorists' competency, or the availability of explosives? What if the bomb didn't go off? How did it get planted? Where's security? Are some areas (or people) more secure than others are? Did all of the students deserve to graduate? What are their levels of competency?

How many new "profiles" does the security company add to its database each year, and where do these come from? If the security company is "padding" its database doesn't that mean that there will be many more "false positives" (people identified as security risks who are not)? Then, couldn't that result in valuable time being spent following the behavior of non-threatening people while the real threats (thieves or dangerous people) go unnoticed?

How many "big" cases does the attorney have to win to be perceived as successful? Does a female attorney have to win more "big" cases than a male attorney? Will a glass ceiling still prevent the female lawyer from advancing into partnership or executive levels? Why was the case brought against these officers? Did they get off over a technicality, so brutality is

Table 8.2   Speculating on the Results of Events

THE EVENT	POSSIBLE EFFECTS OF THE EVENT (You fill in)
The board of directors gives the CEO a compensation package totaling $200,000,000.	
The terrorist's bomb is discovered and disarmed before it can detonate.	
The high school successfully graduates all of its senior class.	
The high school fails to graduate 50% of its senior class.	
In order to "enhance" the database product it sells, the security company adds pictures of people to the database who may be "innocent" but who "look" like they might be criminals or fit a profile.	
The American tourist in Thailand eats his meal with his left hand.	
The lawyer successfully wins the biggest case of her career.	
Police officers accused of brutally beating a black student win their case and are found "not guilty."	

still an issue? If there is a "brutality mentality," is it systemic; can it be uncovered in areas in the community other than the police department?

We began this chapter by claiming that organizations achieve their mission through activities and events. But these activities and events, while seemingly mundane and endless, like the recruiting, hiring, training of staff, the promotion of products and services through advertisements, or the construction of new plants or buildings, always have an effect. They may be dramatic such as when an organization attempts to take over a competitor, produces a product that can save lives, or positions itself so that its actions destroy the lives of people or even whole communities. Most are not.

Terrorists, for example, know this. The short-term energy of a terrorist organization is often summed up in the creation of activities associated with a single, hostile event. One such event, a bombing, is a collection of activities seeking to produce disruptions in the actions of others. That is why the phone call after the bomb explodes is so important. The terrorists know the solution for disrupting the actions of others (detonate a bomb), the decision (do it today) and the action (the bombing) do not complete the event until they associate themselves with it. While bombing may be an outcome reflecting decisions made and actions taken, the bombing itself is only part of a set of operational practices that demonstrate just how different the terrorist organization is from other organizations and the norms of the people bombed.

In other words, the actions and events we see are not the primary issue. At the event's center is the individual's sketch of the event, which reflects the juxtaposition of the organization's structure, processes and practices vis-à-vis the individual's array of potential ways of how to act. It's at this point, where the individuals involved in the event take over and construct an event, that reflects who they are at that point in time and how the event will contribute to the lives of people. Most in organizations understand this. It's why an organization's energy focuses on maximizing the likelihood that those involved in events the organization values as important will perform as the organization wants and needs them to perform. Buildings, equipment, signage, training or educational activities, policies, procedures and processes all aim at helping the organization achieve its mission through the actions of those at the event. Anything else is, in the stricter sense, secondary.

Human decisions enable the terrorist to cross a threshold and commit an act that is a symbolic event. The same logic applies to virtually all constructed events in organizations. At a sales event, the transaction between a customer and the organization's "sales clerk" follows the same model as a doctor's examination of a patient (a medical examination event). Even larger events, like religious or political ceremonies, follow the same pattern. The events are designed to reflect the structure, processes and practices of the organization but the events are nothing without the intervention of people designated to complete the fabrication process.

The following chapter aims at accomplishing two tasks. First, a summary and discussion of features one sees in complex, adaptive systems like organizations is presented. Typically this topic is examined in terms of a system's component parts or elements (e.g., people, groups, departments) linked through various structural features (e.g., a hierarchy, information channels) and operated within the parameters of certain processes, practices, protocols or the like. In this summary systems are approached in terms of factors which contribute to their ability to perform in pursuit of a mission or goals. This enables the reader to build on material already presented and, most importantly, to understand the facets of systems that make them dynamic, functioning entities.

The second objective is more important to our overall investigation of the effects of events on organizations. Here the discussion centers on explaining how organizations work to manage events by attempting to shape behavior to match specific strategies, tactics and activities. This material also builds on previous chapters, but specifically focuses on aspects of performance that illustrate ways success is not always a function of the monetary and physical resources an organization has at its disposal but rather how individuals selectively and personally organize their performance to meet what they believe are the needs of the situation at hand.

CHAPTER 9

The Emergence and Management of Events

EVENT EMERGENCE, EFFECTS AND CHANGE: AN INTRODUCTION TO THE COMPLEXITY OF EVENTS

Events may be the site for organizational performance but they are far from neat, clean phenomena. There are several elements common to all events: first, events are not static but are always in a state of flux. This makes the accuracy associated with the planning for an event very difficult. All planners or those anticipating what's likely to transpire during an event can do is provide a sketch about what might happen or what's likely to happen, for example, based on past experience. Second, regardless of the planning and preparation, event management is constructed by participants on the spot, thus making the event their own and not what others might want or think should happen. This means that any two events are likely to unfold in different ways, even if the same participants are involved. So no two events, regardless of how similar they may appear on paper, are alike across their lifecycle.

Finally, regardless of the similarities among events, each event is unique. The event spectrum discussed earlier illustrates this point and is presented again, below. Some events are familiar or routine, whilst others may come as a complete surprise to those involved. Participant characteristics, their competencies, experience and even their health can influence the way an event unfolds or is managed. Finally, even though some events can be classified by type, for example, a sales event, a fire, a robbery or a graduation, every event has its own lifecycle, characteristics, in some ways its own "personality." Fires are affected by local conditions (wind, availability of fuel, location) and a sales event by the type of store, the participants, or the local economy. So the nature of the event influences the ways events are approached and subsequently managed.

Table 9.1 The Spectrum of Events

1. ROUTINE, ANTICIPATED, EVEN PLANNED-FOR EVENTS WHICH UNFOLD WITHIN THE FRAMEWORK OF GENERAL ACTIVITY	2. UNANTICIPATED EVENTS WHICH EMERGE BUT ARE WITHIN THE FRAMEWORK OF ORGANIZATIONAL OR GENERAL ACTIVITY	3. EXTRAORDINARY EVENTS THAT ARE WITHIN THE ORGANIZATION'S HORIZON BUT MAY BE ANTICIPATED, PLANNED FOR	4. EXTRAORDINARY EVENTS THAT ARE WITHIN THE ORGANIZATION'S HORIZON BUT TYPICALLY MAY NOT BE ANTICIPATED OR PLANNED FOR	5. EXTRAORDINARY EVENTS BEYOND THE SCOPE OF THE ORGANIZATION THAT MAY BE ANTICIPATED OR PLANNED FOR	6. EXTRAORDINARY EVENTS BEYOND THE SCOPE OF THE ORGANIZATION THAT ARE NOT TYPICALLY ANTICIPATED OR PLANNED FOR
FOCUS: maximum control to shape the event so it meets the organization's needs.	FOCUS: bring into control. Manage the event and effects. Possibly add to repertoire.	FOCUS: instill some control. Manage the effects. Search for a cause?	FOCUS: manage the effects and recovery. Consider possible future plans.	FOCUS: since these can't be controlled, emphasis is on preparation and managing the effects.	FOCUS: since these can't be controlled emphasis is on managing effects and recovery.
EXAMPLE: sales or recruiting events, assembly activities, personnel reviews, sales transactions, rituals.	EXAMPLE: customer complaints, employee theft, celebrations, disciplinary actions, loss of key personnel.	EXAMPLE: loss of key person, fire in a manufacturing facility, lay-offs, on-site injury.	EXAMPLE: new technology, loss of key stakeholder, discrimination claims, aggressive driving, defections, sabotage.	EXAMPLE: terrorist attack, regional natural disasters, employee theft.	EXAMPLE: natural disaster (e.g. hurricane), unethical behavior of external stakeholders (lawyers, doctors), stakeholder injuries, terrorist attack.

There are a variety of performance or behavior issues associated with event management. Planning, for example, is an important first activity but it's only a best guess about what might happen in an event or a guide regarding how one might approach an event. Planning efforts can be formal or informal and completed in a protracted or spontaneous manner. The plans produced, too, can be broad sketches about what is expected or very precise specifications regarding the type and nature of programs, their performance criteria, activities, etc. Some events require a detailed, deliberate planning process but if there's little time to plan, spontaneous sketches based on hunches, past experience or anticipations about what should happen in the event can be produced. Some events require that plans be detailed and script the entire event-management process from "A–Z." Other planning efforts allow the event to simply "unfold" and give participants the flexibility to construct the event as it progresses.

Whatever the planning strategy taken to the event, examining how events are managed when they emerge provides a second interesting view of event evolution. The decision to deviate from a plan, for instance, may signal issues with the plan's appropriateness, the dynamic nature of the event or characteristics of a participant. Inappropriate behavior, like failing to follow a plan, or general personal behavior beyond the scope of the plan (e.g., rudeness on the part of a sales clerk) may signal an unwanted pattern or may be just a single incident. An employee's rude behavior (not part of a plan for the typical sales event) is an important occurrence for what it may suggest about the employee. This is true for all performance; performance in a given event is a marker that may provide useful information regarding future behavior and performance. If one observes a good performance, one expects to see the same thing in the future.

Events are all about matching preconceived notions about what should happen with reality. As Figure 9.1 illustrates, people continuously construct and modify their approaches to events and the event process through its entire lifecycle. Assessments can include hunches regarding physical, cognitive and emotional features associated with the event and others involved. These states and other information guide planning, interpretations and insights about the event, its history or situational factors like competencies, attitudes and beliefs of those involved. All in all, we expect things to unfold and people to behave in certain ways in those events. How accurate assessments are before and after the event is important to understand. Equally important, too, is why deviations from our expectations occur and, when they do, how the deviations may

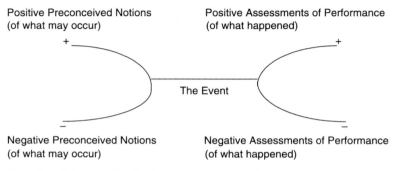

Positive Preconceived Notions (of what may occur)

Positive Assessments of Performance (of what happened)

The Event

Negative Preconceived Notions (of what may occur)

Negative Assessments of Performance (of what happened)

Figure 9.1 Before and After the Event: Exploring Sources for Bias vs. Accuracy.

be managed. Indeed, the emergence of deviations can raise many questions about organizations and their participants and, in turn, set the stage for resistance to any changes the organization or its participants discover are needed.

EVENTS AND SELF-ORGANIZATION

Why, for example, do people who know the rules of the road flagrantly violate those rules, perhaps even engaging in a phenomenon often called "road rage"? Driving is a common event with much of the process routine and predictable. Why then are there deviations from the "driving event plan" as outlined by the state or local government? Or, why would a person who works in a rule-driven and structure-bound organization like the military or a police department behave in ways that are contrary to the employer's most important rules, policies or procedures? This is, after all, what happens when an employee discloses top-secret information, betrays a client's confidence or engages in unacceptable behavior like profiling, evidence-tampering or the brutal treatment of a prisoner.

Most community-type organizations tend to be careful and deliberate in the development of the rules, rituals and processes that define their institutions. So why does a quick survey of behavior in churches or similar institutions seem to indicate that people, regardless of age, sex, education or other variables, are more than willing to pick and choose which rules they'll follow and/or to what extent? Is there something leaders of the institutions impacted by these "rule violators" should know about the violators, the rules or, perhaps, their own organizations?

Why would someone taught to respect life choose to take it, even if it meant taking one's own, through an act of terrorism? Research and studies examining terrorists and their actions expose a variety of issues associated with those moments when, on a given day, peace is disrupted by a terrorist who constructs an event, like a shooting or bombing. The setting of a terrorist act—the market, the school or the office building—was not constructed for a terrorist act, so what is the significance of the deviation from the plan for those settings? Why are these deviations important, and what can we learn from them?

These are the extreme to be sure but, then, consider the similarities between these extreme events and more mundane events. Why, for example, does someone trained to provide good customer service choose to be rude to a given customer or group of customers? Poor employee behavior is a constructed event and the product of the individual's choices. Is the person "just having a bad day" or are there other explanations for the behavior that is observed? Oh, and are any explanations more valid than others?

The answer to all of these questions is linked to the attitudes and beliefs that are linked to personal values which, in turn, are linked to those defined by the organization. The difference here is that the participant may share the same values as those in the organization but not to the same extent as those defining the organization's values; it's a conundrum that fits nicely into situations reflected in complexity theory's concept of self-organization. Moreover, as Figure 9.2 illustrates, it's almost impossible for the individual not to monitor and reflect on events as they unfold. People, in short, are not swept away by events but rather they participate in events to the extent to which they have the capability to do so.

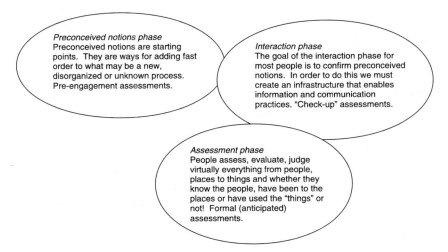

Figure 9.2 Phases of Active and Passive Dimensions Associated with Participation in an Event.

It's important to consider all three phases outlined in Figure 9.2 when looking at events in order to get a fuller sense about the event and behavior observed in the event. In fact, the relationship between the two becomes especially rich as the distinctions between them blur over time as both "feed" off each other in multifaceted and dynamic, non-linear fashions. Consider the example of the speeding car and police officer in Table 9.2. In this scenario the relationship between an event and behavior related to the event doesn't unfold in a strictly predictable manner despite what one might intuitively expect. Rather, it is the shared characteristics of events and behaviors and the fact that each act is motivated by decisions and actions the driver or police officer make and take for themselves. No one is telling the driver or police officer what to do; their choices are their own.

EVENTS AND THE SHAPING OF HUMAN RESPONSE BEHAVIORS

The scenario outlined in Table 9.2 is simple and straightforward. But, even as one reads through it, it becomes clear that there are a variety of ways to "amend" or re-write the event—perhaps based on one's own experience. This is because the relationship among organizations, people and the events that shape their lives is dynamic; it's fluid and totally personal. One can't help but notice two themes that emerge as explanations for why people find themselves where they are in life. Who hasn't heard someone claim that it was events or the circumstances associated with them, rather than anything they did, that accounted for what has happened to them? Their belief is that the event defined their destiny. It's as though the event overwhelmed the individual and his/her capacity to respond so, as the event unfolded, so did the new direction for the individual.

Table 9.2   An Illustration of the Relationship between an Event and Behavior

1. The driver speeds (behavior and event) at 65 mph on a road posted for 35 mph.
2. A police officer sees the speeding car.
3. Officer decides to pursue speeding car. (Behavior—and new event while the speeding event continues.)
4. The driver accelerates trying to escape the police. (Behavior in response to new event and the avoidance is a yet another event.)
5. The police respond by accelerating and seeking help, etc.

Others claim to be in control of their destiny. Their story is that because they are in control, it is their behavior that shapes daily and long-term events in their lives. Events for these people can be viewed as opportunities or, in some instances, as tools used to shape outcomes. If they're prepared, they succeed, if not, they fail. These people describe themselves as "growing from the experience (of the event)." They may see the event as a catalyst that forced them to look at things in a different way or, sometimes, as a way to "clean the slate" so that they could begin again and construct a new life for themselves. It's a "glass-is-half-full" approach toward events and, perhaps, life in general.

Clearly the nature of the relationship between people and events is not as cut and dried as those two interpretations suggest. Optimism can help an individual approach an event or its aftermath, but as many have discovered it takes more than one's outlook on life to negotiate the scope and scale of even some minor events. Indeed, the tendency to explain the relationship between events or behaviors as a simple causal relationship with one or the other as the prime stimulus oversimplifies a very unique phenomenon.

Figure 9.3 provides a sketch that summarizes typical approaches to routine, special and unexpected events. One of the obvious differences among the approaches is that both routine and special events provide those faced with managing them the opportunity to build a plan to guide their action. These plans can serve as guides and may be based on past experience or the experience of others.

Because they're able to build a plan, those faced with routine and special events have some amount of time to prepare. This is an advantage and, coupled with the fact that neither of these two types of event should be emerging as a complete surprise, the preconceived notion of what to expect or how to proceed, based on past experience or the experience of others, should be fairly accurate. This is especially true for routine events.

Unexpected events can have heavy data requirements pitted against limited time in which to act. Those experiencing them have to determine whether they've experienced a similar event in the past, then prepare their own management plan for the event, and then act. That's the ideal. Unfortunately time can be limited so that those faced with the unexpected event simply act (and, if there's time, hope for the best). How can one prepare for unexpected events? What must one do to maximize the likelihood that the unexpected event, all things considered, will be successfully managed? Figure 9.3 provides some insight into how various factors discussed to this point shape behavior in response to an event.

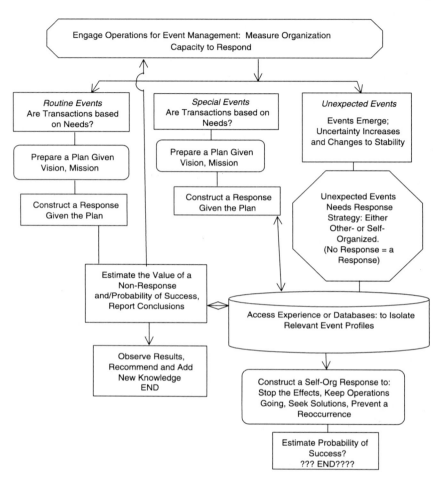

Figure 9.3   The Usual Routine—Operations Management in Organizations: Responding to and Managing Emerging Routine, Special and Unexpected Events.

COMPETENCY, URGENCY AND EVENT MANAGEMENT

Competency and an accurate or realistic sense of urgency are the two overriding factors driving action in Figure 9.3. Competency provides the foundation to accurately manage the event and, in turn, a sense of urgency facilitates assigning the appropriate priority to it. There are a couple of ways to look at the relationship between the two vis-à-vis an event. First, especially in regard to the routine event, is the notion that these events are manageable, the results typically predictable, at least the immediate results. What the individual typically brings to routine events are one's personal competencies: "motivation," "leadership" or, simply, "a sense of urgency." In these routine situations, the opportunity for success rests with the individual. A "self-starter," a "go-getter," a "hustler" are among the labels used to account for those people who take charge of situations, usually on their own and without a lot of direction. In some instances people who display these levels of initiative are sought out as problem-solvers to manage difficult projects or people. Unfortunately, while being a "go-getter" may be a good predictor of the energy one brings to a situation, it may not necessarily be a reliable measure of competence.

A second form of urgency, discerned urgency, is marked by systemic competency: a mixture of common sense and a fundamental know-how regarding the management of certain events. The first of these, common sense, is manifested by a prudent, calculated assessment of the event at hand. Formally, this might be called *risk assessment*; informally it's the difference between trial and error and insight (e.g., Gilhooly 1982). At this level, judgments about how to respond are fast and made along the lines of those captured under the rubric of "rational economics" (Harford 2008). The decision of when and how to act are quickly made but mediated through a convenient, internal cost–benefit protocol.

What makes discerned urgency unique to the individual is the manner in which it nurtured and developed, like a personalized set of practices and procedures. Table 9.3 presents a list of key practices introduced earlier and demonstrates how they might be personalized, manifested or even developed for an organization or individual. Urgency then isn't some mysterious x-factor people are "born with." Urgency, like any competency or trait, is developed. It's an asset for all, not a few.

The second factor, competency, also discussed earlier, is multifaceted and made up of five dimensions: basic skills, professional, administrative and team/interpersonal (social) skills, and a cultural dimension. The assumption is that the individual/organization has sufficient competencies across the five dimensions in order to engage in what Nonaka and Takeuchi (1995) have identified as a knowledge-creation process— in this case a means for determining how best to manage an event.

The steps they outline include sharing tacit knowledge, creating concepts, justifying concepts, building a prototype and cross-leveling knowledge. Obviously Nonaka and Takeuchi are taking a long view of knowledge creation, but it fits this view of urgency and our overall discussion of self-organization in that this process reflects a way to personalize dimensions of urgency throughout one's lifecycle and particularly in terms of events, circumstances or situations one encounters. Nonaka and Takeuchi's steps contribute to our understanding that a sense of

Table 9.3 Ingredients for Managing Events: Key Practices that Drive Urgency and Behavior Generally

CRITICAL PRACTICES AND STRATEGIES	DESCRIPTION	BROAD REPRESENTATIVE INDICATORS	CHALLENGES, RISKS AND THREATS
Communication practices and strategy	Methods, practices and techniques used to transfer, exchange or generally deliver information between or among individuals, groups and organizations.	• Public speaking/ presentation • Good team leadership skills • Good coaching • Mentoring skills • Promotion and public relations • Interpersonal communication	• One-way communication • Closed-door policy • Bias • Miscommunications • Incomplete information
Evaluations practices and strategies	Processes, procedures and practices used to evaluate, assess or appraise performance for individuals, groups, or organizations at the systems level or products, projects or processes at the component level.	• Reliable and valid assessment processes and tools • Consistency • A priori identification/ definition of evaluation criteria • Skilled evaluators • Systemic use of evaluation	• Bias in administration • Poor procedures • Inconsistent procedures • Poor evaluation competencies • Biased evaluation forms, tools
Knowledge practices and strategies	Strategies, practices or procedures used to acquire, build, develop, maintain knowledge and/or skills and competencies.	• Training and growth strategies • Problem-solving skills • Decision-making skills • Needs assessments of jobs	• Competing priorities • Restrictive environment • Limited resources • Limited leadership vision
Relationship practices and strategies	Strategies, practices or procedures used to acquire, build, develop, maintain relationships between or among individuals, groups and organizations.	• Team-building skills • Selection and hiring strategies • Negotiation and bargaining skills • Team work is supported • Customer service is expected	• Few "people" values • Careless hiring processes • Careless job definition • Orientation to individuals

Table 9.3 (Continued) Ingredients for Managing Events: Key Practices that Drive Urgency and Behavior Generally

CRITICAL PRACTICES AND STRATEGIES	DESCRIPTION	BROAD REPRESENTATIVE INDICATORS	CHALLENGES, RISKS AND THREATS
Performance practices and strategies	Routines, processes and/or methods used to introduce, propel and/or guide operations and ensure that performance meets goals, objectives and standards.	• Planning, goal-setting skills • Strategy, tactics planning • Task defined; no surprises • Quality management skills used • Disciplinary processes used • Product quality is expected	• Inattention to detail • Lack of follow-up • Poor coaching skills • Sloppy investigators "react" rather than "think"
Direction and control practices and strategies	Strategies and practices used to identify and define the organization's vision, mission and key goals and objectives. Organization's primary contact point for interaction with other organizations, stakeholders, regulators.	• Planning, goal-setting, design • Vision skills • Skills in negotiation, bargaining, mediation • Direction setting, evaluation • Organization management	• Poor information • Angry regulators • Poor internal communication • Weak management • Poor evaluation • Poor planning
Information practices, evaluation and confirmation practices and strategies	Strategies, practices, tactics for collecting, storing and distributing information. Track sentiments of key stakeholders.	• Maintains information input, storage and retrieval systems • Database research is possible • Research is encouraged • Information is shared • Solid research skills • Needs assessments used • Program evaluations are used • Quality, service is measured	• Availability of information • Accuracy of information • Poor use of information • Information out of reach • Poor research skills • Poor quality research • Bias • Consistency of application

urgency is a process and that this process is defined and used even when conclusions or specifics about how to act are not well-defined or even on the spur of the moment.

Beyond the competency and urgency a third factor, fundamental know-how or tacit knowledge (Von Krogh et al. 2000), serves as a type of "personal translator" or indicator for an individual by facilitating the proper fit of urgency and competency to the event at hand. For Von Krogh et al. tacit knowledge becomes part of an organizational or personal social knowledge "in the form of organizational routines." Here tacit or a fundamental know-how regarding how to proceed materializes through factors like the organization's practices noted above.

Figure 9.4 brings all of the performance factors discussed together in one model. Practices, competencies, urgency and the pre- and post-boundaries of an event illustrate the dynamic nature of successful event management and, also, where and how threats, vulnerabilities and risks can undermine the event-management process. Urgency is a case in point. As attractive as urgency is when described on the printed page, people with this quality are not always liked or appreciated. Be it envy, fear or general ignorance, people and organizations that demonstrate a sense of urgency can be ostracized, scrutinized or generally pestered for not being part of the norm. People may claim they like those with a sense of urgency, and organizations may seek people with this profile because they demonstrate an almost intuitive understanding of what to do and when to do it but, in reality, those with a sense of urgency can, under closer examination, make the others look like underperformers.

The problem of success becomes further complicated because when people and organizations demonstrate a sense of urgency, they seemingly self-destruct. They truly may have the whole picture, as Figure 9.3 illustrates (i.e., they have the competencies, practices, urgency and pre- and post-event profiles that breed success), but, if there are lapses, then something happens. Sometimes the self-destruction occurs because the individual or organization loses focus because of being pulled in too many different directions given its available resources. However, more subtle factors may prevent successful event management by these model individuals and organizations.

The wildcards for their performance equation are the pre- and post-event assessment processes. These are the points where bias can emerge to compromise the likelihood that the right action will occur. It's an ironic twist, because those with the potential and capacity to perform can be, when faced with bias or poor vision, their own worst enemy.

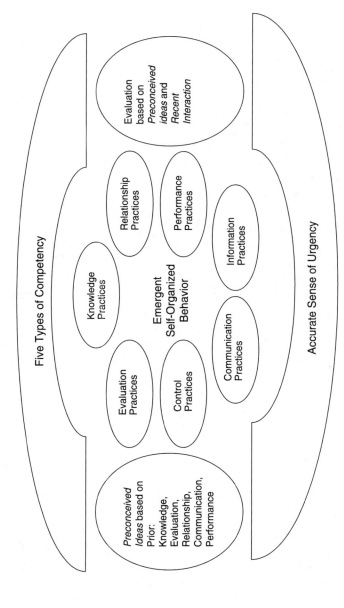

Figure 9.4 Ingredients for Successful Event Management.

Preconceived notions are starting points. Preconceived notions are ways for adding speed and direction to what may be a new, disorganized process, but they can lead to trouble. They are ways of classifying—of controlling the stimuli/information we believe we see, know or may encounter—they can obscure or blind us to key elements of the event or its participants. They help set parameters and objectives for the next steps but when grounded in bias or misinformation their value is compromised and the potential for risk or error increases.

There are a variety of costs potentially associated with every new venture or event. Early costs can include start-up, entry and, of course, switching costs, if one moves from a familiar position to an unfamiliar position. The time it takes to bring one up to the level of familiarity occupied at the former venture is a cost that must be paid. These costs can vary from time to time or from change to change. Once the decision to engage in event management is made, a fourth cost, a volatility/risk cost, appears. Volatility and risk are not constants; they vary over the event's lifecycle, and they tend to reflect the participant's lack of familiarity with the new venture. Poor use of preconceived notions can add to the costs associated with the event-management process.

Perhaps the best way to treat preconceived notions as predictors is by combining them with factors that are already shaping (and potentially straining) available physical, mental and emotional resources. Where the value of preconceived notions is realized is in the interaction phase of the event. Here one has to resist the temptation to use this phase solely to confirm impressions and preconceived notions prior to engaging in the event.

The tendency to use the interaction phase to confirm preconceived notions becomes disastrous when efforts and energy used to confirm what we expect are greater than the desire to get an accurate assessment of what's occurring. Collectively, errors associated with poor conclusions derived during interaction may be labeled as interaction costs and, like entry costs, they contribute to the development of risks, vulnerabilities and potential threats. Obviously, too, they also contribute to the ultimate results of the event-management process.

In order to conduct the event-management process, an infrastructure of key practices like those outlined in Table 9.3 is utilized. Throughout this phase interactions require the individual or organization to deal with diversity even if this means avoidance as a strategy (see Figure 9.3). The goal of the interaction phase is to create a personal management infrastructure that enables the use of strategic practices, skills and competencies with needed levels of urgency to manage the interaction to its advantage.

Events and interactions are rich with potential information. Unfortunately, when faced with the event, it can be difficult to collect the data one needs to formulate the best solution to the problem at hand. Moreover, while formal evaluations most often occur at the end of the event, informal evaluations begin as soon as the event is anticipated. Then, once the event is engaged, a variety of informal, often personal, assessments are instituted to discern how the event is being managed: how "it's going." In the post-event phase participants are free to assess virtually every aspect of the interaction as well as speculate about the future.

Bias can interfere with formal or informal assessments. Prejudices that lead to constructed misinformation or "cover-ups" influence how what is seen is reported; these are acts of prejudicial commission. Sometimes assessments are an attempt to verify our preconceived notions ("See. They are just as I told you they would be"). The inability to see information because of poor competencies, lack of experience or the like lead to visions of what we want to see and sometimes what we can, in fact, see: these are acts of prejudicial omission. Either way, poor assessments can shape both the current and future management of this and other types of event.

EVENTS AND RESISTANCE TO THE EMERGENCE OF CHANGE

Change, however nominal, is a product of events and their effects; in many ways there always is some level of desired change associated with *every* event. Moreover, the relationship between events, people and their behaviors is marked by constant change. There's an ebb and flow among these factors as they are impacted by and simultaneously affect each other. It's not uncommon to talk about events as "unfolding over time" or behaviors that are "infectious" and with influences beyond the immediate setting. Indeed, the metamorphic nature of events and behaviors is one reason careful examination of events and behaviors is so important. Virtually everything about events and behavior has some effect on people and organizations or, as Morowitz observed, "the fitness of a species is not a fixed quantity" (Morowitz 2002: 183).

The potential for behaviors and events to change to something other than was planned, a reoccurring theme in this book, can be a serious threat to the nature and well-being of organizations and their membership. People and their organizations are organized to achieve certain objectives. Yet "things change." Unexpected events can disrupt plans.

New behaviors emerge that require different management strategies, or institutionally planned activities give way to the self-organization strategies of others.

Obviously some change is beneficial to the organization and its participants. Innovation is change that brings about new products or processes. Updating materials, work processes or equipment used to produce products or deliver services can offer an array of benefits, and improving competencies throughout the organization can provide benefits for all.

Still people resist change. When resistance is encountered, those driving the change effort sometimes want to attribute it to those likely to be affected by the change. In some instances associating resistance with the participants and their feelings is a warranted conclusion. If a change is going to result in someone losing her job or suffering some other type of loss, the odds are that she will mount a resistance to the proposed change. Other times, however, the reasons for resistance are not "purely personal" but, in fact, may be linked to those associated with the change process. Those involved in managing the event can forget that they, too, have a role in creating defensiveness and fear among participants.

Table 9.4 presents another view of organizational practices that were discussed earlier, in this instance to illustrate how, when they are poorly designed, they can stimulate resistance to change.

Poor communication practices, for example, can lead to a group of participants that are ill prepared to discuss any issues concerning the proposed change and poor evaluation practices can cause resistance because participants may not know what the criteria for successful change implementation are or how they will be evaluated after the change is in place. And so it goes through the various operational practices and strategies. There's a greater likelihood of resistance if these practices are not in place or are poorly used and, too, there is a strong likelihood that the organization will face increased risk, threats and vulnerabilities as well.

THE GENERAL NATURE OF RESISTANCE TO CHANGE

Regardless of the cause, people resist change. Managers are often told to expect two "facts" regarding their efforts to introduce change in their organization. First, that resistance to change is a naturally occurring phenomenon because of people's general tendency not to want to disrupt the status quo; that it is human to resist change. And second, given that fact, resistance to change is not the "fault" of either the manager or the organization. Our research suggests a broader explanation for resistance to change and, in contrast to the two "facts" presented, we suggest a

Table 9.4   Resistance to Change Possibly Stemming from Key Practices that are Missing, Poorly Defined or Misused

STRATEGIC PRACTICES

Communication management practices and strategy	• Those involved don't know how or have the competencies, courage to express concerns • Reasons or needs for the change; not communicated in advance; it's a surprise • Communications stop after the change is introduced. (How is it going?) • Communicators aren't trained in the program or to communicate • Those expected to communicate the change don't or the wrong people are used • The organization's structure (e.g., open vs. closed) doesn't facilitate communication • Poor communication habits (e.g., meeting for the sake of meetings) or styles remain
Evaluation management practices and strategies	• Those involved (either manager or participant) don't know the evaluation plan • They don't know if/how they'll be evaluated vis-à-vis the change • How will potential for bias be controlled for in the evaluations? • How will evaluations take place? What are procedures? Scope of evaluations is unclear • Poorly constructed evaluations don't make a contribution but do use valuable resources
Knowledge management practices and strategies	• Participants don't know how or have the capability or opportunity to make changes • Competing priorities for time make learning the new change process difficult • Participants aren't given the instruction needed to learn the new changes • One-shot training may be insufficient for complex change(s) • Special trainers may be needed but not used or available • Evaluation programs don't measure learning sufficiently
Relationship management practices and strategies	• Organization's values do not support needed teamwork, effort, etc. to master the change • Existing processes promote behaviors that may not be consistent with new changes • Existing processes (e.g., hiring processes) are not adjusted related to changes • Existing processes (e.g., job definitions) may not be updated to match the new changes

(Continued)

Table 9.4 (Continued)   Resistance to Change Possibly Stemming from Key Practices that are Missing, Poorly Defined or Misused

STRATEGIC PRACTICES

Performance management practices and strategies	• Attention to detail in the plan is missing (e.g., performance standards or benchmarks) • "Change Plan" doesn't cover existing organization problems (e.g., bias, poor processes) • Lack of follow-up after the change is launched can compromise performance • Leadership makes participants manage the change, solve problems, etc. on their own • Sloppy research leads to poor plans for the change program, launch, administration, etc. • Management doesn't demonstrate commitment, capabilities to manage the process
Directional management practices and strategies	• Poorly conceived vision, mission, rules (e.g., who the change affects, how, why) • Bias, prejudice regarding whom the change impacts; who are involved, informed, etc. • Lack of support for the change effort (e.g., poor communication, financial support, etc.) • Turf or political issues lead to poor relations, conflict, perceived favoritism, etc. • Rules (e.g., covering access to information, the change process, etc.) are not consistent • Rules for the change process don't mesh or are inconsistent with current operating rules • Little or no disciplinary systems in place to manage the change process at any level
Information management practices and strategies	• Needed or useful information isn't available • Poor accuracy of information (GIGO: You put Garbage In, you'll get Garbage Out) • Access or use of information is restricted, often when it's not necessary • Access to information requires special competencies or special permissions • Natural and/or fabricated bottlenecks impact the flow of or access to information

strong link between leadership, the use or misuse of organizational practices and resistance to change.

Table 9.4 illustrates why these conclusions seem warranted. The column on the left names seven key categories of practices and strategies for managing organization operations. The category names reflect clusters of related practices discussed earlier. For example, directional practices and strategies reflect the organization's vision and the goals used to direct activities so that the vision is realized. Communication strategies and practices include formal (e.g., newsletters and news releases, meetings) and informal (one-on-one or small group sessions) channels and activities used to disseminate information.

The table is self-explanatory. It can be used as a diagnostic tool applied to existing organization issues or as a guide to illustrate a multitude of ways a change effort can be screwed up. For example, we use preconceived notions for virtually all events: your boss calls you into his/her office for a special, unplanned meeting (search your mind: "What's up?"). You are going to a party on Saturday night at a place where you will not know anyone, but most of them will know each other very well (search your mind: "Why am I doing this? Who will I talk to while I'm there?"). Or, you are going on a job interview, and while you have an impression of the company you are interviewing for you know nothing about the people who will interview you or the particulars regarding the job you will do (search your mind: "What do I need to do to make a good impression?"). In each case, part of your preparation for the event, indeed for some people the only way they prepare for the event, is by preparing a list of preconceived notions. These become the preliminary script to operate from as the event unfolds; they're the guide used to select the "best" operational strategies (Table 9.3) to use for the event.

Obviously, the quality of our preconceived notions can range from poor to excellent depending on a number of factors. Hard factors include personal experiences and competencies, time available, the nature of the event or the people involved. Soft factors can include the biases or prejudices of those involved or the strategies available to manage the event. A mistake some make when formulating their preconceived notions is that they let their impressions serve as a hard and fast template for future plans.

A better approach is to use these "thoughts" as a referent or, at best, guide. This approach is prudent because it does not let the potential for bias to cloud one's ability to see the reality of the event. People with strong prejudices, like racists, let their bias influence their impression of the event, regardless of what the event is actually like. For the clear-headed, the actual event *is* a "reality check." As if preconceived notions were not bad enough, when time is at a premium, strong biases rule in the rush to judgment. Recruiting decisions are a case in point. Many trying to recruit for an organization are eager to see only the best in candidates needed to fill a position, so screening and interviewing events become confirmation events: "This person will do. Let's get going." Unfortunately, the "best and brightest" may not be the best for the tasks at hand. Indeed, some companies expect as much as a 20–30 percent turnover in employees during the first year. Moreover, a rush to a conclusion before the event has actually begun reduces the likelihood that constructive self-organization strategies will be used by the event manager. Since events are constantly changing and different and since no one can accurately and consistently predict how an event will unfold sometimes the best way to enter an event is with an openness to change—to launch an accurate response to what one sees, not what one believes "might happen."

SUMMARY AND CONCLUSION OF PART II

An "event" is any incident, planned or not, that occurs and affects people and/or their organizations. Events are observable, have some element of structure, and are governed by formal or informal procedures; there's a sense of a starting and ending point for any event (for example, Morowitz 2002: 179). The event may be the result of the behavior of others, as in an attack, instances of rudeness or kindness, or it may come from the emergence of a natural phenomenon, like a storm. The event's potential effects often precede its actual occurrence. Anticipation that an event will occur, for example, can shape or bias the ways people think and behave in the event. There may be increased preparation for the event, like the preparation before a major storm, the attack on another organization, or before the initiation of new members. When an event negatively impacts expected operations (e.g., causes action to stop) then potential for disruption and harm to the organization can increase too.

Events are described as "emerging" in order to systematize the study of ways an actual event is different from what was expected. This seems warranted because of several factors, the most significant of which are the perceptions actors engaged in the event bring to the setting. Whether one is a bystander, a target of the event or one expected to manage the event and its potential effects, perceptions of the event unfold as experience with the event is achieved and evaluated; in other words, as the event unfolds.

Regardless of the type, all events have a threshold and subsequent context which must be managed. Thresholds are like a "line in the sand." Events begin and the process of preparation associated with managing the event leads to an inevitable critical tension as one seeks clarification between what was expected versus what is observed and, then, the construction of a potentially new and different response. For example, most people in the fire don't take time to think about how it started, how it will end or even how it will unfold over time—just that the fire (or you!) needs to be managed. Moreover, "managed," in this instance, may or may not have anything to do with controlling the fire towards its extinction; management may simply mean "create a way to escape to avoid danger." In this instance one isn't managing the fire, per se, but rather conditions associated with one aspect of the fire.

One thing that makes events so potentially challenging is that they are defined by several characteristics. Events can vary in size and scope. If someone in a grocery store is shelving stock and someone interrupts with a question that interruption is an event. Hurricanes are great events while a terrorist bombing is, by comparison, a small, localized event. Event size, in some instances, doesn't make the event noteworthy.

Some events are bridged with other events that have their own effects. Speeding is a small event but getting a ticket for speeding is both a different event and one with another set of effects. Both the speeding and ticketing events need to be managed but while they are related they obviously require different strategies for managing them and their characteristics. The act of speeding requires the driver to be alert and cognizant of what it takes to drive at certain speeds. Managing the conversation with the ticketing police officer also requires competencies, but these are not likely to be the same as those required for driving a speeding car.

The most economical way to manage events is by transferring skills used to manage other events. Sometimes the skills needed are learned through training and then transferred to the event as needed. Other times skills learned in other applications are modified to manage the event. When no suitable competency options are available the event may be avoided, which also is an option.

Regardless of the approach strategy used, events are engaged in either an active or passive manner and always managed under the influence of bias and sentiments regarding change. The planning can be structured or informal and perhaps even construed as a combination of planning and spontaneity, unfolding throughout the interactions of those involved or because of circumstances and conditions that emerge.

The approach to an event is devoted to anticipation: the construction of a sense for what to expect for the event. It is at this point that a sketch regarding prefabricated reactions is developed for what we "know" about what is to occur. But what if you do not have access to useful information? That's easy, it turns out we fabricate a conclusion as a composite of what we have experienced, believe may occur or, perhaps, just how we feel at the moment. What's important is that it doesn't matter where we get the information. While some information may be better than none, regardless of the source, detail or quality, the interpretation of what is useful or reliable rests with the individual.

This sets the stage for the self-organization of a response to an event at hand. The middle event phase, defined by matching preconceived notions or expectations with what we see before us, with "reality." Again, information is the driving factor here and, again, it doesn't matter what the true quality of the information is that we are immersed in because all of this "real time information" is still subject to filtering through our preconceived notions and biases. From an economic point of view we're simply trying to come to a conclusion efficiently so we can move on to whatever is next on our agenda. So we construct an answer for the question we might ask ourselves or, most probably, that someone might ask us: "So, what did you think?" That is, "Were your preconceived notions confirmed or not?"

The end phase is where our "final" evaluations occur. In truth we're conducting evaluations and assessments throughout the process but it's at the end when a "final, final" conclusion is rendered. Again, accuracy appears to become "the mind of the beholder." If you don't want to like a person before meeting him or her then the event is biased against you changing your sentiments. In fact, if we are really biased against liking the person it's possible we'll manage the interaction phase in such a way that that is the only conclusion possible.

Arnold's (1969) discussion of the relationship between the emotions one feels and the action one may take illustrates the very personal nature of this dynamic evaluation process. Arnold writes that:

> emotions are chameleonlike and change with every new aspect that is evaluated. However, certain appraisals become habitual. The resulting emotions become more intense and are more quickly aroused because of affective and motor memory. They become emotional attitudes. When emotions are acted out repeatedly, they soon become what could be called emotional habits.
>
> (Arnold 1969: 183–184)

If there is a singular importance to evaluation vis-à-vis the event's last phase, it rests in the ways this phase sets the stage and links to future events. A given event is not a discrete phenomenon. Behaviors exhibited during the event are likely to have been stimulated by other action(s)/events and are very likely to stimulate behavior toward future events/actions. If you shout at someone, they may behave coolly toward you, behave in ways that show they are afraid of you, or behave in hostile, aggressive ways toward you. Regardless of the choice they make, their behavior, feelings or emotions can be linked to your behavior, your feelings, your emotions. Behaviors don't exist in isolation so appraisals people make of the people and situations they experience pull them to or push them from future experiences (Arnold 1960: 172).

The next three chapters bring this discussion of organizations to a new level by examining what, in effect, all the fuss is about. The focus of these chapters centers on ways to restructure organizations to maximize performance and generally improve operations, particularly through the use of complexity theory and application of concepts such as "emergence" and "self-organization."

PART III

Designing a Framework for Organizational Effectiveness

Sometimes an organization's leadership realizes there are benefits with letting the membership operate without direction; in other words, to let them self-organize a response to events, problems or situations they encounter. There are examples of this strategic use of people for both the individual as well as group levels, two of which are described below.

For example, one classic tool for stimulating innovation and/or product development in a self-organized manner involves the use of skunkworks teams. These teams are formed within the overall organization and illustrate key features of self-organizing teams. According to McConnell, a skunkworks effort takes a "group of talented, creative product developers, puts them in a facility where they will be freed of the organization's normal bureaucratic restrictions, and turns them loose to develop and innovate" (McConnell 1996: 306). McConnell continues by saying that "management doesn't want to know the details of how the skunkworks team does their job; they just want to know that they're doing it. The team is thus free to organize itself as it sees fit" (1996: 306).

Management has a key role, however, in the success of these teams but, as Wheelwright and Clark point out, "the issue in creating high-performance development is not senior management involvement, but senior management leadership. It is not activity, but effective action, that makes the difference" (Wheelwright and Clark 1995: 21). Competent senior management has both a vision for the organization vis-à-vis its future and a vantage point from which to see the organization as a whole.

One example of the use of a skunkworks team in a manufacturing organization occurred in Warminster, Pennsylvania, at Fischer and Porter Co. Fischer and Porter manufactured technical meters and instruments used to measure the flow of fluids in large-scale industrial settings, like water purification facilities. The creation of a skunkworks at Fischer and Porter involved the formation of a team to drive the development of new ideas and solutions for one of the company's products. According to the retired Chief Executive Officer, Jay Tolson (2009), the organization's R&D department was encumbered by a structure built around formality and accountability, measured through routine checks and balances and defined follow-up procedures. The vision for the new skunkworks team was for something very different.

The team was a collection of individuals from across the organization. Prospective members needed core talents and competencies in key areas, complete separation from their former department and a willingness to be part of a stand-alone team that would not function like a typical department. According to Mr. Tolson, the team's objective was to turn ideas into innovation and innovation into product development. The team would have the materials and people resources it needed at its disposal and was expected to operate without dictated goals and objectives; there was no one looking for mistakes or monitoring their performance. "We didn't have to," Mr. Tolson said. "They made their own rules" (Tolson 2009). Their relationship with the CEO was nominal and coordinated through a monthly, two-hour meeting where issues, plans and, of course, progress could be discussed.

Another illustration of an organization's planned use of self-organized behavior comes from a retail environment. In this case, the company is Best Buy, the nation's leading electronics retailer. Best Buy's ROWE (Results Only Work Environment) program emerged out of efforts to improve its working environment. Initially, "two HR subversives who started a stealth movement among Best Buy's headquarters employees to work wherever and whenever they wanted" led the change effort (Conlin 2009).

ROWE's premise is that work is measured in output, not hours, and that performance should be based on results, not the amount of time one spends at the office. As an article in *Business Week* magazine pointed out, "Best Buy was afflicted by stress, burnout and high turnover. The hope was that ROWE, by freeing employees to make their own work-life decisions, could boost morale and productivity and keep the service initiative on track" (Conlin 2006).

According to Timothy Ferriss (2007), author of *The 4-Hour Work Week*, productivity as a result of ROWE is evident. "Six months after teams go live, they are asked how much more productive they perceive they are on a scale of 0–100%," Ferriss wrote in his blog. "Then managers are asked how much more productive the team is according to actual business results. If perception and reality match, that's a winner. Under this model, ROWE teams show an average increase in productivity of 41%. It makes sense" (Ferriss 2008).

The Fischer and Porter and Best Buy examples illustrate ways organizations can create an environment that fosters self-organized behaviors associated with complexity theory. The organizations described allow individuals and teams to self-organize to meet different needs and for different purposes. Moreover, the examples stand in contrast to those other types of self-organized process discussed where an organization's participants take it upon themselves to construct responses to situations that may or may not be of benefit to the organization.

It should be evident that phenomena explained by complexity theory can materialize in any organization. Emergence and self-organizion of behavior in response to events can occur at any time, in any organization. In the next three chapters the topics presented examine ways organizations can use what's been discussed in earlier chapters to construct organizations that can use facets of complexity theory to:

1. maximize desired performance; and/or
2. curb performance that is undesirable or generally not meeting the organization's operational or performance needs.

Obviously, the discussion and material are presented against a broad backdrop of ethics. What's proposed isn't offered as a way to introduce social engineering designed to control worker behavior. It's an attempt to use available tools, resources and information to clean up or generally improve organizational operations and environments in ways that benefit the maximum number of stakeholders.

CHAPTER 10

Framework for Organizational Effectiveness
The Organizational Level

In Chapter 9, Figure 9.4 provided a sketch of components contributing to successful event management in organizations. It's a summary of ways an organization's systems can help shape individual behavior to produce desired results. But, as we've seen, there are limitations to the influence an organization has on its stakeholders and, regardless of the detail provided in Figure 9.4, it is only a superficial picture of a truly remarkable phenomenon: organizational dynamics. In this and subsequent chapters complexity theory is used again to reveal more robust strategies for thinking about and maximizing individual and organizational effectiveness.

For example, Table 10.1 lists characteristics of what we see as two unique types of system one can associate with organizations. One, Complex Adaptive Systems (Arthur et al. 1997; Johnson 2001; Levin 1998; Miller and Page 2007) is familiar to those who study and do research related to complexity theory. The interactions among components or system members lead to the emergence of behavior or events or patterns in these organizations and these in turn influence the further development of interactions and, subsequently, other patterns, events or behaviors (Miller and Page 2007: 233–244; Sole and Bascompte 2006: 13–14). The second, Competent Adaptive Systems, is offered to extend facets of Complex Adaptive Systems and complexity theory to those situations where self-organized behavior is a primary part of an organization's generic makeup. As Table 10.1 illustrates, these systems reflect or have the same features as Complex Adaptive Systems but assume that competency and operational practices are fundamental to the system's function.

Both contribute to our understanding of organizations and, at times, each can be viewed as related to the other. However, the emphasis on systemic competencies and use of practices is a way to link the

Table 10.1   A Comparison of Complex and Competent Adaptive Systems and the Formation of Behavior and Patterns within an Organization

GENERAL FEATURES OF A COMPLEX ADAPTIVE SYSTEM LEADING TO BEHAVIOR	GENERAL FEATURES OF A COMPETENT ADAPTIVE SYSTEM LEADING TO BEHAVIOR
1. Localized interactions: most interactions are with/near others	1. Maximized contact: open information and communication channels
2. Absence of top-down control: local ownership of decisions	2. Empowered control: local ownership of decisions
3. Prominent network construction: form directs content	3. Open Access Construction: virtual networking
4. The capacity to adapt: capable of adapting to different conditions	4. Embraced innovation and entrepreneurial activity
5. The capacity to evolve: new characteristics can emerge	5. Evolution and change: unlimited emergence and self-organization
	6. Systemic practices that support and reinforce interaction
	7. Dynamic, enriched competencies (Five Dimensions)

Competent Adaptive Systems model to dynamic social systems. Information in Table 10.1 illustrates how each approach differs in accounting for human behavior. In the Complex Adaptive System the referent is largely local while in the Competent Adaptive System the referent is diffuse, systemic in nature.

ELEMENTS OF A SYSTEM AND ITS STRUCTURE

Both systems have advantages, so while there's not a lot to be gained by wondering if one is better than the other, there are some benefits in exploring the capacity of each to stimulate performance. The first three characteristics of these systems outlined in Table 10.1 focus on the impact of structure on organizations and their operations. Camazine et al. (2001) might describe Complex Adaptive Systems as environments where behavior or "pattern formation occurs through interaction internal to the system, without intervention by external directing influences" (Camazine et al. 2001: 7). They see systems lacking self-organization as vulnerable to having "order imposed on them in many different ways, not only through instructions from a supervisory leader but also through various directives, such as blueprints or recipes, or through pre-existing patters in the environment" (Camazine et al. 2001: 7).

Johnson (2001), on the other hand, sees Complex Adaptive Systems as fostering self-organizing behavior, where events are addressed "by drawing on masses of relatively stupid elements, rather than a single, intelligent 'executive branch.'" He describes them as:

> bottom-up systems, not top-down. They get their smarts from below. In a more technical language, they are complex adaptive systems that display emergent behavior ... In these systems, agents residing on one scale start producing behavior that is one scale above them: ants create colonies; urbanites create neighborhoods; simple pattern-recognition software learns how to recommend new books. The movement from low-level rules to higher-level sophistication is what we call emergence.
>
> (Johnson 2001: 18)

Johnson sums up what may be the heart of the matter for complexity theory and self-organized behavior. For Johnson, a system is self-organized when it has multiple agents dynamically interacting in multiple ways, following local rules and oblivious to any higher-level instructions. But for Johnson the behavior wouldn't be considered emergent "until those local interactions resulted in some kind of discernible macro-behavior" ... "a higher-level pattern arising out of parallel complex interactions between local agents" (Johnson 2001: 19).

The characteristics used to describe features of a Complex Adaptive System parallel those used to explain the nature of a Competent Adaptive System. The difference is that in Competent Adaptive Systems the characteristics outlined above are interpreted as both process elements and features or characteristics of a system's structural makeup. At the descriptive level a competent adaptive organization's localized interactions may be the obvious point of origin for the emergence process but not necessarily the foundation for emergence.

Viewing localized interactions as an enabling feature, however, allows one to examine and test the many different features that can define interaction patterns and the manner in which they, too, emerge. For example, localized interactions in these systems rely on a range of management strategies (e.g., information, communication and knowledge management) and these are utilized, promoted and valued over more typical variables like position, title or role. In other words, one is not likely to see people "standing on formalities" in a Competent Adaptive System, where the focus is on action, not who's most important or needed to "OK" what action to take before that action can commence.

In comparison to traditional approaches to an organization's use of strategic practices in Competent Adaptive Systems these become drivers as well as facilitators for the organization and its membership. Competent adaptive organizations embrace an open-access approach to practices and are places where participants keep current on their use, particularly in ways they affect one's role in the organization.

An absence of top-down control is a second descriptive feature of these organizations. In these organizations the manner in which control and/or direction materializes across the organization seems to be more situational than institutional, more a guide than a rule, especially in competently adaptive systems. In competently adaptive systems/organizations people operate with the potential of being a leader/manager/supervisor/follower to some extent and over some period. Everyone is, literally, a manager, at least over one's own job, assignment or area of responsibility.

This leadership latitude makes everyone responsible for the mission, as well as activities that may be associated with achieving the mission. In short, everyone is responsible for his/her own assignments and everyone is a "follower" or non-leader participant to some extent as well. This isn't a semantic exercise; regardless of the organization, everyone reports to someone.

Certain military units, terrorist groups, sports teams and entrepreneurial companies are examples of this organizational feature. But this feature isn't reserved for small organizations or organizations with a finite mission. During the 1970s many manufacturing organizations began giving employees on a production line the authority to stop production if quality seemed to be falling below acceptable standards. These are not "leader-less" groups, but rather instances where roles in the organization have a level of flexibility so that traits typically reserved for a leadership position are distributed across all positions.

One of the reasons these first two features can work in harmony is the way practices, processes and interactions are networked— configured and linked—in the organization. When roles and processes are well defined and integrated effort can be configured so that it streams in the direction it's needed. In other words, neither a rigid top-down nor bottom-up directional format governs the organization or its membership. Rather, energy and effort emerge and follow the best or an ideal course given the conditions (e.g., people, events, needs) of the moment. (Some might even conclude it's a classic illustration of complexity theory in practice.)

Even the term "networking" seems too rigid to describe the exchange of information or communication patterns in these dynamic organizations. Networking implies a state defined by linkages, protocols (e.g., for turn-taking or other communication behaviors) and/or a sense of priorities, gatekeeping or other control mechanisms. In the dynamic organizations we're describing there's an atmosphere of spontaneity sparked by a fluidity of thinking about ways, how and when to proceed or act in a given situation or for a particular event. In these instances, planning and procedures are used more as guides than in a prescriptive sense. This gives the organization and its participants greater latitude and also greater responsibility for their actions.

RESPONSIVENESS, FLEXIBILITY AND CHANGE

A fourth characteristic of these systems is adaptability, specifically the flexibility to change and be changed over time. This responsiveness to and capacity for change is vital for managing unexpected emerging events or unanticipated requirements for the management of events as they unfold. But it's not just change for change's sake; it is very much the right change given the need at hand.

A fire event is a case in point. Sometimes the best response to a fire is to attempt to put out the fire. Other times the best response is to leave the fire and let someone else manage it. Organizations and people are malfunctioning when their systemic makeup prevents them from making a needed or most appropriate change. This becomes more serious when malfunctions are an integral part of the organization such that the systemic configuration of policies, procedures, culture, etc. promotes resistance to change. When this occurs not only performance is affected but sometimes the worst of people and organizations surfaces to do real damage. Consider resistance to Best Buy's ROWE initiative described earlier.

Conlin (2006) reported that while the company's CEO bought into the program, other executives didn't:

> Many execs wondered if the program was simply flextime in a prettier bottle. Others felt that working off-site would lead to longer hours and destroy forever the demarcation between work and personal time. Cynics thought it was all a PR stunt dreamed up by Machiavellian operatives in human resources.

This level of resistance isn't uncommon but again, as Conlin (2006) discovered, things can get worse because "as ROWE infected one department after the other, its supporters ran into old-guard saboteurs, who continue to plot an overthrow and spread warnings of a coming paradise for slackers."

Managing these types of resistance requires well-conceived responses because resistance in these instances is yet another form of self-organization in a complex environment. If an organization's systemic makeup seems to foster resistance, "quick fix" solutions can increase threats, risks or vulnerabilities for the organization. A prescription for change in these instances often is best if it's local or at least regional in scope, narrower in nature and inclusive but not necessarily a concerted effort to get at the root cause of a problem.

Change is a part of the lifespan of all organizations. Sometimes the change is nominal, seemingly unobtrusive and local in its effect while other change is sustainable, protracted and, often, integrated on a wide scale and within the fabric of the organization's systemic nature. But, regardless of the pervasiveness of the change's scope and scale all change has an effect so no change is inconsequential.

ORGANIZATIONAL SYSTEMS AND LONG-TERM CHANGE

Table 10.2 outlines two more views of change. The first column lists key features of change, the second column evolutionary change and the third, spontaneous change. Evolutionary change is change that an organization can or, one might expect, will experience as a manifestation of the organization's lifecycle.

The third column, spontaneous changes, reflects those that emerge as a function of events. A perceived need (e.g., the need to improve quality) may require a change in a manufacturing organization's production processes or the skills of those assembling the product. A sports organization loses a key player to injury and needs to introduce a substitute. Design and implementation of the change needed are products of human intervention.

Individuals initiate some spontaneous changes. People choose to change their lifestyle, their weight and their knowledge of a subject matter or their skill levels. Particular incidents may make the need for change apparent (e.g., substance abuse, health, a grade in a class, or a performance review), but it is an individual who initiates and implements the change needed. Still other spontaneous changes are products of natural phenomena. Accidents may come without warning, and while warnings may accompany an approaching storm, any warnings may be mediated by the individual's interpretation of the storm's intensity and personal resources to "weather the storm."

There's a natural tendency to locate decisions regarding the need to change—the types of change needed, or how the change will be introduced—with designated "decision-makers." But, as we saw above, the true locus of control for decisions regarding organizational change in the adaptive organization may be widely distributed throughout the organization. The restaurant or bar's business is to serve food and drink

Table 10.2 Evolutionary and Spontaneous Change

	EVOLUTIONARY CHANGE: CHANGE EVENTS EMERGING AS A LOGICAL PART OF THE ORGANIZATION'S LIFECYCLE	SPONTANEOUS CHANGE: NATURAL OR HUMAN-CAUSED CHANGE EVENTS
General characteristics	Range from beneficial to non-beneficial and which is often a result of other conditions. Can result in a wholly different direction for the organization.	Range from good to not, from planned to unplanned. One result, effects of the change, can be difficult to predict.
Locus of control	Typically at the top, however, in social movements the top may have little or no control.	Control is typically at the site of the change event.
Phases	Always a beginning, middle and "end" with these considerations.	Inception, growth, occurrence, end, *post hoc*. The change never stops.
Focus: areas where change management is concentrated	Systemic. Range across hard (bricks and mortar) and soft (vision, mission, processes and practices) sides of the organization. Processes, practices, mission.	Specific. Primary focus is on the occurrence and *post hoc* period.
Magnitude: minor to large	While the process may be subtle the effects typically are not. In part because they're systemic. Magnitude is measured in two areas: the likely size of the change and the size of the impact from the change event.	Magnitude is measured in three areas: the likely size of the event, the size of the event and the size of the impact from the event.

in order to make money, but it is the bartender or waitress who can "change that strategy" if he/she determines the prospective patron already has had too much to drink.

The army general in, say, Washington, D.C. decides that the village in Iraq must be taken but the local commander disagrees and chooses not to do so because the target village is not the "best" military target. The school board decides books chosen for school students to read in the high-school English class aren't appropriate and bans them, but a teacher disregards the ban and introduces the books to the students anyway. The coach tells everyone on the team that in the last few seconds of the game the ball must get to Harry to take the final shot, but Joe has the ball and decides he can make it.

These examples may be construed as resistance to authority or as how determining the "right thing to do" may be more a product of one's interpretation of the context in which the decision is being made than the context for which the decision is designed. A more realistic conclusion might be that the ultimate locus of control in event management rests with those at the event. They may try to do what they're told but in the end they simply do what they can.

RESPONSES TO WIDE-SCALE EVOLUTIONARY AND SPONTANEOUS ORGANIZATIONAL CHANGE

This discussion of the role of change and organizations provides an opportunity to review that important aspect of performance management vis-à-vis change. For example, because evolutionary change tends to be widespread, the nature and effects of this level of change can be difficult to address, let alone manage or reverse. This is due to several reasons, any one of which can encumber participants of the organization. Evolutionary change is gradual and effects are sometimes almost imperceptible. Because of this it may be very difficult to launch attempts to manage the change once it is recognized without creating a significant strain on available resources. How easy, for example, would it be for Russia or China to revert to their Communist ideologies or economies? In the 1960s colleges around the country abandoned a standing philosophy of *in loco parentis* in which they operated in place of the parents when students were in school. The change altered campus life throughout the United States. The nature of this change affected everything from curricula and housing policies to dress codes. This isn't to suggest that such changes were bad for the institutions' participants or that they should be guarded against. It's just that, like other change, evolutionary change requires competence, energy and effort.

RESPONDING TO SPONTANEOUS CHANGE

In contrast to evolutionary change, rapidly occurring, spontaneous change, like the quick mobilization to deal with a fire, may result in a "temporary" shift in participation roles and privileges (e.g., the suspension of protocols or rank), but that's it. After the event, things revert to a point near where everyone began. The end is anti-climactic. The *post hoc* period tends to focus on two elements: why and how the event occurred and how the event's ramifications will continue to influence others.

As Table 10.3 illustrates the emergence of the spontaneous event produces a dynamic state for organizations and their membership.

Table 10.3 The Spectrum of Events

1. ROUTINE, ANTICIPATED, EVEN PLANNED-FOR EVENTS WHICH UNFOLD WITHIN THE FRAMEWORK OF ORGANIZATION OR GENERAL ACTIVITY	2. UNANTICIPATED EVENTS WHICH EMERGE BUT ARE WITHIN THE FRAMEWORK OF ORGANIZATIONAL OR GENERAL ACTIVITY	3. EXTRAORDINARY EVENTS THAT ARE WITHIN THE ORGANIZATION'S HORIZON BUT MAY BE ANTICIPATED, PLANNED FOR	4. EXTRAORDINARY EVENTS THAT ARE WITHIN THE ORGANIZATION'S HORIZON BUT TYPICALLY MAY NOT BE ANTICIPATED OR PLANNED FOR	5. EXTRAORDINARY EVENTS BEYOND THE SCOPE OF THE ORGANIZATION THAT ARE OR MAY BE ANTICIPATED OR PLANNED FOR	6. EXTRAORDINARY EVENTS BEYOND THE SCOPE OF THE ORGANIZATION THAT MAY NOT BE ANTICIPATED OR PLANNED FOR
FOCUS: maximum control to shape the event so it meets the organization's needs.	FOCUS: bring into control. Manage the event and effects. Possibly add to repertoire.	FOCUS: some control. Manage the effects. Search for a cause?	FOCUS: manage the effects and recovery. Consider possible future plans.	FOCUS: since these can't be controlled emphasis is on preparation and managing the effects.	FOCUS: since these can't be controlled emphasis is on managing effects and recovery.
EXAMPLE: sales or recruiting events. Assembly activities.	EXAMPLE: customer complaints, employee theft, celebrations.	EXAMPLE: loss of key person. Fire, for example, in a manufacturing facility.	EXAMPLE: new technology. Loss of key stakeholder. Discrimination claims. Aggressive driving.	EXAMPLE: terrorist attack, regional natural disasters.	EXAMPLE: natural disaster (e.g., hurricane). Unethical behavior of external stakeholders (lawyers, doctors).

Everything that happens is unique to both. The spectrum of events illustrates that not all events are the same. Organizations and people have more control over some events than others. Some are pleasant, others not. Some events are more likely to occur than others and some "just happen." What's common about all events is that there are effects associated with them and these are what define the event's saliency for organizations and people.

As the event spectrum illustrates, a plane hijacking is an extraordinary event but one that an airport or airline (the organization) might have actually planned for or at least have provided its staff with some training instructions should one occur. So, in this instance, determining whether the factors that led up to the event, and that might follow after the immediate threat and event have ended, aren't the most relevant issues. What makes one's position in the beginning, middle or end of the event important hinges more on the needs *now, where you are in the event.* Someone building a program to prevent future hijacking might see the preliminary stages of this type of event as most important. A mediator or negotiator might find the middle stages most important, while a lawyer or insurance adjuster might be more concerned with the end stage where damages occurred. Lastly, with all this said regarding the hijacking event the same is true regarding the hijacker's behaviors.

Clearly, events and behavior don't unfold in a neat, linear fashion. Rather, it's as though events and behavior associated with them spawn and nurture twists, turns and new directions for those involved. The initial event becomes new events and new behaviors and these, in turn, produce more events/behaviors.

A second characteristic of events and behaviors is the role and manner in which transition points and thresholds define or shape them. Transition points and thresholds give events and behaviors their distinctive traits and significance. Changes an organization experiences may require whole new sets of competencies and technologies. Moreover, not paying attention to what is happening as changes occur also can increase reaction time when action is required.

TARGETING OPERATIONAL AND ORGANIZATIONAL PRACTICES IS CRITICAL FOR ORGANIZATION-WIDE EFFECTIVENESS

There may not be a "silver bullet" for use in the face of an impending threatening event, but operational practices are the next best thing to have as part of a planned offense and defense. The seven categories of practices are ways to extend an organization's structure so everything from planning and design to hands-on management of routine, day-to-day events occur in ways that are of benefit to the organization. Moreover, opera- tional practices are critical when unanticipated, risky or threatening events have the potential to disrupt organizational performance. These practices have been presented and illustrated in earlier chapters. A brief summary of each is presented here to reframe them in terms of the structural features of organizations.

Evaluation management practices are among the most important and least often used, at least to the extent to which they can be used. Moreover, when they are used they often suffer from poor design, devel- opment and implementation, which makes them a waste of time and, in many respects, an unethical use of the people who use them or are evalu- ated by them (Tafoya 1984, 1978). Evaluations include formal and infor- mal examinations and assessments that estimate or determine value, effectiveness, performance, or other criteria so that judgments or con- clusions are possible. Evaluations are tools organizations can use to anticipate and/or possibly prevent damage from exposure to risks, threats or vulnerabilities.

Knowledge management practices include expected pedagogical activities (training, teaching, mentoring and observation) and the devel- opment of ways of thinking designed to advance learning, understand- ing or competencies generally. Fundamental features of knowledge management practices aim at ensuring competency and skill benchmarks are in place to enable performance beyond intuition or inspirational starting points. Having appropriate competency and skill benchmarks in place begins with effective hiring programs. When candidates enter an organization, knowledge management processes continue through orientation programs and training and development programs. Advanced knowledge management practices include the use of databases or online training and information management, so that individuals push their own self-study opportunities. Beyond these, knowledge management aimed at achieving system-wide or specialized development includes mentoring, succession planning or specialized training, often particu- larly designed to reduce risk, manage threats or address vulnerabilities.

Communication management practices enhance skills that facilitate the transmission and reception of information (e.g., in listening, speak- ing and writing). These efforts can include developing process rules and practices to guide or regulate the flow of information and are evident in events, activities, materials and programs. Communication practices are among the most important in an organization because they transcend all other practices. All practices are inter-related but only communication practices are essential to all other practices.

Communication is the single most important way cults, religions and political organizations convey their messages to potential and existing stakeholders. Communication also is the single most important factor behind terrorist organizations' operations. Terrorists do not necessarily bomb a building to destroy property or assassinate a political figure to remove that person from the mainstream. Often terrorists commit their acts as a communication strategy to demonstrate they exist—that "this act" is a sign of their reach, that "these are people or ideals we don't like" or that "this behavior or action demonstrates how pervasive we are as a force." The role, structure and practice of communication are what separate the terrorist organization from the petty thief or mob.

Effective communication skills and strategies mark the stream of activities associated with the efforts of lawyers or doctors, as individual contributor organizations. The individual contributor utilizes other organization practices but communication is the pivotal practice.

Organizations cannot manage day-to-day or extreme events without communication. They use communication to define, establish and build their brands and they use communication again when their brand is threatened, or after "brand bruising events." The Tylenol scare in 1982, the Exxon Valdez oil spill in 1989, the My Lai massacre in Vietnam in 1968 and the Abu Ghraib prisoner abuse incident in 2005 are events whose memory lasts in the minds of the public. The memories last not only because of what happened but also because of how communication activities associated with these events were managed. Effects associated with some events are long lasting and can extend their potentially damaging influence beyond the activities immediately surrounding the event. Ramifications associated with the Tylenol event, for example, are evident to this day—whenever one opens a bottle of water, vitamins or, of course, Tylenol. Despite the impact of the event's effects, Proctor and Gamble's credibility and professional image managed to negotiate this disaster in large part because of the communication program used.

Regardless of the benefits and value of communication practices one does not have to look closely at most organizations to see how often these practices are underutilized, abused or generally ignored. Communication may flow only one way, usually down the organization with few feedback mechanisms. The use of special languages or codes, often to protect turfs or positions, can also hinder development of a useful communication environment. Indeed, when poor communication patterns exist often it's people, rather than programs or practices, that lead to communication problems.

Size can be an issue in defining an organization's communication environment, but size is not as significant a factor as it was in the past. Computers and personal handheld devices like cell phones, for example, add speed, accessibility and flexibility to communication. These advancements dramatically reduce the impact an organization's size may have on communication flows. An organization's use of intranets, for example, can reduce the costs associated with producing and disseminating newsletters, updates and follow-ups to meetings, further reducing communication obstacles in even the largest organizations.

Information management practices are a different story. Despite the logical relationship between communication and information, information is easier to control in most organizations. Organizations and people tend to control information when they cannot trust that the information will be secure without its being controlled. Trade secrets, plans regarding new product releases, acts of aggression against an opponent, or the rituals of a secret society are examples of information controlled by organizations. Information control in these instances is a way to manage risk and threats and/or to reduce the organization's vulnerabilities.

All practices can tell insiders and outsiders a lot about the organization. Information management practices are an illustration. Some in organizations see the control of information as a badge of rank or an indicator of power, a way of saying "I'm in and you're not." Using information in this manner communicates something about the organization's culture and creates the potential for communication breakdowns during critical events like emergencies or a crisis. Think about what happens when someone leaves the company and takes the password to their computer with them. Performance at that workstation suddenly comes to a halt.

When access to information is limited or controlled there's a sense that there are gaps separating groups of the organization's membership. It also may suggest that a "gatekeeper" manages the flow of communication between or among groups or the membership as a whole. Organizational behaviors like these run contrary to the philosophical and practical nature of information management practices that seek to maximize information availability.

Creating barriers to information flows can slow or prevent the transmission of information. This can be a critical problem during emergencies. In some instances barriers between groups can lead to the development of informal networks like "grapevines" or "rumor mills." There is an old notion in information theory that people will get the information they need or want even if that means they have to create it.

When these types of environmental practice shape information management, a variety of problems can emerge, not least of which is differentiating between truth and rumor.

Unnecessary barriers stifling the flow of information can lead to increased tensions or divisions between or among groups in the organization. Clearly, controlling information in some instances is necessary, but making non-critical information privileged ties up process flows with extra bureaucracy and can create division among people supposedly pursuing the same mission. It's insulting when people know information is not "secret" or sensitive but they still can't have access to it. Creating a "we/they" hierarchy or a sense of favoritism can be more damaging than the loss of key equipment or materials. In fact, all of these negative control mechanisms can materialize into vulnerabilities for the organization during times of crisis, an emergency, or even the handling of day-to-day matters as petty power struggles risk the efficient flow of operational processes or procedures.

Information, as a composite of facts, attitudes, opinions and beliefs, is critical for effective response and recovery processes. During a crisis, information communicates not only the people, equipment and material needed to re-establish key processes, but also how quickly they're needed or how great the emergency. One needs only to look at the Hurricane Katrina/FEMA fiasco of 2006 in terms of information issues and the important role of this one operational practice quickly becomes apparent.

One expects information management problems to arise and potentially impact physical operations during a hurricane. Transmission lines may be down and people may be more concerned with finding shelter than talking with someone. The information problems that occurred after Katrina, however, seemed more perverse. After the hurricane people were unable to get answers to questions, and the information they received was incomplete and, sometimes, even inaccurate. All of this and the hurricane itself had passed! Katrina is one of the best examples of the role of people in whether communication and information flow successfully or not.

Communication and information management around Katrina also demonstrates another phenomenon that can emerge in organizations. People in organizations don't need to be threatened by terrorists or attacked by an opponent or enemy to experience life-threatening, organization-damaging events; sometimes they can let their organizations operate as designed, and catastrophe can follow. Perhaps the most ironic information-related learning point to take away from Katrina was that the events in New Orleans occurred to the same generation of Americans who experienced the attack on the World Trade Center and who claim to fear even potentially greater, more traumatic events in the future. Katrina was an opportunity to practice wide-scale disaster management on a real-time, real-life event, and it failed.

The ongoing competition between terrorist organizations and national governments offers information and communication case studies. In events related to these conflicts, national governments need and rely on pre- *and* post-event information *and* information management processes, while the terrorist organizations need pre-event information *and* information management processes. Terrorist organizations are in the "delivery business"; they do not need to wait for a response. Indeed, while the natural tendency is to react to the terrorist event—for example a bombing—often more is gained by examining information management across the terrorist's "event spectrum": the pre-event, event and post-event periods of activity. How do terrorists control information, and what information is controlled? What information do they need and how do they get it? What information do they fabricate and how do they distribute it? Moreover, what information don't they need and why not? All of these questions tell something about an organization's behavior given its information needs and information management strategies and practices. And this is just one of the key practices successful organizations use to maximize their performance.

Once information flows are troubled or disrupted other management practices and behaviors must engage for successful event-management processes to begin or continue. Some organizations like doctors, lawyers or consultants are dependent on information. Without critical information these organizations can develop increased risk exposures and become vulnerable to errors or poor judgment associated with incomplete or unfulfilled information needs. Information is needed to assess situations, set priorities, design plans of action, to evaluate the progress of plans, and to assess the success of plans and procedures after the event is brought under control.

Directional management practices are another category important to all organizations. One facet of directional management is the devices an organization uses to define its purpose or aspirations. The mission, or purpose, often appears as a "mission statement" and can be formally and publicly presented or kept as a secret known only to insiders. Sometimes organizations don't feel the need to state their mission; it's just "understood," like the mission of a local business (e.g., a laundry or local lawn-care company) that seeks, simply, to "make a profit while managing risk." Whatever the case, and however formal or informal, the mission provides direction by focusing efforts toward an achievable point, usually with a defined timeframe in mind.

Unions, religions, secret societies, special project teams and special interest groups typify organizations that are defined in terms of a particular mission. Their mission may range in focus from one that's precisely stated to one that's vague or less defined. Mission statements that define a point in time or specific benchmark can be modified or changed to reflect the organization's achievements or new interests.

Some organizations do not define their mission in a temporal sense or link it with attainment of an "achievable" target. For these the goal is not a place in time but a "way of being." A religious order's mission to "serve God" is ongoing; it is not viewed as a point or mark one achieves but is "renewed" from moment to moment. Organizations with this type of mission are almost impossible to stop because the mission is an ideal, often best understood through the personal interpretations of each member of the organization.

Directional management practices are linked to equally personal organizational concepts like values, culture or behavioral ethics. These philosophies, conceptions or principles can be traced back to the mission but are structured to embrace, reflect and advance the personal philosophical nature of the organization *and* its membership. These become the foundations upon which the organization's image, brand and/or reputation are grounded and the base upon which individual performance is constructed and evaluated. Once the directional practices are in place at the strategic organizational level, tactical directional factors, like the definition of goals, objectives and activities can be delineated, thus setting the stage for the development of performance management practices.

Performance management practices reflect policies, procedures and/ or routines used to support the establishment and execution of behavioral and performance parameters for individuals or the organization. At this level the organization translates values and ideals into measurable goals, objectives and activities. An expectation that the racetrack "pit crew" should be "fast" translates into "seconds," a measurable indicator of "fast." A notion that the product should be well made becomes stipulated as a measurable "level of quality." Expectations that staff should be courteous become measurable benchmarks of "service standards."

Performance standards are like the base of a pyramid with the organization's vision and mission at the top (see Table 1.1, p. 6). Next are goals. Within each family of goals are sets of measurable objectives and, finally, these turn into actions, activities or events. Ideally, rules or established protocols guide the development of performance standards. Moreover, performance standards are not meant to be a form of punishment or secret; they should be communicated to those expected to perform within the standards established. Finally, since performance standards are associated with areas of responsibility, assessments or evaluations of an individual's performance can be based on the appropriate performance standards.

Relationship management practices seek to produce a state or feeling of nearness between or among individuals and/or organizations. If successful, relationship practices allow one to speak about or assess these relationships using labels like "quality," "value" or "importance." Once established the parameters of a relationship can be used to delineate skills useful in developing or maintaining them (for example, decision-making, problem-solving, negotiation, bargaining or conflict resolution).[1]

Efforts to manage risk and threats are a natural part of relationship management practices. Organizations build or repair relationships with adversaries, form alliances with other organizations that may have needed resources, or engage in conflicts with those with whom they have poor relationships. Internally, organizations use relationship management for mundane issues associated with pecking order, turf issues, in/out-groups, seating order, or to establish protocols associated with the organization's hierarchy. In some instances relationship management practices even can stipulate if or how relationships develop and the events or programs used to initiate or develop those relationships.

Some programs, like customer service, quality or warranty programs are developed to anticipate or prevent problems from developing in the organization's relationship with stakeholders. Process assessments of or around interactions or transaction points between the organization and its stakeholders can be used to improve events or service delivery, especially when these assessments are based on established performance criteria. Should conflict events emerge, there is a wide array of tools and programs to manage them or their effects. For example, counseling, punishment, surveillance and investigations are examples of often used options.

Practices are dynamic tools. They simultaneously extend an organization's structure to all areas but they also have the unique capacity to imbue people, those accountable for the organization's performance, with a personal template for behavior.[2] In the first instance the practices reflect "what" or "how" things are done but in the second instance they reflect "a way" things can be done. The extent to which these two themes emerge rests, again, with people: those leading the organization and those doing the work.

Many organizations make the mistake of taking time and resources to identify and develop core practices and then, once they are developed and launched, they are placed safely on a shelf. There is a level of efficiency and economy associated with this approach but the returns tend to be short-term. Treating practices as though they are set in stone can lead to increased risk, threats and vulnerabilities for the organization and its membership. The introduction of new materials, equipment, legislation, competencies and the like can change the processes associated with their use, so one should expect that key practices should change as well. Improving communication around the use of a particular practice can improve the skill or competency associated with the practice as well as the opportunities to use the practice for the organization's benefit.

Certain organizations need practices to be centrally located to be of strategic benefit. Those organizations have naturally high control needs (e.g., security, military, terrorist, penal systems, cults, gaming, research and certain religious organizations). In most other organizations decentralizing responsibilities makes them "everyone's responsibility."

CHAPTER II

Framework for Organizational Effectiveness
People and Performance

Performance is not treated the same in all organizations. In enterprises, companies like General Electric or Microsoft, for example, we are accustomed to hear people talk about profits or losses, production rates or new product releases. Millions of dollars in stock value can hinge on a penny's profit or loss when earnings are reported. The same is true for individual contributor organizations like tennis players, doctors or lawyers where win/loss records, patient recovery rates or the ratio of cases won or lost are suitable benchmarks for gauging performance in these organizations. But what about organizations that do not measure gain in terms of profits, sales or win/loss records?

STIPULATING PERFORMANCE EXPECTATIONS: IN EFFECTIVE ORGANIZATIONS PEOPLE KNOW WHAT'S EXPECTED OF THEM

What is a good performance indicator for a religious community like a synagogue or parish? Or what about charitable organization like a food bank, a social organization like a Girl or Boy Scout troop, or a terrorist organization? What are the benchmarks for successful performance for these? They can't easily demonstrate their capacity to perform according to conventional production or service standards. Some organizations, like a military unit or a police SWAT team, may never be called in to demonstrate their performance capabilities so how can one be sure they would perform against expectations when called into action? A software development team may only see its product developed and released after many years of research and work. Is that when its performance should be evaluated? What about the period in between? And how does a financial advisor, priest, lawyer, judge or doctor demonstrate a fairness or ethical profile? In many of these organizations things are done either right or not.

What about other performance issues, like how people behave toward one another? Should institutions stipulate and measure how priests, lawyers or doctors perform ethically regarding their parishioners', clients' or patients' confidentiality? Labor unions do not exist in the United States and elsewhere because their members like to pay dues. They exist because the risks, threats and vulnerabilities in the workplace demand someone represent workers and their needs. Unions focus on the performance of others, not necessarily their own membership.

At the heart of this discussion is the fact that poor performance places the organization at risk because of what did or did not happen. Consider, for example, the use of the scale below (Table 11.1) for evaluating an employee's performance. It not only presents a range of acceptable and unacceptable performance, but also a numerical value with each scale position. This makes it possible to compare scores across a variety of organizations or on different categories within the same organization. But this scale has one other feature that makes it particularly useful: it includes a statement that explains something about the way the score was established.

It's not hard to image the same scale, with some modifications, used in a religious organization to evaluate a novice, in a school system to evaluate a student or teacher, in a charitable group to gauge its fundraising efforts, or even in a terrorist organization to evaluate the performance of a member. It is not even necessary to use the scale on paper. Most of us conduct informal evaluations of things around us every day using "mental scales" like the one below. It is a simple exercise of assigning a specific value to what is observed and comparing that to what is expected.

We resort to scales such as these because they allow for a way to quantify consensus about what's expected, what various levels of performance look like and, of course, what's observed. These types of rating are also popular because they provide a baseline, a common understanding among participants about what to expect of all people and especially for routine, key events. They also allow for score comparisons across people or situations. The need for evaluation is critical even when the nature of organizational effectiveness is hard to pin down. Where, for example, does one draw the line between the organization's general role in performance and the performance of individuals? Is a sales clerk's rudeness representative of an organization's failure or simply one employee's? If one person's carelessness causes a workplace accident, is that a reflection on the organization or just the individual? If a police officer brutalizes a suspect or a priest violates a parishioner,

Table 11.1   Rating Scale Illustrating Performance Expectations

EXCEPTIONAL PERFORMANCE	EXCEEDS EXPECTATIONS	MEETS EXPECTATIONS	DOES NOT MEET EXPECTATIONS	FAILURE. DOES NOT ACHIEVE MINIMALLY ACCEPTABLE RESULTS
5.0 Far exceeds normal expectations. Consistently seeks new opportunities to improve. Self-directed. Reliable.	4.0 Achieves results beyond expectations. Requires less than normal direction and supervision.	3.0 Consistently meets expected results on time and at established standards. Competent performance. Requires normal supervision.	2.0 Missed or incomplete goals and objectives. Performance needs improvement. Close supervisory guidance required.	1.0 Inappropriate workplace behavior; work performed in an unsatisfactory manner or other deficiency identified. Fails to meet key goals or objectives. Immediate remedial action is required. Monitoring, even restriction of privileges possible. Continued privileges subject to early and considerable performance improvement.

where is the responsibility grounded? When, or how, does one person's poor performance reflect organizational ineffectiveness?

Similar questions arise when looking at different types of organization. Are the standards of performance for a terrorist organization different from those of the security organizations whose job it is to limit the terrorist organization's effectiveness? Why do organizations with all the right resources seem to fail when confronting an unexpected event or crisis? Is there a way to account for the success of one organization over another, even when both seem equally qualified? What is there about one culture that makes it attractive and another that appears unattractive or undesirable, and how do these judgments influence interactions with either culture?

Scales are useful for periodically measuring the performance of individuals or small groups but they are not particularly useful when looking at the behavior of organizations as a whole; they are just too general. The same is true for discussions of organizational performance that center on holistic terms like "results" or stop their analysis of performance with cursory examinations of the effects or consequences of effort. Organizational performance is more than knowing how the behavior of individuals affects the organization. Things get "sticky" when one tries to explain organizational performance as the sum of the performance of its components or parts. At both the macro and micro levels, organizational performance is best measured in terms of results, but to truly understand performance the nature of the results observed must be closely examined. This, then, is the focus of the performance evaluation.

PERFORMANCE EXPECTATIONS VARY BY ORGANIZATIONAL TYPE

Perhaps a good way to begin examining the issue of performance in organizations is to look at the underlying expectations associated with the organization. In this case, we begin with the four types of organization presented in this book. The first of these types is the "enterprise." Familiar examples of the enterprise include retail stores, for-profit corporations and the like. But they also include organizations like factories, mills, workshops, studios, repair centers and laboratories.

The Enterprise Organization Type

The dominant characteristic of the *enterprise* is its three-part focus on growth (financial or otherwise), meeting stakeholder needs and simultaneously managing risks, threats and vulnerabilities. The enterprise pursues its mission via measurable targets. Policies and procedures are important to the enterprise. In fact, in some instances it appears as though the policies and procedures both define and drive the enterprise.

Evaluation and performance standards are an important part of the enterprise's efforts to achieve its mission. These, when linked to production, products, services and procedures, help establish the true focal point for performance in the enterprise: *individual accountability*. Clear and unambiguous definitions of tasks, their requirements, and links to organization objectives, become the basis for knowing one's personal responsibilities and accountabilities.

Leadership's role is to guide the use of resources vis-à-vis the organization's vision and mission. The vision, designed to display the organization's image of itself at some point in the future, reflects the interests of stakeholders (e.g., customers, clients, competitors, regulatory agencies) and the organization's scope of operations (e.g., the marketplace). Similarly, the organization's structure, its policies, job descriptions, project plans and the like serve as guides for individual behavior and performance. It's safe to say in most cases the enterprise "operates by the book."

Participants know that in the enterprise performance means "getting the job done." You can be part of the organization as long as you do what is expected for as long as you are needed (or affordable). If the organization no longer needs what the individual has to offer the individual should not expect to stay. There are no promises in the enterprise. Skills and competencies, communication with others and day-to-day activity *must* produce results. Relationships in the enterprise are "business relationships." There are few surprises. The individual knows what to do and does it.

Threats, vulnerabilities and risk can be widespread and attributable to internal and external factors. They may be naturally occurring—the result of changing stakeholder needs, the introduction of new technologies, failing to keep abreast of the times or changing conditions, or a natural maturation of the organization's culture. They may be warranted, as in the case of complaints or fines resulting from poor working conditions or carelessness. They may be unexpected—an attack by competitors, for example, through a threat of takeover.

The Community Organization Type

The *community* organization's dominant characteristic is its almost singular focus on a vision and mission. These are *the* reasons, often the only reasons, the community exists. Growth, too, reflects a focus on the mission. Members can be added whether there is any apparent need for them or not. In fact, many members may not have any specific role in the community. They add "size" to the organization and sometimes revenue, but that's the extent of their "performance." If there are expectations for members it is that they follow the community's policies and procedures—that they maintain a clear alignment with the community's vision and mission.

The community's members often see themselves in pursuit of an ideal, a philosophy. Cultures take a similar orientation: "Here's who we are. It's who we have always been. It's who we will always be!" The community welcomes anyone interested in its beliefs or "reason for existing." If the participant has specific skills, the community will try to use them. When focused performance is needed, this can materialize as energy and effort. The community needs membership to recruit others, to promote the organization's ideas, or, sometimes, simply to be a presence—to make the whole place seem like one big family.

It is not that there are no boundaries or structure in communities because there are. But everything—skills and competencies, communication with others and, in the end, performance—is linked to the relationships participants have with each other and the community's mission. Control and direction in the community are defined in terms of the vision or mission and manifested through rituals, orientations and instruction and, of course, policies and procedures. Policies and procedures, in the community, are very useful ways to manage entry to and exit from the community in addition to handling day-to-day affairs. One rule that often guides a community's policies is that deviation from the vision is not tolerated.

People and relationships are important in communities. People get things done acting, thinking and working as a community. The community often may measure success and disappointments as a community. Networks tend to be reinforcing. They are used to educate, nurture, monitor and, if needed, participate in the evaluation and management of participants. Leadership is most important to the community. In some instances, however, the leader is perceived as the personification of the ideal, and this, in turn, can make some communities vulnerable to dependencies or a "follower relationship" between the leadership and membership.

Communities tend to be insulated from many external threats because of their internal focus. Vulnerabilities typically are associated with things that challenge achieving their mission. Communities become most at risk when the pursuit of their mission brings them in conflict with broader, mainstream institutions. This is especially likely when organizations outside the community perceive it to be a threat to the norm or mainstream expectations.

The Team Organization Type

Like the community, the *team*'s focus is the achievement of the mission, only in this instance, participants and their skills are very important. The membership's competencies facilitate the team's efforts. Communities also rely on people to achieve the mission but membership selection in the community does not place as much emphasis on skills as in the team. The team's mission tends to be more time-bound than the community's and skills can facilitate quick action. A baseball team wins a title (this year), a project team completes its work and submits a report (when scheduled) and the surgical team successfully completes the operation (and moves on to the next patient.) In these instances, being part of a team is the way to get things done

If someone "makes the team" or proves he/she can deliver, he/she is accepted. Others are outsiders. It is important to keep up one's skills in order to stay. Performance allows you to participate. Skills contribute to the team, communication centers around the team and performance reflects the team's work. Individual performance is important. It is possible to be a star, but performance with the team is most important. Sure, the organization has a mission but so does the team. Participants may work for the organization, but their team, be it a department or group, is their primary relationship.

Operational practices (e.g., information, communication or relationship management practices) are important for the team, particularly given the time constraints that can define their efforts. Indeed, for some teams (e.g., military, police or medical) there are few tolerances for variance beyond defined practices. Team practices in regulated disciples, like sports, law or medicine, may be defined and monitored by outside agencies.

While relationships are important, there are opportunities for individuals to flourish, if not shine, in comparison with others on the team. This is because of the team's dependence on skill to achieve its mission. In enterprise and community organizations, things like technology or sheer numbers can mitigate or augment the efforts to achieve a mission, but teams succeed in large part by the competencies of their members. Leadership, in this instance, serves to maximize the talent of individuals, given the mission or challenges at hand. In short, teams are organizations where people are allowed to participate because they can make a contribution to the team.

A vulnerability that affects teams is loss of key personnel. A team that does not maintain the competencies needed to perform is also at risk, particularly when competing teams are available to do the work. Because many teams are expected to operate within rule-governed environments, a team's or a team member's failure to honor expectations also can lead to penalties or losses.

The Individual Contributor Organization Type

Performance of an expert, the star or "the authority" is the primary driver of the *individual contributor* organization. The individual contributor organization may have a vision and mission but it is performance, particularly in contrast with the other three types of organization, that sets it apart and makes it the "one to choose" in special situations. Professionals like doctors, educators or lawyers and those who work in trades like antique restoration, artists or architects are typical examples.

The individual contributor is largely self-directed. Like other organizational types, he or she can exist as a self-sustaining entity or be part of a larger organization, like a surgeon with a private practice who is affiliated with a hospital, a designer with an affiliation to a particular department store, a lawyer within a firm or a key software engineer within a company. Individual contributors tend to work alone. They know what is expected and do it. If they don't have to interact with anyone else, they don't. In many ways, individual contributors are their own bosses. They have the skills to get things done on their own, with or without others, although they may be assigned to a particular department or group when part of a larger organization. They are a natural resource.

Competency is critical for the individual contributor organizations, and that is reflected in their operational practices. Pharmacists, mechanics, accountants or real-estate agents are subject to rules and regulations that ensure that professionals have certain levels of competency before they offer their services. Competencies not only help the individual contributor perform as expected, but they enable him/her to enjoy a certain degree of independence. Independence comes at a price, however. The individual contributor organization is vulnerable to economic conditions, the strength of the relationship they have with key clients, or the need for competent, available support staff. Anything that prevents the individual contributor organization from functioning, like loss of a key individual, is a representative risk.

Operational practices designed to organize and manage performance facilitate not only the achievement of an organization's mission and goals but can also be used in specific applications associated with day-to-day events and activities. Operational practices are primary contributors to an organization's ongoing functioning. Practices play a role in different organizational features. Table 11.2, for example, illustrates how organizational practices can contribute to the development of one performance feature important in relationships: trust. In this illustration, the column on the right lists activities that can contribute to, and the absence of which can cause harm to, the development or improvement of relationships in organizations.

In Table 11.3, another use of organizational practices is illustrated. Here different operational practices (listed in the column to the left) are utilized in a problem-solving application. The table illustrates how general use and maintenance of organizational practices can be tools or aids when doing research, solving problems or making decisions. So an organization's development of good relational practices can help a problem-solver identify and work with others who might be able to solve the problem.

Competent use of information and communication practices may mean that the organization has access to databases for use when solving

Table 11.2 Using Operational Practices to Build Trust

STRATEGIC PRACTICES	REPRESENTATIVE ACTIVITIES ASSOCIATED WITH THE USE OF ORGANIZATIONAL PRACTICES TO BUILD TRUST IN KEY RELATIONSHIPS
Communication management practices and strategies	• Communicate clearly and consistently. • Ensure staff have communication competencies needed.
Evaluation management practices and strategies	• Establish stakeholder relationships needs. • Establish performance benchmarks for ALL involved in the relationship. • Evaluate staff for threats to relationships (e.g., bias, discrimination). • Evaluate operational procedures for effectiveness (consistency, reliability).
Knowledge management practices and strategies	• Ensure staff have the capacity to perform and opportunity to learn. • Educate stakeholders on their responsibilities to the relationship. • Provide resources (e.g., databases and materials) for stakeholders.
Relationship management practices and strategies	• Establish critical "relationship building behaviors" as goals. • Build programs to build "relationship awareness." • Hire people who fit "relationship building profiles." • Define "relationship management" elements of jobs, tasks, responsibilities.
Performance management practices and strategies	• Define skills and competencies required for relationship building, maintenance. • Define key organization processes that can impact relationships. • Target coaching skills that may be needed to support development efforts. • Build investigative processes to use in evaluating relationship performance. • Ensure consistency and reliability of processes.
Information management practices and strategies	• Ensure the accuracy of information available to stakeholders. • Ensure systems are in place to use needed information. • Ensure the accessibility of information. • Bias, consistency of application, bottlenecks.

problems or generally doing research. Indeed, people involved in managing information resources may become extensions of the problem-solving effort with an informal seat on the problem-solving team. This often happens in organizations that allow "cross-functional teams" to develop when trying to solve problems or make decisions.

The ways organizational practices are managed can improve a participant's sense of belonging to the organization; it's right for me, it's safe and it's "healthy." Practices typically have a proactive or preventative tone to address threats, risks or vulnerabilities so that by having them in place, it's conceivable that the emergence of potential destabilizers is reduced or at least better prepared for, should they occur. Indeed, having key practices in place can appear as evidence of responsible management to regulators, adjudicators or the public in general should problems occur. The prudent use of organizational practices also can communicate something about the management's commitment to the organization and mission.

Structure, as discussed, provides the framework for organizational operations. As such, organizational structure facilitates the organization's efforts at maintaining direction and control, for example, through the development and use of rules. Organizational practices are a manifestation of rules and a means for further defining the organization's physical structure by delineating its subtle infrastructure. In this sense, operational practices are the tools for use in defining "how" to achieve direction and control given the organization's rules and structure. Organizational practices are important in their own right as a means for facilitating direction and control, but they are critical for managing risks, threats and vulnerabilities inherent in the operation of an organization.

Organizational practices are "ways of behavior" that can shape individual and group performance. Since organizations exist to achieve their mission, they must do so while simultaneously managing exposures

Table 11.3 An Example Illustrating the Inter-Relatedness of Operational Management Practices and their Use in a Problem-Solving Application

Step 1
An issue or problem is recognized

Step 2
Interpret the issue/problem
The problem is defined and priorities recognized in terms of risk, time investment and knowledge needed/possessed, etc.

Step 3
A response strategy is prepared based on what you know about the problem and key stakeholders
~ Use one of the response strategies in Step 4 ~

Table 11.3 (Continued)   An Example Illustrating the Inter-Relatedness of Operational
Management Practices and their Use in a Problem-Solving Application

A. RELATIONSHIP AND KNOWLEDGE MANAGEMENT PRACTICES	Step 4a You take action: use prior knowledge or get additional information (e.g., from databases). END	Step 4b You choose to let someone else do it (pass the problem off—use a proxy). END (for you)	Step 4c You delay: acquire the knowledge needed to act. CONTINUE	Step 4d You take no action (maybe it will go away). END

B. INFORMATION MANAGEMENT	Step 5 Seek relevant information. Set up formal search processes to gather needed information. Seek out reliable resources within the organization for information.

C. EVALUATION MANAGEMENT	Step 6 Evaluate: verify information is relevant and valid.

D. PROCESS MANAGEMENT	Step 7 Adapt information and build a strategy and/or conduct additional research. Verify the "legality" of the possible solution.

E. EVALUATION, INFORMATION AND PROCESS MANAGEMENT	Step 8 Trial run to test the solution (some form is always appropriate).

F. PERFORMANCE MANAGEMENT	Step 9 Take action. Implement the plan, strategy and tactics.

G. EVALUATION AND INFORMATION MANAGEMENT	Step 10 Evaluate. (How did it go? Report final information.)

H. COMMUNICATION AND KNOWLEDGE MANAGEMENT	Step 11a Develop BKMs (best known methods) for use in the future. END	Step 11b Add knowledge and experience to your personal skills. END

resulting from risks, threats and vulnerabilities that are a natural part of the organization's nature or that can emerge in the course of the organization's operation. What makes risks, threats and vulnerabilities most challenging for organizations is that they can emerge from within and outside the organization. It is through the competent use of organizational practices that threats, risks and vulnerabilities can be addressed and managed.

CHAPTER 12

Framework for Organizational Effectiveness
Urgency and Competency at the Individual Level

The scope of the previous chapters has concentrated on the role of structural elements that facilitate organizational performance. Form, without content or defined functions, seldom produces an effective device, idea, person or organization. One key facet of the formation of content is the "urgency" people and organizations bring or assign to the seriousness, insistence, exigency or sheer need to act.

URGENCY IS A PERSONAL, PROACTIVE PRECURSOR TO ACTION
So special, in fact, is urgency that some would say few examples, if any, exist of people or organizations that demonstrate this unique quality—especially over long timespans. The individual with a high sense of urgency can face a variety of challenges that may have nothing to do with the position one has or the work to be done. "Burnout" or accelerated exhaustion can result from the individual's poor management, usually attributable to the supervision received. For example, most people with a high sense of urgency often are the first to be assigned more work—not because it's wanted or warranted but rather because people know this is someone to be counted on to get the job done. The group manager may have others to choose from but that doesn't mean they're ones to count on to perform.

Those with high levels of a sense of urgency also create problems for themselves. Not pushing back when they have already got too much to do, poor time management, or an inability to set priorities (not everything demands a high sense of urgency) may be linked to personal management issues of some with a high sense of urgency.

The high-urgency individual can face other, sometimes truly peculiar, challenges, such as being ridiculed for doing the work others can't (or won't) do. This may be an indication of an environment that is out of control but it still can have a potentially negative impact on the person "just trying to get things done." When one hears labels or comments attached to the high-urgency member like "brown nose" or "he thinks he's so much better than us," it makes us stop and wonder if the organization's membership really understands:

1. the broader mission; and
2. their role in achieving that mission.

When people can be ridiculed for "working too fast," "working too hard," "working too much" or labeled "teacher's pet," "not a team player," because they're quick to respond to even the most undesirable task, there's a problem in the organization's environment.

But urgency is a valuable commodity in an organization. Urgency is what turns intent into action. The problem with urgency is that it's often not well received by those who don't demonstrate it. Organizations without a sense of urgency can have short lifespans or go through painful periods as they try to figure out how to manage any of a number of different types of problem they may face. Poor organizational design can lead to problems but so, too, can a failure to prepare an appropriate response to emerging crises and events in a timely fashion.

The state of urgency also can be compromised when the organization's vision changes. If an organization is the target of a takeover, the membership may not align itself with the new vision, and this may affect their allegiance and, in turn, sense of urgency about participating in efforts to achieve this new vision. Sometimes the potential for a disruption in an organization's state of urgency comes from within, as when competing groups struggle for dominance. Divisions between labor and management, turf battles between departments, or "over-the-wall" communication patterns and styles can disrupt efforts to build a state of urgency.

This "cutting one's nose off to spite one's face" mentality can appear across organizational types. Enterprises can find production lines disrupted with "work slow-downs" or the use of rumors, innuendo or simply fabricated allegations of impropriety or conditions that lead to long investigations. The right "claim" of workplace safety violations or environmental damage can stop the efforts of the largest organization.

Urgency plays an especially important role for the other three organizational types. The individual contributor stays ahead by being faster, smarter, more ingenious than the others. This person has a need to perform in ways that demonstrate he/she is a viable alternative to what exists. So, to that end, reputation is critical for the individual contributor organization, and anything that can damage, taint or bring into question its quality can disrupt or even threaten its existence. This is especially true when these organizations are so heavily dependent on the efforts and activities of a key personality.

Because urgency often is the hallmark for the individual contributor and team organizations, anything that disrupts the state of urgency can literally bring their efforts to a halt. Prevent the right type of resources from reaching the team and its ability to contribute can be affected. Get the team's key player sidelined for an important game and the opponent gains an advantage—a gain realized without having to add additional resources or without the burden of an extra expense. It's like a "double benefit."

The fabric of a community organizational type also is dependent on and vulnerable to a loss of urgency. Many times community organizations exist as an extension of larger, more mainstream organizations, so much of their performance occurs because the parent or mainstream organizations permit them to act. The relationship between the two organizations is important, for sometimes community-type organizations have to scramble for funds, membership and other resources and anything that hinders efforts toward those ends can be damaging to it or its efforts. This is especially true when volunteers make up the membership. Keep them idle for long periods and their willingness to stay can be compromised. They are there to work, to help achieve a vision they believe in, so if there is nothing to do why stay?

As an organization matures it may not have the same needs, values or interests of earlier periods. This can present a real dilemma for some participants. Engaging in new activities with the same sense of urgency used on past activities can be hard to do when one does not like the changes that have occurred. So, when attitudes are displaced by rapid growth, the luxuries of extra time or, simply, the emergence of a new environment, a door opens for a potentially new use for urgency and that is to resist change or to bring about a direction that is closer to one that's familiar. Urgency now becomes a driver for efforts to self-organize around a different vision.

So, while some change may be inevitable, it may also benefit organizations to make sure participants recognize how widespread changes are aligned with the organization's vision. This may be especially important for those who identify as strong proponents of the organization's operational activities.

Urgency is not a given; it is a personal trait that can be turned off or on. It may also be of benefit if the organization's leadership understands ways in which its environment supports or encourages a sense of urgency.

Consider the organizations listed in Table 12.1. Notice how urgency can be defined across different organizations. While some boxes in the table already have some contents filled in, what else could be added to balance the role of urgency vis-à-vis the usual topical areas one associates with an organization? What are examples of ethical behavior one would expect to see, and how might these behaviors correlate with the urgency states in the automobile industry, among lawyers, the army, television news, unions, or a hockey team? What about quality? What is the relationship between quality levels and urgency and how might these vary for a religious organization, television news, unions, or a doctor? When does one sacrifice one dimension or another?

Table 12.1   Organizational Performance Factors by Organizational Type

	REPRESENTATIVE URGENCY	REPRESENTATIVE QUALITY	REPRESENTATIVE SERVICE	REPRESENTATIVE ETHICAL BEHAVIOR
Automobile manufacturer	On-time production	Reliable product	Make to meet various stakeholders' needs	Make safe products
Religious organization	Respond to threats to authority	Keep doctrine accessible	Timely response to parishioner needs	Don't harm parishioners
Lawyer	Timely filing of briefs	Good legal research	Good representation	Don't violate confidences
Terrorist group	Secrecy at all costs	Ensure bombs work as designed	Security for membership	Don't violate trust
Army unit	Fast deployment	Well-trained soldiers	Go where needed Go when needed	Honor codes of conduct
Colleges	Respond to campus security needs	Good instruction	Wide array of courses for students	Honor system
TV news	Fast coverage	Intelligent newscasters	Local area coverage	Tell the truth without bias
Unions	Fast "strike" mobilization	Good contracts	Good representation	Systemically support membership
Football team	Scout upcoming opponents	Winning season	Good ticket prices	Do not steal opponents' signals or game plans
Doctor	Covers emergencies	Excellent diagnosis	Good listener	Protect patient confidentiality

Completing a matrix like the one in Table 12.1 can be instructive for the membership of an organization. Completing it helps ask questions such as "How important are these issues to us?" "What does it take for us to assure these factors are delivered?" "What might our key opponents' profiles on the same factors be?" It's common to hear an organization's leadership ask participants to demonstrate a sense of urgency when doing their work or when meeting with customers or clients, but in what ways could the leadership demonstrate a sense of urgency when doing their work? How can the organization's leadership demonstrate a sense of urgency regarding product quality, safety, employee health, compensation (their employees', not just their own) or security?

Urgency, quality, service and ethics are learned traits; they are within the scope of all people. We all have seen the least urgent, worst worker, rudest person, most unethical politician do it right. The question is: "Why not all the time?" Examining the effects of the choices people make regarding their organization vis-à-vis their own behavior is central to understanding the role of urgency to performance and, in turn, self-organization.

THE FIVE DIMENSIONS OF COMPETENCY REVIEWED IN TERMS OF URGENCY

Urgency is only one of the key tools or traits that drive performance. Competency is the other one. There are a variety of ways to think about competency. Schools, for example, focus on having fundamental skills in math, reading, speaking or writing. These are among the important skills within organizations but others are also important. Where do customer service skills fall into a competency profile or skills in people management or leadership? What about skills needed by an accountant or a technician like an electrician or engineer? What are the skills needed by those doing fundraising, by receptionists or waiters?

Five important competencies needed to perform as expected in an organization that were discussed earlier can be summarized as follows. The first of these are *specialized competencies*, those directly related to one's primary job or assignment. These are the central reason individuals are recruited to be members of an organization. *Managerial and/or administrative capabilities* are a second category of competencies associated with all jobs, tasks or activities. A third class of competencies, *basic skills*, are part of all positions within an organization. *Social and interpersonal skills and competencies* also are associated with all jobs, tasks or assignments. Finally, *cultural competency*, one often overlooked and under-studied, is particularly important.

Finally, two last points regarding competency and competent performance in organizations merits mentioning. First, while "professional competencies" may lead to a candidate's selection, people are usually promoted and given expanded responsibilities because of proficiency in the other four competencies. The reason is that while all competencies are "enablers," specialized competencies have their greatest "enabling capacity" for the individual's professional area while the other four (the administrative, basic, interpersonal/social and cultural) enable the individual to contribute *in conjunction with* others. The other four competencies, in effect, expand the individual's overall "competency capacity" and, subsequently, expand the potential to make an impact across the organization or its membership. The engineer hired because of excellent technical skills who can't present ideas in a clear, organized fashion may remain in a position as a lead engineer but not be picked as head of the engineering department or as part of a key inter-departmental team designed to roll out a new product.

So, too, the "nuts and bolts" administrator who "doesn't have time for customers or their problems" can stay behind the scenes but not up front with the public. The risks are too high. The professional fundraiser who is great at helping the community raise money but can't work well with the office staff stays in the development role but may not be selected to be the group's executive director. In the end, those who have strong specialized competencies but low levels in some or all of the other four competencies may keep their existing role or job title but not be given expanded responsibilities. They become, in short, individual contributors.

In addition to reflecting a range of skills or capabilities, competency also can be used to describe a general state or condition of an individual or organization as a whole. When one person is perceived as "more competent" than another in a particular role, competency becomes a tool to predict the individual's ability to perform, based on past performance. Referring to someone as competent also makes a statement about the individual's ability to manage changing situations.

The ability to adapt to changing situations becomes very evident when the situations are complex and/or increasingly risk-laden. When we speak of competencies in terms of the complexity of a job or task needing to be done we're speaking of the individual's potential to make a contribution to the organization; it's a projection of the individual's future value. You prove your value to the organization when you handle an important task well. Table 12.2 compares levels of competency with the complexity of different tasks and activities. When examined in this fashion the true "worth" of a task, activity or job isn't necessarily dependent on the field or profession. Under the right conditions fashion design can be classified in the same category as brain surgery since both are highly complex tasks requiring people with high competencies in their field.

When, however, one adds levels of risk or volatility to the nature of the task or assignment, as illustrated in Table 12.3, brain surgery

Table 12.2 Levels of Competency and the Complexity Associated with Different Tasks and Activities

COMPETENCY REQUIRED TO SUCCESSFULLY COMPLETE THE ACTIVITY	LEVEL OF COMPLEXITY ASSOCIATED WITH AN ACTIVITY		
	LOW COMPLEXITY ACTIVITY (EASY, UNCOMPLICATED ACTIVITY TO DO)	MODERATE COMPLEXITY ACTIVITY	HIGH COMPLEXITY ACTIVITY (COMPLEX OR DIFFICULT ACTIVITY TO DO)
High competency needed	• Play championship bridge • Form a union	• Psychiatric counseling • Cross-cultural communication • Blue-collar crime	• Haute couture design • Brain surgery
Moderate competency needed	• Terminating an employee • Yoga • Gardening • Traffic officer	• Make counterfeit money • Flying a commercial jet • Downsizing an organization • British black-cab driver • Computer programming • General practitioner (medical doctor)	• Terrorist act • Air traffic control
Low competency needed	• Launch a boycott • Sell illegal drugs • Membership in the military • Fashion modeling	• Work stoppage, strikes • Police investigator	• Weaving • Hair stylist

Table 12.3   The Related Volatility/Risk Associated with Poor Performance: Competency Under Stress

LEVEL OF VOLATILITY/ RISK COMPETENCY REQUIRED	LOW VOLATILITY/ RISK IF NOT DONE WELL	MODERATE VOLATILITY/ RISK IF NOT DONE WELL	HIGH VOLATILITY/ RISK IF NOT DONE WELL
High competency	• Play championship bridge • Form a union • Haute couture design	• Psychiatric counseling • Cross-cultural communication	• Blue-collar crime • Brain surgery
Moderate competency	• British black-cab driver • Yoga • Gardening	Computer programming	• Terrorist act • Air traffic control • Police investigator • Terminating an employee • Flying a commercial jet • Downsizing organizations • General practitioner (MD) • Make counterfeit money
Low competency	• Weaving • Hair stylist • Fashion modeling	• Illegal drug sales • Work stoppage, strikes • Traffic officer • Launch a boycott	Membership in the military

maintains a high complexity/high risk rating while a haute couture designer's classification falls, by comparison, to a high competency/low risk rating. Obviously we're talking about risk in terms of the different degrees of loss that may be associated with poor performance. It's often a life-or-death scenario for the brain surgeon. The important thing to take away from this discussion is the relative nature of competency vis-à-vis the task or work to be done and the risks associated with poor or sub-par performance.

The ability to manage changing situations can be a critical capability for most organizations. An accountant with strong accounting skills, for example, who can manage routine accounting matters and, if necessary, adapt to a surprise audit adds value to the organization. Or, a person with strong customer service competencies who can manage routine transactions makes one type of contribution and, then, in those extreme situations triggered by rude or perhaps even hostile customers makes a second, potentially more valuable contribution. So, too, in our terrorist organization, if the bomb fails to detonate or the ideal target does not appear as expected, the more competent bomber knows how to identify a secondary target or to use back-up devices to detonate the bomb. Our conclusion: competency is a key ingredient in mission, goal and task achievement.

URGENCY, SERIOUSNESS, INSISTENCE, EXIGENCY

Competency is a very personal trait that can be of great value to an individual or organization. The competent individual's greatest potential or "magnitude of effect" appears through either individual action or when personal competencies create ways for others in the organization to act. Action is an organization's lifeblood but the potential for action is one thing; doing something with that potential is another.

Some individuals, for example, "do what they're told" and that's it! No more, no less. Others do "enough to get by." Time is spent talking about action or searching for a shortcut, but not doing the work. Still others "extend" themselves when the boss is around or when they want something. (Ever notice how behavior changes in organizations around the time performance evaluations are being prepared?)

On a more positive note, however, there are those who seem to always be first in line to "volunteer" to do more work. Finally, too, there are those who consistently go beyond what is expected. They are sometimes referred to as "value-adders" because the work they do not only completes the assignment, it actually "adds value" to the organization and its efforts.

Value-added performance can be the difference between a satisfied customer and one who selects your restaurant as the *only* place to "go for an excellent meal," your research firm as *the place* "to get the kind of help needed to finish that project," or your law office as *the best place* "for advice on a critical problem." But this raises a question. If all employees or participants in an organization have comparable skill and competency levels and have received the same type and amount of training, why are some participants more approachable, more helpful, or more likely to have a higher sense of urgency than others? These people seem to demonstrate they not only have the capacity to act but that they also know the urgency behind the assignment. They anticipate it, prepare for it and they seek out solutions for the situation they are facing.

Columnist Todd Archer (2008) noted the role of urgency when he wrote about the Dallas Cowboys football team's preparations for a game with the Washington Redskins. Even if their quarterback Tony Romo couldn't play because of a broken finger, the Cowboys thought they would easily defeat the Los Angeles Rams team that only had one win at that point in the season. They didn't. However, in preparing for their next game, with Washington, Archer wrote, "the players and coaches talked about seeing a sense of urgency, a resolve, up-tempo practices with a purpose" (Archer 2008).

Later, after Dallas won the game, another columnist, Steve Wyche (NFL.com) said offensive lineman Leonard Davis reported "the Cowboys played with a sense of urgency, unlike the team had for some time." But the level of urgency seems to be evident throughout the team, as Wyche wrote that with "a loss possibly burying Dallas, urgency was a must. Then, again, urgency was a must a few weeks ago, when owner Jerry Jones told coach Wade Phillips to fix the defense he felt was underperforming. . ." (Wyche 2008).

Those who appreciate the role a sense of urgency can contribute to an organization don't hesitate in telling others. Ray Dean's advice to those seeking good contractors is a case in point. Good contractors (our individual contributors) "demonstrate who they are and what they are about throughout the process starting right at the beginning." "Companies," he wrote, "that ask intelligent questions, offer insightful suggestions and show a sense of urgency and concern are the ones with whom you want to do business" (Dean 2008: 50).

Those in the fields of security and defense are acutely aware of the role urgency plays in achieving their missions. They know that a solution is what is needed, not just effort. Moreover, they know that their role is in either providing the solution or creating conditions so that those with the solution can be connected to the problem. "We're working this one with an incredible sense of urgency to get it out into the fight," Rear Admiral Mark Kenny, Director of the Navy's new "Irregular Warfare Office" said about a new technology called "The Sea Stalker" the Navy is developing. This technology will be added to the capabilities of ships the Navy considers "premiere counterterrorism tools" (*Defense Daily* 2008).

People demonstrating a capacity to see and/or understand the importance for action are labeled as having a sense of urgency. But having a sense of urgency is more than just taking or thinking about taking action; it's not just a "shoot from the hip" approach. A sense of urgency is really a three-dimensional approach to action beginning with a systemic orientation to situations—to an assignment, a problem, an issue or action, generally. Second, a sense of urgency is knowing that something not only needs to be done, but that there is a timeframe within which a goal must be achieved. Finally, a sense of urgency is rich with vision. There is a sense of what the final product should look like given the situation at hand and, of course, how to translate vision into action and action into a final product.

Those who demonstrate they have a sense of urgency about action are often labeled as "doers," "go-getters" or, sometimes, "real leaders." But labels that describe the flurry of activity one sees surrounding these individuals really misses the most valuable point: a sense of urgency emerges as an extension of the mind used strategically. The potential value of someone with a sense of urgency is so important to some organizations that this trait is treated as though it is a tangible, observable characteristic that should be considered a prerequisite for certain jobs or candidates. Leaders and managers like this characteristic in their followers or staff because a sense of urgency marks a person who can be counted on to know what to do, where to do it and when to act without having to be told.

A sense of urgency is such a powerful concept that some believe it's a behavior their entire membership should demonstrate; that everyone in the organization should possess this unique quality and that it's essential for the organization's performance in achieving its vision. A company's sensitivity to its market, its ability to meet customer needs in a timely fashion, or to keep abreast of changing conditions or competitor advances are offered as measures of a company's sense of urgency. David Blumenfeld's review of TECO Peoples Gas in Florida is a good illustration.

TECO's employees work with natural gas so the working environment can be very dangerous. To keep them aware of threats and risks associated with their environment, TECO's management made safety one of the company's core values. Simply labeling safety as a core value, however, doesn't mean people will think in terms of safety when they do their work, just as naming integrity, respect for others and customer service as other core values doesn't mean that employees will translate these key behaviors into action. A solution? Add a fifth value, an organizing value, to its list of core values for people associated with the company: a value named "achievement with a sense of urgency" (Blumenfeld 2008: 59). Finally, to help employees keep these values with them throughout the day, North Division Manager at TECO, James Farris, had the values printed on coins the employees could carry with them so the values would be "something more than a poster that [employees] would see a couple times a day" (Blumenfeld 2008: 59).

Companies with a high sense of urgency can rise to be leaders in service, product development or commercialization. Stakeholders have learned to expect these companies to lead in the design and development of products that meet customer needs, time-to-market and performance standards that aim to deliver products and services when customers need them, or a vision of the future that anticipates new needs or demands for products and services. Teams with a high sense of urgency are the ones people believe they can always count on to complete a mission successfully. These are the SWAT and "emergency response teams" organized to handle only special issues or circumstances. Like the employee with a high sense of urgency these are special organizations.

HOW DOES ONE "GET" OR DEVELOP A SENSE OF URGENCY?

Change is a major issue for organizations, so much so that whole portions of the book have been devoted to the role of change and the emergence of events organizations are expected to manage. When change occurs in either planned or unplanned form, a sense of urgency is a key prerequisite for successfully managing it. Urgency is such an important factor in change management that Kotter, in his book *Leading Change*, sees it as the first step in his "eight-stage process of creating major change" (Kotter 1996: 21). For Kotter and others, a sense of urgency "does not imply ever present panic, anxiety, or fear. It means a state in which complacency is virtually absent, in which people are always looking for both problems and opportunities, and in which the norm is 'do it now'" (Kotter 1996: 162).

Clearly, managers and leaders like to have people in their organizations operate with a sense of urgency. But, if you can't recruit all those you need with this special trait, why not develop them from within? According to Kotter's latest book it's possible to develop this important trait, but before we outline how this might be done, there are some myths about urgency that need to be addressed. Myths cloud action by cloaking potential action with miscellaneous, often unwarranted ideas that prevent people from seeing the truth regarding a matter at hand. Consider the first myth.

Myth one: "Some people have urgency, some don't." If anything this is a rationalization to account for why people we believe should be effective performers are not or why everyone just can't be like "so and so." One way to demonstrate the weakness of this myth is to watch people, especially those one doesn't believe have a sense of urgency, at different points in time. Watch them when it's mealtime after a long day of work, when there's a fire in the building, when it's time for a "bio-break" during a long training session or at the end of the day when "it's time to get out of here!" Regardless of the way they performed at other times, at these moments one can see that anyone has the potential to demonstrate a sense of urgency. These moments demonstrate that people learn how to move from their current state to a "state of urgency" *if that's what they want to do*.

There's an important distinction to be made here, however. Sometimes what people may be seeing in others is "energy" and not a sense of urgency. Urgency is more than activity; it's focused direction and action for the right reason. Managers have to be wary of what Kotter calls "false urgency," especially in the face of complacency. Far too often, he believes, managers think they have found a solution for complacency:

> when they see lots of energetic *activity*: where people sometimes run from meeting to meeting, preparing endless PowerPoint presentations; where people have agendas containing a long list of activities; where people seem willing to abandon the status quo; where people seem to have a great sense of urgency. But more often than not, this flurry of behavior is not driven by any underlying determination to move and win, *now*. It's driven by pressures that create anxiety and anger. The resulting frantic activity is more distracting than useful. This is a false sense of urgency that may be even *more* destructive than complacency because it drains needed energy in activity and not productivity.
>
> (Kotter 2008: 5–6)

A true sense of urgency also implies the construction and use of a plan, regardless of the plan's sophistication. Focus, action, development and use of a plan are all learned skills that contribute to defining a sense of urgency. Finally, the fact that people can turn urgency on and off when it suits them illustrates it is not a trait, skill or competency one is born with—one learns to "be urgent," "when to be urgent" and "how to act urgently."

Myth two: "Urgency can't be defined: it looks different for everyone who has it." Like many myths this one is partially reasonable and partially not. For example, urgency does look different from person to person and situation to situation, but that is to be expected. After all, urgency wisely used has to be adapted to the exigencies of the situation, much like competency. Even as urgency is modified and adapted to meet a situation's changing needs, the phenomenon is still defined by certain constants clearly associated with a sense of urgency.

Focus and intensity are two regularly appearing characteristics that define urgency, as are tenacity and determination. What is most important when defining urgency is that the degrees of focus, tenacity and intensity match a given situation and people involved. In fact, knowing how to manage urgency and its characteristics is one of the ways a sense of urgency correlates with competency. A highly competent person understands the levels of urgency to apply to the situation.

Beyond what the individual brings to the situation, the organization also establishes levels of urgency through training, practices and guidelines for behavior. Soldiers are expected to demonstrate urgency in attempting to recover their wounded comrades while a terrorist on the other hand might see the loss of one's life as inconsequential when compared with the urgency of bringing a message of defiance via a suicide bombing.

Less extreme situations make the same point. For example, in Table 12.4, "typical performance strategies" are matched with "urgency performance strategies" at key points for a given situation. The material in that table illustrates that while there is a difference between the two strategies, operating from a "position of urgency" should not put an organization or its stakeholders at risk. Indeed the mandate for all organizations—advance the organization and its mission while taking care to manage risk and exposures—is evident in both strategies. It is the approach that differs.

Myth three: "If a person has a sense of urgency in one setting, you'll see the same behavior in other, similar settings." This myth has been partially addressed in myth two, but it merits attention for a different reason: human behavior is a dynamic process and not some linear string of events. There is no one reason someone behaves in a particular way. Nor is there any one "cause" that leads to the development of a behavior or, in this instance, a sense of urgency. A crisis, a threat, or just a "personal desire to be more responsive" each could influence a person to demonstrate a sense of urgency in the ways they approach things. It's also impossible to predict that a person who displays a sense of urgency will do so in different situations. What stimulates a person to behave one way at one time may not have the same effect in the future.

A reason people are often unable to explain the behavior they see versus behavior they expect is because they take a simplistic, linear orientation to behavior. They want to believe that "X" happened so "Y" should occur. The officer told the soldier to "guard this door" so ... The mother told her son "to come home right after school" so ... The dentist told the patient to "brush after every meal" so ... The terrorist leader

Table 12.4   Performance vs. Urgency Strategies

TYPICALLY ACCEPTABLE PERFORMANCE STRATEGIES	URGENCY PERFORMANCE STRATEGIES
BEFORE STARTING ACTIVITIES	
There are goals for performance.	Don't let others put limits on the ability to perform.
Learn what is important by being told.	Transfer learnings about "importance" to other situations.
Know the boundaries; the limits.	You know boundaries are not fixed limits; you see and figure out when it's possible, when to move beyond.
Training and education are necessary to do some things.	There are lots of ways to get the knowledge needed.
Wait to be told; to start.	Fill in gaps in activity with something of benefit.
DURING THE WORK	
People are not always good communicators so don't expect to be told everything needed to do the job.	Use many channels to get the information needed.
Life is not fair; be careful.	"Unfairness" and bias do not mean that all of the doors are shut.
Avoid risk.	Manage challenges to risk.
Only a few people can get ahead.	If you can't perform here, go somewhere else.
Do what you are told.	Aim for the objective behind the activity, the goal behind the objective, the mission behind the goal, the vision behind the mission.
Do things as you are told.	Learn to think; think about what you're doing.
Do what needs to be done.	Do what must be done.
Do what must be done.	Anticipate how to "add value."
AFTERWARDS	
Change is part of the job.	Make change work for you.
Know when you're beat.	Don't stop looking for "a way to the job done!"
Quit on time.	Get the job done!
Look for feedback; it helps to know what is done is as expected.	Know how to measure your own performance, to make change.

told the suicide bomber to "detonate the bomb once the bus was half full" so …

So, what? What will *actually happen* in these situations? And if what one expects to happen does not, why not?

A linear orientation to behavior assumes that certain behaviors cause certain effects. This isn't supported in real-life situations. Sometimes you respond aggressively to the behavior of an aggressive driver, sometimes you don't. Or, you might respond one way at one time when someone is driving aggressively and have a totally different response at another time. When one examines behavior and assumes a certain outcome is "inevitable," the potential for error increases. A manager who tells employees to improve customer service may find that some employees interpret this to mean show up for work, to be friendly and smile, to offer to be of service and so on, often regardless of the training the employees received. In short, there's seldom, if ever, only one response to a request, to an idea or to an order.

Not only may the conclusion one expects to see not happen, but the scope of the effects which do occur may last long after the event has ended. Anyone who has ever recalled the pain or happiness associated with a past event, especially one that happened years ago, knows the reality of long-term effects. Effects can linger long after the event: long after the award was won, a compliment was made (or not made), the bully's insulting voice has died away, the accident caused by the careless driver, or the bomb debris is cleaned away. Because effects associated with behavior or events do not end once the behavior ends, a simple linear explanation does not provide the best foundation for understanding the event. Linear orientations assume that if there's a stimulus, there's a response but, in reality (and some say this is what makes life both interesting and difficult), for any stimulus there may be any number of potential responses and many of those unplanned or unanticipated.

A "process orientation," in contrast to a linear orientation, to examining behaviors often gives a more accurate view. A process orientation begins with speculations about the number and types of possible variables that may describe the system studied. The sample questionnaire below (Figure 12.1) presents a series of responses one might see associated with a particular situation, in this case a terrorist incident. The range of responses fills the page but, in fact, with a little thought it is possible to add more. Additionally, the way you answer each question can reflect the level of intensity you associate with the possible response. Someone else might answer every question differently. Some of the responses listed refer specifically to you, the respondent, while others are general. Some

The situation: imagine you have just heard about a terrorist incident—a bombing here in the United States. You don't know all of the details but it is clear people were hurt and it's another illustration of *terrorist activity* in today's society. Please read each of the possible products, outcomes of impacts possibly associated with the event, and circle the number that you believe best indicates the likelihood each may occur.

This will escalate into more terrorist activity.		People will want to retaliate, to be aggressive toward the terrorists.	
There's a strong likelihood this will occur	There's little or no likelihood this will occur	There's a strong likelihood this will occur	There's little or no likelihood this will occur
10 9 8 7 6 5 4 3 2 1		10 9 8 7 6 5 4 3 2 1	
The terrorists will get caught.		People who believe they have seen the terrorists will report them to the police.	
There's a strong likelihood this will occur	There's little or no likelihood this will occur	There's a strong likelihood this will occur	There's little or no likelihood this will occur
10 9 8 7 6 5 4 3 2 1		10 9 8 7 6 5 4 3 2 1	
The public will just ignore what is happening. They'll learn to live with it.		Terrorists will be punished.	
There's a strong likelihood this will occur	There's little or no likelihood this will occur	There's a strong likelihood this will occur	There's little or no likelihood this will occur
10 9 8 7 6 5 4 3 2 1		10 9 8 7 6 5 4 3 2 1	
A lot of time will be spent talking about the problem but nothing will happen.		Someone will get hurt.	
There's a strong likelihood this will occur	There's little or no likelihood this will occur	There's a strong likelihood this will occur	There's little or no likelihood this will occur
10 9 8 7 6 5 4 3 2 1		10 9 8 7 6 5 4 3 2 1	
Hearing about terrorist behavior has a greater effect on my overall behavior than hearing about terrorists being prevented from acting.		Terrorist behavior has a way of changing everything for me. It can really ruin the day!	
Strongly agree Strongly disagree		Strongly agree Strongly disagree	
10 9 8 7 6 5 4 3 2 1		10 9 8 7 6 5 4 3 2 1	

Figure 12.1 Accounting for the Causes and Effects Associated with a Terrorist Event.

outcomes are probably more likely to happen, while others may be less likely but still possible. Some are more immediate, others not. Some speculate about what is happening now, others speculate about the future.

The process orientation does not assume there is a predictably direct relationship between an event and a stimulus, but rather that as a stimulus is experienced and interpreted, other factors can enter or emerge to influence the outcome. In other words, in addition to any primary stimulus contributing to an event's occurrence, a process orientation understands that what is observed may be a product of not only certain stimuli but also conditions around the event as it emerges. So, the setting—who's present, their attitudes, opinions and beliefs—also can shape the interpretation of what behavior ultimately does emerge. Possible responses to the survey mentioned earlier illustrate this point. Perceptions of a "terrorist event" or "terrorist behavior" can be influenced by who is completing the survey (e.g., a terrorist, a politician, someone in law enforcement, a victim), where the event occurs (e.g., a religious center, a battlefield, a shopping mall) or one's feelings or sentiments about, for example, the terrorists' cause or motives.

A process orientation also helps avoid assuming a simple straightline relationship between a stimulus and potential results because both the "sender" and "receiver" can and do influence each other, often simultaneously. Matching aggression-with-aggression versus "turning the other cheek" are real-time orientations *and* responses that can influence the emergence and unfolding of virtually any event. So, if an event occurs in the absence of other behaviors, is it still a stimulus? Would someone speeding and moving from lane to lane on a highway where there are no other cars be considered an "aggressive driver" causing an "aggressive event"? Someone looking at behavior with a process orientation might conclude that "conditions are right for an aggressive event to emerge" but also would stop short of concluding that what's observed is causing such an event.

Again, what may seem like splitting hairs or semantics is not meant to be. The driving behavior just described may be viewed as perfectly appropriate, almost natural, on a racetrack or if the driver is rushing to a hospital because of an emergency. An observer might interpret the driving as excessive, even dangerous, but the "aggressive driving" label might not even enter the mind of the racecar driver or the driver trying to get to a hospital quickly.

Process orientations allow room for perspectives a linear orientation cannot readily allow for or accept. Researchers use a linear approach to focus, clarify or explore the potential causes or effects of events. The linear approach is a valuable tool when exploring effects of a particular drug on cancer or the role of certain chemicals in contributing to pollution. However, in society, a fanatic, a racist, an extremist, a die-hard zealot or even a revolutionary are labels used to describe people with a linear orientation to events, their causes, or their effects.

Finally, while a linear orientation tends to be definitive and assumes "an" end result, process orientations see effects of events as continuous and ongoing. Think back to when you were in the fourth or fifth grade in school and a teacher pulled you aside to talk about your work in class. Whether the teacher's comments were positive or negative, the teacher's behavior, even after the passage of time, left you with impressions you can reconstruct long after the event occurred.

The event's physical nature may have ended but its effects can linger. So, organizations that want you to have a "good shopping experience" are hoping the positive effects of that experience not only stay with you for a long time but also increase the likelihood you'll come back, tell others of your good experience, or think of them again before your next shopping event. In short, the store realizes the long-lasting nature of an event's effects and hopes to use them to benefit the store in the future, as you recall and relive the event in your mind.

Looking at behavior as a process rather than a linear event creates an opportunity to utilize a broad range of factors when developing plans, organizing responses, or when engaging in problem-solving or decision-making activities. Both approaches are tools that can make a contribution to understanding what's occurring or what may occur in the future, but they do it differently and with potentially different results. Moreover, knowing when and how to use each approach is necessary when applying them to the study of organizations, behavior in organizations or the role of events on organizations.

THE DESIRE TO ACT: MAKING URGENCY WORK

Still, despite the theory, how does one stimulate the development of a sense of urgency in people and then make sure this "drive" works the ways one wants? John Kotter has outlined a two-part process for building urgency in his recent book, *A Sense of Urgency*. Kotter's strategy reflects a perspective he claims "is rarely acknowledged in the classroom or boardroom" (Kotter 2008: 45). It is that underlying a "true sense of urgency is a set of *feelings*: a compulsive determination to *move, and win, now*. When it comes to affecting behavior ... feelings are more influential than thoughts" (2008: 45). He believes that facts and data are helpful in understanding why an urgent response may be necessary or what risks may result from a failure to act. But Kotter's approach adds a new dimension to building a winning strategy for building a sense of urgency. He supports building a strategy that wins over the hearts and minds of participants by revealing emotionally compelling needs that excite and arouse determination.

He believes a sense of urgency results from strategy that aims at creating action that is "exceptionally alert, externally oriented, relentlessly aimed at winning, making some progress each and every day, and constantly purging low value-added activities—all by always focusing on the heart and not just the mind" (Kotter 2008: 60). The role of this strategy serves at least two fundamental purposes: it provides direction and it sets the stage for explaining how one can build and maintain a sense of urgency. The directional component defines the need for an urgent response. In contrast, the process component explains the needs and benefits from being committed to the challenge at hand, how a committed individual or team energetically works and how the individual or team uses management practices to build and maintain levels of urgency to meet emerging challenges. In this instance, the building and maintaining of urgency process levels demand strong communication, information and knowledge management practices, among others.

Tactics, on the other hand, focus on the details, the how, for achieving urgency. Kotter outlines four he believes are useful in achieving a strategy that focuses on the heart and not just the mind. The first he describes as "bringing the outside in." The aim of this tactic is to address a natural tendency of organizations to be so internally oriented that they cannot clearly see consequences associated with problems that need to be addressed and also to disrupt the levels of complacency that subsequently may come to dominate an organization's participants (Kotter 2008: 64–68). Bringing the outside in strives to help the participants become more externally oriented in general and to develop a better sense of the issues at hand by pulling in, again from outside the organization, data and information specifically related to the challenges to be faced.

The second tactic is to "behave with a sense of urgency." This tactic has intuitive appeal and appears across a variety of situations. When behaving with a sense of urgency, one is focused and quick to respond in meaningful ways. Urgency requires communication, and communication patterns must support frequent interactions among those involved. This communication must be frequent, open and passionate about the issues at hand. Those with a high sense of urgency match action with plans and talk and, importantly, involve and engage others in the state of urgency that grips the organization and its membership. Urgency is not one person's responsibility; it is everyone's!

Kotter's third tactic is a challenge most have heard: find opportunity in crisis. What makes Kotter's discussion useful in this instance is his distinction between the ways people look at an emerging crisis. Those who see crises as "rather horrid events" define one perspective. These are crises that "can hurt people, disrupt plans, or even cripple an organization or community beyond repair" (Kotter 2008: 119). The tactics that surface and reflect this perspective regarding crises can be described as "crisis avoidance or, if necessary, crisis management and damage control" (2008: 119).

A second perspective sees crises as "not necessarily bad and may, under certain conditions, actually be required to succeed in an increasingly changing world" (Kotter 2008: 120). This perspective sees a crisis as a tool for jarring the organization out of a sense of complacency, to push people to act, especially when not acting may result in true tragedy. Either approach to a crisis can be useful if used prudently, however, there are risks with both. As a guide for using crises to create a true sense of urgency, Kotter offers eight tips, each of which should be adhered too. The potential benefit of keeping these tips in mind is so important they are summarized below in Table 12.5. They merit attention, thought and action.

Kotter's fourth tactic to build a sense of urgency in an organization is a must! This tactic's focus aims at identifying and eliminating resistance to efforts to build urgency in the organization. Kotter believes the person who resists change is "more than a skeptic. He's always ready with ten reasons why the current situation is fine, why the problems and

Table 12.5   Kotter's Principles to Follow When Viewing a Crisis as an Opportunity to Create a True Sense of Urgency

---

"Always *think of crises as potential opportunities*, and not only dreadful problems that automatically must be delegated to the damage control specialists. A crisis can be your friend.

Never forget that crises do not automatically reduce complacency. If not monitored and handled well, burning platforms can be disastrous, leading to fear, anger, blame and the energetic yet dysfunctional behavior associated with false urgency.

To use a crisis to reduce complacency, *make sure it is visible, unambiguous, related to real business problems, and significant enough that it cannot be solved with small, simple actions.* Fight the impulse to minimize or hide bad news.

To use a crisis to reduce complacency, *be exceptionally proactive* in assessing how people will react, in developing specific plans for action, and in implementing the plans swiftly.

Plans and actions should always focus on the others' hearts as much or more than their minds. Behaving with passion, conviction, optimism, urgency and a steely determination will trump an analytically brilliant memo every time.

If urgency is low, *never patiently wait for a crisis* (which may never come) *to solve your problems.* Bring the outside in. Act with urgency every day.

If you are considering creating an urgency-raising crisis, *take great care* both because of the danger of losing control and *because if people see you as manipulative and putting them at risk, they will (quite reasonably) react very badly.*

If you are at a middle or lower level in the organization and see how a crisis can be used as an opportunity, *identify and then work with an open-minded and approachable person in a more powerful position* who can take the lead." (Kotter 2008: 142–143)

---

challenges others see don't exist, or why you need more data before acting" (2008: 146).

There's some real benefit from studying the distinctions Kotter makes between a skeptic and those he calls "NoNos" and we encourage you to read his entire treatment in his book, *A Sense of Urgency*. His book and others illustrate that there are more ways to develop urgency within an organization than to simply attempt to recruit it. Beyond what's offered in Kotter's book and elsewhere, systematic efforts to develop and reinforce a sense of urgency in individuals and the organization are possible if certain fundamental steps are taken.

For example, knowing what it is you want to be urgent about, when and how often is a good place to start. Emergency rooms use triage procedures in order to prioritize injuries while simultaneously maximizing the efficiency of their operations. Quality and service are key by-words used by other organizations to signal areas where special attention is required. If a general state of urgency is not warranted then knowing when one should move to this heightened state or condition is important. For example, if "customer service" is the stimulus then when customers are present one should expect to see employees behaving differently from when they are not around.

Let the tendency toward urgency work. If employees are empowered and want to run with their new capabilities then let them, with one caveat: have procedures in place to guide or focus their efforts and energy. Suicide bombers are successful not only because of their efforts, but because they are extensions of an organization that functions holistically to ensure that its mission is achieved. The suicide bomber illustrates excellent use of a person who's an example of some now familiar management themes. Suicide bombers receive the training and instruction needed to do their assignment (they're enriched), they have the directions and equipment needed to act (they're enabled) and they are allowed to take charge of the situation as they see fit (empowered). Once released on their mission these individuals don't need someone with them to tell them what to do and when to do it. It's as though the bomber is at one with the bomb being carried. It is an efficient, prepared system equipped with appropriate procedures and guidelines that help all involved know "THE MISSION" and how a sense of urgency helps achieve it.

Eliminate naturally occurring obstacles to urgency. This means deal with deficiencies in the organization or its membership. This includes factors in the community (managers who fear being outpaced by "star" employees or jealous peers) and the enterprise (equipment that doesn't work or can't be relied on to work when it must work). Using the key operational practices as a template to audit the organization helps identify potential obstacles.

Manage the system and its elements. Acting with a sense of urgency often creates new processes, guidelines and rules, some of which the participants devise for themselves as they go along. As the ways things are done in a system with a sense of urgency change, the fundamentals associated with the organization also may need to be modified. Processes that govern the ways things are done frequently undergo significant change, so, while those "doing the work" may find their roles and responsibilities undergoing major changes, those responsible for the organization as a whole may not.

THE LOGISTICS OF MAKING URGENCY WORK

There is no quick fix possible when trying to build a sense of urgency in an organization. A "Triple-E" approach to urgency assumes that when people are enabled, empowered and enriched (e.g., trained) they are better able to prepare for and respond to emerging events. The plan is simple: give people the training needed (they're enriched), add processes that allow them to use the training (they're enabled) and tell them they can use the new skills and competencies (they are empowered). Then people will see what needs to be done (they'll have vision) and they will act (urgency).

But, like so many good ideas, this fell by the wayside, often because Triple-E lacked management's understanding and support. Management failed in some cases to integrate Triple-E throughout the organization, creating uneven participation in the program (e.g., the belief "it's only for those at the bottom"), and in other cases failed to integrate Triple-E with key operational practices. When committing to a program like Triple-E the organization's leadership must demonstrate its support in a variety of ways.

When organizations do successfully launch change programs (like Triple-E, business rules, Total Quality Management or Urgency), they work best when they are fully integrated into all facets of the organization. That is, they are no longer discrete "programs" but are processes that change the "way" things are done systemically. Failure to integrate such programs increases the likelihood that they will add to the already dynamic, confusing, troubled environments they are designed to improve. If this happens, mismanagement can create significant potential for increased risks and dissonance resulting from stress or the conflict associated with introducing change when a crisis is evident. It is no wonder people avoid change; change introduced without proper preparation and full integrated into the system is just confusion.

Organizations are systems *and* processes, so every element of the organization, every department, team or division, continuously and simultaneously affects all other organizational elements. The enterprise dimension continuously and simultaneously affects the community, groups/teams and individual contributors while the reverse also is true: those elements continuously and simultaneously influence every other dimension and the enterprise. Therefore, participation that is selective or partial when it should be "system-wide" creates an imbalance and the potential for problems like emerging resentment ("Why not them, too?") or division ("Do they think they're better than us?").

One often sees defective social behaviors like oversights or miscommunications in organizations with low community and high enterprise profiles. In these organizations elitist, ego-driven behaviors can surface and contribute to "we"/"they" displays among organization members. The sense, for example, that one individual or sub-group/team is better or more privileged than another can make it virtually impossible to launch change and process improvement programs successfully. If those in the "preferred" classes do not have to participate, then those who do may feel as though they are being targeted, perhaps for a remedial program, and that the organization's problems are a result of things they do poorly. On the other hand, if those in the preferred groups are the ones selected to participate then those on the outside may see this as "just another perk" they are not entitled to receive.

Finally, one logistical factor that influences the ability to build urgency is the extent to which key operational practices are used when designing and implementing urgency efforts. These practices are common to all organizations and are a key part of the organization's enterprise dimension. Once in place the effects on communication, information flows, knowledge development, evaluation management and utilization can be immediate, especially when developing a sense of urgency is the goal.

Practices that focus on communication, information and knowledge are enriching and enabling practices. Practices that focus on evaluation, relationships and performance lean toward being empowering practices. The former contribute to the development and use of skills and competencies and the latter to the use of skills in doing one's work or in working with others. Organizations and individuals with a sense of urgency use all of these practices strategically and tactically. Individuals, for example, use the practices to "get the job done." For the individual they help identify and communicate intent, means and targeted or achieved results. The practices are tools one uses to get results alone or with others.

Organizations derive benefits from the use of these practices in many ways too. When these practices are in place and used effectively, urgency is a way of being in the organization; it is as though the organization cannot help but anticipate and be responsive to its needs. Things happen not only because people want them to but also because the system, through its practices, guides the organization and its elements to action. It's almost as though one has no choice and can only be urgent in the ways things are done. If communication, for example, is expected, then one communicates (or receives a poor evaluation for not communicating). If evaluation is expected, then one performs knowing that evaluations will occur. These practices are not in place to punish or to create bureaucracy but to demonstrate expectations about what one is to do, how one is to do it, when things are to be done, etc.

Table 12.6 illustrates ways a sense of urgency can influence both individuals and the organization as a whole. It illustrates that sometimes focusing on building urgency within individuals, in fact, may be misguided—for example, when attempting to construct "readiness states" in response to a crisis. This use of urgency tends to end once the crisis is past or, generally, diminish over time, simply because it is not a "natural" way for most organizations to be. The readiness efforts or "readiness posture" is, after all, artificial or what Kotter (2008: 32–33) might call "false urgency."

Organizations with a true sense of urgency, however, are always in a virtual state of responsiveness. The organization's personnel do not have to be "turned on" because "being on" is how they operate. Terrorist organizations, SWAT teams, emergency departments (e.g., fire or hospital emergency rooms) illustrate the point. If one thinks of these organizations and compares how they operate with the information in Table 12.6 it is easy to see how and why their performance, day in and day out, exceeds that of typical organizations.

The irony is that because individual and organizational "urgency states" are linked to standard practices and procedures they do not typically add to the organization's operating costs. In contrast, pseudo-urgency states, for example, used because of "a possible threat" or when a "crisis is at hand," can add costs. Pseudo-urgency states require not only changing the ways things are done but they usually require a whole other system be learned and used in conjunction with the existing operations.

The recent "Terror Alert Level" system the United States implemented is a case in point. The primary audience for the system, the American public, often didn't know what the system's elements meant,

Table 12.6   A Sense of Urgency and Critical Operational Practices

CRITICAL OPERATIONAL PRACTICES AND DESCRIPTION	IMPACT ON, FOR EXAMPLE, A SENSE OF URGENCY FOR THE INDIVIDUAL	IMPACT ON, FOR EXAMPLE, A SENSE OF URGENCY FOR THE ORGANIZATION: CHALLENGES, RISKS AND THREATS
Communication practices and strategy are used to exchange information between or among individuals, groups and organizations.	Communicate goals, issues and processes. Used to build relationships, to confront issues. Communication reduces avoidance strategies and conflict.	Communication is expected. Communication practices show up in programs (e.g., mediation and bargaining), processes and procedures.
Evaluations practices and strategies are used for research and systematic evaluation of performance, projects or processes. Evaluation practices help planning, decision-making and problem-solving.	Focus is on performance not personalities. Individuals know how efforts, strategies, relationships are assessed. Evaluations look back and ahead. Evaluation criteria make goals meaningful, encourage communication.	Evaluation practices underscore risk-taking and goal achievement. Goals are achieved against defined performance criteria and through prudent risk-taking. "Tempered urgency."
Knowledge practices and strategies are used to acquire, build, develop and maintain knowledge, skills and competencies.	When one has needed skills and competencies one can act. Practices help problem-solving, decision-making. Knowledge enables move beyond thinking to action.	Knowledge practices add depth to the organization. A key practice for the Triple-E: enabling, enriching, empowering.
Relationship practices and strategies are used to acquire, build, develop and maintain relationships.	Relationships and networks are critical for urgency. Relationships expand competency capabilities.	Good relationships promote urgency. Some programs include customers; urgency expands the organization's reach.
Performance practices and strategies are used to introduce, propel and/or guide operations and ensure that performance meets goals, objectives and standards.	Urgency is part of all personal and group/team planning, goal-setting, design and mission activities. Urgency found in priorities, strategy, tactics and tasks. People know what's expected, when.	Urgency requires attention to detail, plans for evaluation and follow-up activities. Consistency and reliability increase with solid performance practices.
Information, evaluation and confirmation practices and strategies support infrastructure, and information management practices facilitate all strategic practices. Both formal and informal.	Information is critical for urgency. It's used to define issues, to seek out solutions and problem-solving channels; for confirming and evaluating progress and results.	Priorities, needs, conditions are communicated via information channels and networks. Practices facilitate progress assessments. Availability, accuracy and accessibility of information are critical for urgency.

what triggers a move from one readiness level to another, or what current levels were (James 2004; Kremer 2006; Anonymous, *Tribune Business News* 2009; Shapiro and Cohen 2007). These conditions were only aggravated when it became clear people were not sure if the system was politically motivated or what to do if there is a crisis (Chabot 2008; Haberman 2007; Hall 2009; US Federal News Service 2007). Individuals, groups/teams and organizations with a true sense of urgency operate in a state of readiness as a matter of course. Their sense of readiness is not artificial, not a political ploy.

MAKING COMPETENCY MEANINGFUL: CHOICE-MAKING AND ACTION

The value and recognizable features and benefits associated with a sense of urgency rely on several factors: the speed with which things begin and end, the scope of effect resulting from action, or the depth of potential benefit or effect. A widespread sense of urgency can breed strong community ties within the organization, partially because a wholesome sense of urgency requires teamwork, cooperation or collaboration. Because urgency has the potential for touching the entire organization, the benefits of this behavioral characteristic can extend beyond immediate tasks and clearly speed the spread of urgency to other plans and programs designed to address an emerging crisis.

Those with a sense of urgency also may recognize the residual values of urgency to the organization. Having doors or communication channels open is a benefit. The development and use of new and existing networks are benefits. People develop and use new, strong skills and competencies, and because urgency works best when the organization as a whole is prepared to support urgency, growth can become pervasive. So, while an impeding crisis may be impacting one area in particular, raising a sense of urgency throughout the organization can galvanize and focus any systemic response to the event.

Urgency behaves as a linking function connecting competency, the skills and capabilities to perform, and the action taken. Intuitively one wants to believe that competency is urgency's enabler but urgency's contribution to making a mission clear and meaningful is a separate value. The result, if both competency and urgency are at their strongest, can push optimal problem-solving and decision-making throughout the organization.

The staging associated with creating a workable sense of urgency culminates in the choices made regarding the crisis at hand. Indeed, it is something of an understatement to say competency and urgency play a critical role in the decision-making associated with an event. It can be at once truly heartbreaking and disorientating for participants when they see that for all of the talk and drum-beating regarding acting with a sense of urgency, the response to a crisis can end with cowardly decisions.

An organization's membership is not dumb; after all, they're the ones smart enough to do the organization's work day in and day out. So, when a choice or decision comes down that's supposedly crafted to best meet the organization's needs given the crisis, they ask the bottom-line questions: what's the quality of the choice(s) made and are quality levels high enough to meet the risks, threats and vulnerabilities related to the crisis at hand? Is the best alternative chosen, given competency and urgency resources available, or has a choice been made to please certain members of the organization?

The thrust of this chapter is to examine the role a sense of urgency plays when constructing a response to an event, but all of the urgency in the world doesn't matter if the result is a poor choice or decision. Choice-making behavior is a product of conscious decisions which, themselves, may be a product of perceptions based on little valid or reliable information. Often the best choice might not be the one made. A lot depends on the circumstances, motives and perceptions of the impact(s) the choice might have. Choices do have an effect, however, and these effects are not linear and cannot be completely controlled or predicted by the decision-maker.

While having a defined and developed set of organizational practices provides certain guidelines for choice-making behavior, the choices made cannot prevent errors from occurring or even guarantee the quality of decisions and choices that are made. In the best of all worlds an array of factors, among them the competence, urgency and credibility of the decision-maker, all contribute to defining the best choice produced.

PART IV

Summary and Conclusions

CHAPTER 13

Self-Organization and Beyond

The sum total of an organization's effort to design, build and maintain itself and its operations can be summarized as its "effectiveness profile." This profile is construed to be a composite of three factors: levels of performance, preparedness to act and overall capability. From one perspective, the profile reflects how well the organization's structure and systems contribute to its effectiveness on a day-to-day basis and, on another, the organization's potential for future performance as defined by the competencies and focus of its membership. The assumption of both is that a sufficient level of preparedness should help the organization achieve its objectives.

However, readiness to perform and performance are static indicators of effectiveness. The organization's overall actual performance is the wild card as the strength and capacity to perform are fluid and change daily. Loss of a key employee means work that is thought to be important enough to be done by one person may not be done or may have to be done by others. Lose a key piece of equipment or a valued customer, face a threat of legal action, a defective product or a service that causes damage and an organization's capacity to perform shifts from what is expected to something the organization's membership didn't expect to have to do for that day.

Readiness is both a key operating organizational dimension and a "fail-safe" should a crisis emerge. At the individual level readiness is reflected in wide-scale flexibility, demonstrated in the capacity to adapt to changing situations. At the individual level, plans meet reality and the successful individual is the one most able to invent a proper response to circumstances as they arise. At the organizational level, readiness is often anything but flexible. Systemic readiness means structure; processes and procedures are in place to shape, guide or direct performance.

Here then is the point of resolution where the role of complexity theory as a tool can offer insights into organizational performance: people at all levels in organizations plan for or anticipate an event, but it is not until the event actually emerges that one can gauge how accurately the plan truly matches what is observed. Complexity theory facilitates efforts to anticipate the emergence of events, the examination of how and why they emerged and the results associated with the events' emergence and management. It's not a "silver bullet" for members of an organization or researchers, but it helps!

An organization has a mission, policies and procedures and it engages in hiring practices, training and development and evaluation through various departments or areas. All of these efforts are in place to increase the likelihood events are managed in ways that benefit (or at least don't harm) the organization. Despite these strategies and efforts, there are times when even routine events are poorly managed. Using complexity theory in a way that is sensitive to the social dynamics of human organizations (perhaps better called "social complexity theory") assumes that there is a separation at the event between the organization-driven vision of what should happen and self-organized individual-driven construction of what will happen. It is not simply that "people trained to respond in a particular way, don't" but, rather, that "people trained to respond in a particular way, *choose not to*."

THE SETTING AND SELF-ORGANIZATION IN HUMAN SOCIAL SYSTEMS

Self-organized behavior occurs in all types of organization and across all types of event. Key factors contributing to self-organization in an organization have been discussed throughout the book. These are summarized in Table 13.1 for your reference.

Sometimes the organization's environment has features that can facilitate or inhibit the self-organization of unwanted behavior. Two of these features, conditionality and constraints, are a blend of factors that stipulate under what conditions behavior can occur and an acceptable range for the behavior when it occurs (Ashby 1962). Aspects of conditionality and constraints will materialize differently because of any number of factors, such as a particular organization's structure (e.g., whether an enterprise, community, team or individual contributor as described), the overall complexity of the moment and the general influence and makeup of the actors involved.

Recalling the early work of Kenneth Boulding (1956), one of the benefits of modeling and systems theory is that they help uncover gaps in

Table 13.1   Factors Contributing to the Process of Self-Organization (referenced from Chapter 1)

1. Localized interactions. An organization's participants involved in self-organization activity tend to focus their interactions among themselves.
2. With localized interactions there is a reliance on local information.
3. There is an absence of well-defined top-down control.
4. The self-organized behavior forms patterns, again without external guidance.
5. There is variability within critical areas of the organization.
6. There is evident use of positive feedback regarding actions and can lead to the development of behavioral rules for the self-organizing system.
7. Adaptations. There is variability in the adaptation process within organizations.
8. Finally, there is the capacity for change.

our existing understanding of a field of study. To those ends, this chapter's focus aims at illustrating the dynamics associated with those times when anticipated conditions and constraints meet the reality of an event.

Most organizations use their structure and procedures as boundaries to increase the likelihood that desired behaviors occur and, simultaneously, to reduce the likelihood that undesirable behaviors emerge. However, people in organizations, regardless of their training or preparation can, and do, construct their own behaviors. Sometimes this happens naturally. Complex behavior in organizations has a tendency to *evolve into a critical state* where minor disturbances induce *events of all sizes* (Bak 1996). At other times the emergence of behavior seems spontaneous, marked by "opportunity"—the metaphorical opening of a door or window that allows the self-organization to begin.

The emergence of these behaviors typically follows an identifiable set of steps or stages triggered by a particular stimulus. The organization is out of balance or, as Bak et al. (1989), Jensen (1998) and others have suggested when organizations are far-from-equilibrium, they can spontaneously drive themselves to a critical point leading to spatial and temporal fluctuations of all types and sizes. The culmination of these fluctuations, in turn, can stimulate additional behaviors that, in turn, lead to newer emergent behaviors.

From the observer's vantage point some event stimuli become "slope clearing events" as they overload local control mechanisms (or good processes), competencies and certainly any plans or guides for action. Consider Figure 13.1. This overview of the self-organization process illustrates three key points regarding self-organization. First, an event places participants in a position of making a response (avoidance is a

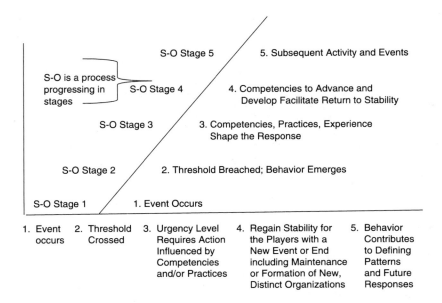

S-O Stage 5   5. Subsequent Activity and Events

S-O is a process
progressing in   S-O Stage 4   4. Competencies to Advance and
stages   Develop Facilitate Return to Stability

S-O Stage 3   3. Competencies, Practices, Experience
                           Shape the Response

S-O Stage 2   2. Threshold Breached; Behavior Emerges

S-O Stage 1   1. Event Occurs

| 1. Event occurs | 2. Threshold Crossed | 3. Urgency Level Requires Action Influenced by Competencies and/or Practices | 4. Regain Stability for the Players with a New Event or End including Maintenance or Formation of New, Distinct Organizations | 5. Behavior Contributes to Defining Patterns and Future Responses |

Figure 13.1 A General Model of a Self-Organization Process.

response). Second, actions taken, in part, by the manifestation of thresholds that, like a metaphorical "line in the sand," trigger the emergence of behavior. And third, the process of emergence in response to an event may reflect not a single emergence or instance of self-organization but a number of emergences, triggered by the need to cross thresholds and move further into the event-management process.

In Figure 13.1 the event occurs at point 1, but the overall complexity of the event-management process is overshadowed by elements that follow. In short, designed conditions and constraints for the system give way to exigencies of what becomes a "series of moments."

Since self-organization is not a point in time but a process, each response following the initial event adds complexity to the setting and this complexity, in turn, can increase a participant's exposure to risks, threats and vulnerabilities. Combatant organizations devote hours to training before a mission is launched to reduce the complications and complexities that may arise once the mission is launched and the opponent is engaged. The temptation to think that training is a panacea for the changing nature of events seems to stem from the notion that the self-organization process evolves in an orderly, linear fashion. This is seldom the case. For example, what starts out as aggressive driving, a student/teacher confrontation, or a routine traffic incident can quickly change with the presence of an unexpected stimulus, like a gun. This is an extreme example of situations changing but, as we've seen in the United States, it is not unrealistic. So what happens to the participants when conditions or the stakes change in the interaction? What new requirements or resources are needed and how should an organization prepare its membership to deal with these challenges?

After the attack on the World Trade Center some airline pilots wanted permission to carry guns in their planes' cockpits. After the tragedy at Virginia Tech some argued teachers should be allowed to carry guns to protect themselves and their students. Regardless of how we feel about these reactions, what they illustrate is how an organization's membership seeks ways to improve their advantages in the face of changing conditions. Even if these requests for guns and training in their use were supported, they would not guarantee that complex situations like those prompting the requests wouldn't emerge again or spin into different directions once the initial event emerged.

How events are managed as thresholds are crossed can affect the tone and direction of a participant's reactions for the rest of the process. Table 13.2 illustrates this point. Often there are formal and informal rules to guide behavior in various situations. "Turn taking" is an informal rule associated with conversations. You say something, I respond and so forth. Two drivers approach a four-way stop at the "same time" and one of those drivers is to the right of the other. That driver is expected to move through the intersection first; it's an informal rule.

But people don't always honor rules, formal or informal. When drivers are stopped at a red light and the driver across the intersection makes a quick left turn in front of the other driver as soon as it turns green, that turning driver has violated the rule that says, "the person proceeding straight through the intersection has the right of way over the person on the opposite side who wants to make a turn."

We regularly see examples of people who violate formal rules on the highway or in the workplace or when they discriminate against someone because of age, race or sex.

The model also suggests that thresholds can be affected by conditions or behaviors related to the event. Rules, personal values or biases and assessments of the existing conditions act like modifiers to shape interpretations of events and to guide behavior. They are referent points and an important part of the event-management process.

The process of seeing and breaching a threshold is unique because it communicates something deep-seated about the participants. When a consumer is buying something and the merchant says, "If you pay cash I

Table 13.2   Competencies Associated with the Self-Organization of Emergent Events—Three Examples

EVENT EMERGENCE RESULTING FROM A VIOLATION OF "RULES"	THRESHOLD CROSSED	COMPETENCY UTILIZED IN MANAGING KEY PRACTICES TO ADDRESS SITUATIONS
Driver cuts you off on the highway	You interpret as "aggressive driving" directed at you	*To manage aggressiveness:* • Communication management • Information management • Control management • Evaluation management
The teacher asks student to stop talking in class	Teacher interprets student's response as "rude"	*To manage rudeness:* • Communication management • Direction management • Control management • Relationship management
A police officer pulls a driver over for "failing to stop at a stop sign"	Driver accuses officer of "profiling"	*To manage defensiveness:* • Information management • Communication management • Relationship management • Direction management

won't charge you sales tax," the act sets up a unique relationship opportunity for the participants. The statement tells the consumer something about the merchant's value system and invites the consumer to collaborate with the merchant in behavior that is illegal. Moreover, if the consumer agrees with the merchant's offer then both gain insight into the consumer's value system as well. The two may never see each other again but for that moment they have constructed a relationship that may or may not be like any other relationship they have with others.

Finally, negotiating the emergence and management of thresholds and events requires successful utilization of key competencies. Every event is a learning opportunity for those involved; events are personalized laboratories for participants to test what they know against what's demanded by the situation. The spectrum of events presented earlier illustrates the range of events, from routine to extreme, that one can encounter. The process of event management begins before the event as anticipations guided by preconceived notions set the stage for action. To paraphrase Axelrod, foresight, for example, may not be necessary to build an accurate management strategy, but without foresight or its corollaries the event-management evolutionary process can take a very long time (1984: 188).

And time is always a key variable in the event-management process. As events mature, they require participants to devote their time to a variety of activities and, importantly, to make sometimes continuous assessments of and changes to their performance vis-à-vis the event. Knowing what didn't work in managing the event is one learning opportunity but the potentially greatest benefits come from knowing what did work. Isolating what did not work, a deficiency analysis, tells the participant what needs to be learned before another similar event emerges.

Knowing what worked not only marks content that doesn't have to be learned, it also signals that the participant is immediately ready to advance and, should a similar event arise again, to quickly build an appropriate response. In other words, the participant's "time-to-productivity" is reduced because it's not necessary to negotiate some learning curve as part of the event-management process. It's like a military commander who separates troops into two different groups: those with battle experience and those without battle experience. Those with experience can be placed on the front line, ready should an attack occur, while those without experience can be placed as a "rear guard" position that, in turn, becomes a learning situation to improve their readiness (good luck!).

The management of events offers a classic opportunity to use and assess a full range of personal and organizational operational practices. Information management practices provide participants with data about the situation and stakeholders. Information practices are critical for all events. The same is true for evaluation and knowledge management practices. Evaluation practices provide needed assessments regarding the progress of the event-management process or particular details about what's occurring, like the quality and quantity of information received. These and other practices, when used in conjunction with the competencies and sense of urgency one brings to the event, are strong indicators of the success one might associate with the process.

Individual competencies often are suggested as the best predictor of success for those involved in managing an unfolding event. But, it's important to recall that competency is a multidimensional construct that helps define "one's ability to do the job" but not necessarily how one will behave when faced with actually "doing the job." In Table 13.3 the events outlined earlier are presented again with special consideration for the types of competency one might see associated with an event-management

Table 13.3 Self-Organization of a Response to Emergent Events—Three Examples

EVENT EMERGENCE (BECAUSE OF A VIOLATION OF "RULES")	THRESHOLD CROSSED	URGENCY LEVEL REQUIRES ACTION	REGAIN STABILITY TO "ADVANCE" THE EVENT OR "BREAK OFF"	BEHAVIOR CONTRIBUTES TO DEFINING PATTERNS AND FUTURE RESPONSES
Driver cuts you off on highway	You interpret as "aggressive driving" directed at you	You catch up and "offer a rude gesture"	Non-verbal argument develops or the two "break off" the situation	Both participants learn something about how to respond in the future
Teacher asks student to stop talking in class	Teacher interprets student's response as "rude"	Teacher takes the student aside	Teacher explains the problem for the student; sends to principal's office	Both participants learn something about how to respond in the future
Police office pulls driver over for "failing to stop at a stop sign"	Driver accuses officer of "profiling"	Police officer interprets this as a personal insult but remains focused on matter at hand	Driver is issued a ticket and leaves	Both participants learn something about how to respond in the future

strategy. This discussion is particularly interesting because it illustrates how organizational or personal practices and core competencies can be linked to the management of events and behaviors, whether one's own or those of others. In the aggressive driving incident, for example, "aggression," "communication management," "information management" and "control management" tactics appear to lead to negative results.

In contrast, in the "rude student" and "profiling traffic officer" scenarios we see similar competencies and practices emerging, only there they are used in positive *and* negative ways by the participants. The student and driver use communication to attack, while the teacher and officer use the same competencies to control the setting. Notice, too, how particular competencies can be used in combination to achieve a goal for the situation. Both the teacher and officer use communication and control management competencies and practices together to bring order to their events.

We do not know how any of these situations turned out, but one can speculate about potential outcomes for them. The extent to which competencies and practices are strong or high, or when they are moderately or poorly developed, will affect an event's results. For example, in their recent book, *How to Break a Terrorist*, Mathew Alexander and John Bruning (2008) offer alternative approach strategies for interrogating terrorists.

The strategies they recommend are positive and proactive and parallel the relationship, communication, evaluation and information practices and competencies presented earlier. Their discussion centers on how the positive use of practices, combined with interrogator competencies, can make a terrorist more willing to participate while negative use of management practices can push the terrorist away from the interrogator.

Several factors can affect an individual's choice of strategies and/or personal competency levels and just possessing the core competencies in the five areas outlined earlier doesn't guarantee success. The key is how the competencies are used in combination with available operational practices and, of course, balanced against the urgency of the situation.

Tables 13.4 and 13.5 show how examining different situational factors can contribute to the development of self-organized behavior. In these examples, the makeup of one's position or occupation, competency requirements and the impact of three common conditions, an individual's emotional, physical and cognitive characteristics, are examined as contributors to self-organized behavior. In the tables ten positions, representative of those experienced in modern society, are described.

Next, as the information in Table 13.5 illustrates, when an individual's occupation is examined in terms of ways they can be shaped by the

Table 13.4 People, Positions and Events in a Typical Modern Society

---

1. A union organizer: this person has a mission: insists on change in the organization and cooperation from co-workers.
   Significant extreme event: threatened with a violent response by the company.

2. Suicide bomber (at the direction of another): has a goal, knows what to do (sometimes not why or when).
   Significant extreme event: possible detection by authorities.

3. Assassin: has a goal. Knows what to do and how. Usually trained.
   Significant extreme event: detection by authorities.

4. Expert cross-cultural communicator tourist has a vision of "how to behave" in cross-cultural interactions.
   Significant extreme event: hostage-taking terrorist event.

5. Evangelical crusader: emotional attachment, proselytizer, "lives the mission."
   Sample extreme event: hostile attack by competing group.

6. A racist. Knows what not to like. Knows how to "communicate" feelings or sentiments.
   Sample extreme event: possible discovery by authorities.

7. Shop owner. Knows products and services, the market, the customer.
   Sample extreme event: armed robbery.

8. Brain surgeon. Completes often long, complicated operations in a very complicated body area.
   Sample extreme event: patient suffers heart attack during operation.

9. Professional basketball player. Competes against the best opponents. Long season, many games.
   Sample extreme event: player is attacked by fan of opposing team.

10. Jet airline pilot. Manages take-offs and landings. Significant responsibilities for passengers, crew and equipment.
    Sample extreme event: crash landing.

---

disposition or general cognitive, emotional or physical skills required to perform the job, one gets yet another view of potential causes of self-organization within particular settings. The tasks required of a suicide bomber, for example, don't require much in the way of cognitive competencies or capabilities but completing the task of carrying and detonating a bomb can require a strong emotional makeup, or at least a certain amount of resolve and courage.

The least taxing of the positions outlined appears to be the "evangelical" crusader. On the other hand, successful cross-cultural communication may require strong cognitive competencies and the brain surgeon requires high core competency levels across the board (professional, basic skills, team, etc.) and an overall strong cognitive, emotional and physical profile.

Table 13.6 presents yet another view of potential products, outcomes and impacts associated with spontaneous, self-organized behavior. In

Table 13.5 Comparison of Different Positions Given Cognitive, Emotional or Physical Requirements for Successful Performance across a Range of Events

	COGNITIVE SKILLS NEEDED (the intellectual capacity required to act or perform successfully)	EMOTIONAL SKILLS NEEDED (feelings, sentiments or general emotional makeup required to perform)	PHYSICAL SKILLS NEEDED (the strength, stamina or physical capacity to act)
Very high core competency requirement levels	8. Brain surgeon 10. Airline pilot	2. Suicide bomber 10. Airline pilot	9. Professional basketball player
High core competency requirement levels	4. Cross-cultural communicator 5. Evangelical	1. Union organizer 6. Racist 8. Brain surgeon 9. Professional basketball player	8. Brain surgeon 10. Jet airline pilot
Moderate core competency requirement levels	1. Union organizer 3. Assassin 7. Store owner 9. Professional basketball player	4. Cross-cultural communicator 5. Evangelical	1. Union organizer 3. Assassin
Low core competency requirement levels	2. Suicide bomber 6. Racist	3. Assassin 7. Store owner	2. Suicide bomber 4. Cross-cultural communicator 5. Evangelical 6. Racist 7. Store owner

Table 13.6 the ten positions presented in Tables 13.4 and 13.5 are listed again but, in this case, rather than behavior resulting from directed planning, behaviors that might emerge as a result of self-organization are presented. The list of "representative self-organization acts" in the table is interesting, but what is most likely to stand out is that this list contains only the most obvious effects associated with each position. What would be most interesting is if the list of potential spontaneous, self-organized acts for each position contained three or four examples. Then it would be possible to see a range of potential effects associated with unplanned self-organizations. This might be more dramatic.

When the model presented above is examined in light of the information in these tables, one can see that the self-organization process is a process defined by attempts to maintain balance and control as time

Table 13.6   What Spontaneous Self-Organization Opportunities Might Look Like for Select "Occupations"

THE POSITION	REPRESENTATIVE SELF-ORGANIZATION ACTS
A union organizer	Tries to get workers to "walk out" before being represented
Suicide bomber	• Premature detonation (not according to plan) • Deciding not to detonate
Assassin	Deciding not to shoot the target
Cross-cultural communicator tourist	• Intervenes in a cross-cultural dispute • Volunteers tour information
Evangelical	• Offers personal interpretation of the Bible • Speaks on behalf of the Church without permission
Racist	Creates racist act without direction
Basketball player	Takes a risky, perhaps low-probability shot at a critical point in a key game
Brain surgeon	Attempts an unorthodox surgical procedure
Jet airline pilot	Decides to "bring the plane in" after being told not to do it now
Shop owner	Resists a robbery attempt

passes and events unfold. Urgency is matched against new developments, and both are influenced by competencies one brings to the situation. And then, as if to really spice things up, the setting's physical, emotional and psychological demands permeate the process in a purely stochastic manner.

REPAIR OF THE OLD OR MAINTENANCE OF THE NEW ORGANIZATION

There are several differences among the four types of organization introduced in this book. The community organization, for example, tends to evolve over time, partially because a community is characterized by hard-to-define-values, ideas or ideals, the meaning and saliency of which often only evolve along with the community and its membership. The others organizational types, in contrast, frequently are constructed by design.

An enterprise organization is a nuts-and-bolts operation, grounded in rules, procedures, policies and structure. These are tangible, measurable organizational features. Teams and groups, too, are established in terms of predetermined models and requirements. Size, for example, is a defining and limiting feature of both teams and groups. Teams and groups exist to accomplish defined goals, objectives and tasks and these, too, are tangible and measurable. Material traits or conditions also define the individual contributor organization. There are specific competencies, goals, objectives and tasks to be possessed and maintained.

When self-organizations occur within an organization change also occurs. In many instances, the introduction of change can modify existing practices, processes or procedures or, in extreme instances, cause splits within the parent organization. When this happens the ramifications can be significant. One significant change that sometimes occurs is that after the self-organization processes have occurred a new organization may emerge in response to the changes taking place.

An enterprise might move from being a privately held company to a public company with stock sold to the public at large. A volunteer fire department might evolve into a fully funded organization and now operate as a department with the local municipality. Whatever the case, the change can lead to new stakeholders, new expectations for performance and, in fact, an organization with a new and different vision and mission for itself and its membership.

When new organizations emerge they have two distinguishing features. First, the emerging organization typically still has some relationship with the former organization. The relationship may be harmonious, as when a group spins off to form a new venture or when distant locations are set up as offices or production centers. These are regular strategies companies use to facilitate the development of new markets, religions to set up new proselytizing centers or to increase membership, and military organizations to set up posts in different areas as a means for expanding the protective perimeter of the government they serve.

Other times the relationship is adversarial, perhaps in direct conflict with the former parent. Unions, cliques, special interest groups, new sects or wide-scale social movements often emerge as new organizations with unique links to the former parent. If the new organization is positioned as an alternative to what the former parent offers the relationship may be hostile or cold at best. Sometimes the new organization serves as a safe haven for those who need a place for comfort within the parent or as a way of contrasting the newly emerged organization with the alternative "old" organization, "old" way of thinking, "old" way of believing or, simply, "old" way of living and doing things.

A second, important feature of these new organizations is that they need to be organized, nurtured and maintained if they are to be successful. The post-emergence period is a critical phase of a new organization, one in which it is expected to perform in ways that meet participant needs and expectations while also learning how to function as a stand-alone entity. It's a period of invention. Processes, procedures, rules and practices are defined and developed to match the new organization's vision and mission. When the organization is a product of self-organization, the emergent structural and process features can occur hand-in-hand with the clarification of a vision, mission and values.

Questions during this period deal with fundamentals like, what's necessary to survive, who among us has the competencies to do "x" and, of course, whom can we count on for help? These types of question reflect both the organization's desire to advance and its simple need to survive—to make it through another day. They also illustrate the dynamic nature of complexity vis-à-vis organizational theory. Whatever the context, the actors, the needs or issues the evolutionary nature of organizations continuously responds to the change that's all around it.

CHAPTER 14

Conclusion
Open Issues and New Directions for the Application of Complexity Theory to Organizations and Organizational Research

Camazine et al. describe emergence as "the process by which a system of interacting subunits acquires qualitatively new properties that cannot be understood as the simple addition of their individual contributions" (2001: 31). Camazine et al. never specify the makeup of these "qualitatively new properties" but we see them as including people, processes, materials and changes to the physical, emotional and cognitive states of both people and the organization's environment. This orientation opens the door to a variety of topics or issues for future research. These include the following.

AN AUTONOMOUS AGENT, AN AUTONOMOUS ORGANIZATION, AN AUTONOMOUS EVENT

Stuart Kauffman, one of the early and prolific writers on complexity theory, began his book, *Investigations*, with a quote from Immanuel Kant which summarizes the spirit of the human self-organization process. For Kant, wrote Kauffman, an "organized being is then not a mere machine, for that has merely *moving* power, but it possesses in itself *formative* power of a self-propagating kind which it communicates." Later, Kauffman added to this notion and introduces his concept of an autonomous agent:

> I have tentatively defined an autonomous agent as a self-reproducing system that carries out at least one work cycle ... A next step is to realize that only well-known autonomous agents ... do actually carry out linked processes in which spontaneous and non-spontaneous processes are coupled to build constraints on the release of energy. The energy, once

released, constitutes work that propagates to carry out more work, building more constraints on the release of energy, which when released constitutes work that propagates further.

(Kauffman 2000: 101)

The individual, engaged in self-organizing processes, is the center-piece of this book. This is a person whose actions take charge of situations so they meet personal needs brought on by a particular moment or event. This orientation can present a dilemma for the organization. How does the organization as a whole manage self-organization when it occurs and, then, the results of these self-organizing efforts?

Is the individual, as an autonomous agent, capable of producing only one type of self-organization process or, are there different types, for example, formal and informal self-organizing processes that need to be addressed? What about the quality of processes created? Are some autonomous agents better at self-organization or more inclined to self-organization processes than others? Are there cultural or, as suggested earlier, possible competency requirements that can be associated with the agent's efforts?

A NEW TAKE ON THE GENESIS OF BEHAVIOR

One topic that surrounds discussions throughout the book concerns the genesis of human self-organized processes. What stimulates self-organized behavior to materialize, to emerge in organizations? Some psychologists suggest all behavior begins in response to a need, as need-fulfillment, but is that an established link that holds for all self-organization behaviors? An observation by Miller and Page illustrates the concern of some researchers. They write that much of

the focus of complex systems is on how systems of interacting agendas can lead to emergent phenomena. Unfortunately, emergence is one of those complex system ideas that exists in a well-trodden, but relatively untracked, bog of discussion. The usual notion put forth underlying emergence is that individual, localized behavior aggregates into global behavior that is, in some sense, disconnected from its origins. Such a disconnection implies that, within limits, the details of the local behavior do not matter to the aggregate outcome.

(Miller and Page 2007: 44)

Clearly, behavior is not disconnected from its origins, especially in an organizational context. First, context is important. A well-defined organization can place certain constraints on self-organizations, can enable them and/or can directly or indirectly influence or contribute to the nature and type of self-organization that may occur. Perhaps it's time to move beyond descriptive studies that seek to identify things like "those low-level routines [from which] shape emerges" (Johnson 2001: 19) and investigate:

1. the nature of the self-organization process(s); and
2. particular features that stimulate, nurture and sustain the process as it unfolds.

Events, for example, play a role in our lives; they happen all around us day in and day out. Some are naturally occurring, like weather events, but others are the product of human actions and it's the role of people in these events that can make life interesting. When and why are people rude, hurtful or kind? Why do people make conscious decisions to self-organize to do wrong, to be evil, to be ill prepared, or do good? Research in self-organization may be able to help turn these types of philosophical question into studies that open doors to an improved understanding of human behavior. Axelrod's (1980) treatment of cooperation, Krugman's (1996) look into economics or Rapoport's (1970) early study of conflict in his book, *Fights, Games and Debates*, are easy stones in the pond. Each offers levels of precision and thought to use for building future studies about the nature and foundation of self-organization within different social contexts.

IS SELF-ORGANIZATION PREDICTABLE?

Well, here's a hot topic. Predict a dynamic process? One obvious thing we want to explain is why self-organization occurs or does not occur when the proper criteria are in place. Is self-organization a foregone conclusion if certain criteria are in place or does something else have to act as a catalyst for self-organization to occur? If the criteria are in place, does the individual also need certain characteristics (e.g., competencies) to proceed or to be successful? Are certain environmental conditions necessary for emergence and self-organization? In short, what role do systemic features within which the behavior emerges play in the self-organization process?

There are at least two contributions prediction can make toward our understanding of complexity theory generally and the self-organization process specifically. The first is linked to a need to reduce possible negative effects associated with poor planning. Prediction helps take the mystery or magic out of the emergence of phenomena around us.

This mystery is appealing to a certain extent for, as Miller and Page point out:

> part of the innate appeal of emergence is the surprise it engenders on the part of the observer. Many of our most profound experiences of emergence come from those systems in which the local behavior seems so entirely disconnected from the resulting aggregate as to have arisen by magic.
>
> (2007: 45)

But there are costs with only seeing something emerge and not knowing why it occurred, if it will occur again and, of course, what is likely to happen next. For example, Krugman suggests that the "initially disordered structure organizes itself, because a disordered structure is unstable when subject to random shocks" (1996: 47). In other words, prediction may be useful in helping to reduce ambiguities associated with the unknown.

Predicting self-organization processes is possible if one addresses the process from different directions. For example, Holland (1998) uses the "transition function" to predict change in a model from one point in time to another (Holland 1998: 47–49). The role of transitions was noted in the models presented above because, as Johnson has noted, they mark the move "from one discrete state to another" and, importantly, they signal that these moves are "not gradual but sudden as though a switch were thrown" (2001: 63–64).

But what may be most interesting about attempts to utilize predictive tools in studies of complexity, emergence and self-organization is the range of opportunities possible beyond those noted. There appears to be a greater likelihood of self-organized behavior occurring in poorly rather than well-structured organizations. Indeed, given the typology of organizations presented (i.e., the community, enterprise, team or individual contributor) self-organization may be germane to some organizations simply because of their purpose or the way in which they are designed. So, self-organization may be more likely to occur in some organizations and, if one understands the organization's role in defining the results of activities or efforts, it's also likely one may be able to predict the products, outcomes and impacts of those results.

WHAT IS SUCCESS?

What is a successful self-organization? Is there a way to judge that one self-organization is better than another? Does it matter? In biology if we are studying the development of, say, an appendage like a finger, a

typical example of self-organization in these studies, what do we conclude if the final product is defective? Is that merely self-organization
with a poor end result?

As we noted earlier, Krugman concluded that self-organization "is
something we observe and try to understand, not necessarily something
we want" (1996: 6). This notion seems especially true for those instances
when self-organization yields undesirable results. However, sometimes
organizations try to stifle self-organized events that the organization's
leadership sees as unwanted but that, on a different stage, might be
considered desirable or even encouraged.

Whistle-blowing, creativity, defiance of "unjust" laws and sometimes even change itself, are examples. But are these examples of good
self-organizations or deviant behavior? Pushing our understanding of
self-organization and complexity theory into different contexts helps
clarify our definitions of success and, importantly, those instances which
could be accepted and encouraged without necessarily having an expectation of "success" attached to them.

The question of success is open for all studies of self-organization
regardless of the context. What, for example, can complexity theory tell
us about the genesis of disease on a societal level, the collapse of the
banking or automobile industry or a competitive engagement between
two teams or adversaries, like a terrorist or criminal organization and
the police? In the context of success even evil can be done well.

In fact, viewing adversarial relationships from complexity theory's
objective perspective may provide helpful clues to nagging problems facing
people and society today. Our studies ask questions like "Why does a
driver choose to be aggressive?" or "What goes through the mind of the
suicide bomber before and at the time the trigger is pulled?" As potentially
tragic as these self-organized events can be, they are successes for some of
those involved. In light of the previous section can they be predicted and,
in turn, the level of "success" limited or prevented?

Since self-organization may be interpreted as an ongoing measure
of every part of every activity, what can complexity theory contribute to
our understanding of what the profile of successful systems, like organizations, could look like? Which practices are critical to an organization
and should practices be conceptualized in different ways? Are there
core practices for use in everyday matters and other, supplemental practices, for use in critical emergent situations? Should the definition and
interpretation of an organization's lifecycle be amended to include
periods of wanted and unwanted self-organizations or the role and
impact of ecological succession? It is quite possible that the concept of

an organization's lifecycle is an anachronism—after all the term's use is usually after the fact, to provide a descriptive tale about "what happened."

ARE THERE BOUNDARIES TO SELF-ORGANIZATION OR IS THE DEPTH OF THE PROCESS YET TO BE PLUMBED?

Axelrod's (1984) book, *The Evolution of Cooperation*, is a perfect place to start this last segment of the chapter. His study of self-organization and cooperation is both a solid example of research in the field and an illustration of how good research can open the door for research in other areas. For example, what if we take Axelrod's treatment of cooperation as a process and recast it instead as the rubric for, say, the phenomenon of cooperation. Now we can explore issues like the role of cooperation in the self-organization of communication environments or for building trust.

What does cooperation contribute to the self-organization process and to relationship-building? Once these parameters are established concepts like self-disclosure, trust and risk-taking might be added to gain a fuller understanding of the development and nurturing of relationships. Our early studies on self-disclosure helped identify categories of secrets and their risk level, but we could only speculate on what effects self-disclosure, a self-organized phenomenon, might have on relationships (Norton et al. 1974).

Lieberman et al. (1973) for example, reported the "stranger on the bus" phenomenon as a device people would use to disclose their innermost secrets to pure strangers. Self-disclosure in this instance was a purely self-centered act; it wasn't used to build a relationship, just to reduce the stresses an individual might carry because of the risk (e.g., fear of rejection) associated with telling one's secret to another, say a friend or associate. But self-disclosure is part of a healthy relationship and, too, a good illustration of self-organized response to a situation, so how might self-disclosures be effectively handled given what we're learning about both processes?

There's been a lot of controversy regarding the treatment of prisoners vis-à-vis the self-disclosure of information, so is it possible that our understanding of complexity theory might better enable those in a position expected to secure this type of information to get it without the use of force or deception? Can complexity theory contribute to efforts aimed at making people more humane toward one another?

WHAT ABOUT THE FORMATION OF NEW ORGANIZATIONS?
BIG AND SMALL WORLDS AND THEIR OLIGARCHIES

What can be gained by applying complexity theory to our understanding of power, authority, influence and conflict on one hand or problem-solving, invention, innovation or peace on the other? Simply stated, a lot. There are obvious moments in an organization's lifecycle. Complexity theory as it's applied helps us understand:

1. why certain organizations exist;
2. how they exist; and
3. what can be done to grow or stop or terminate organizations.

We reported, for example, on one effort to stimulate innovation in an organization by creating conditions and an environment which fostered self-organization; this is an example of the three points just presented being used at an organization's microscopic level. Typical issues for researchers engaged in this level of organizational change and design are reflected in questions like "Can self-organization become a sustainable feature of an organization as a whole?" or "What happens after the exercises in self-organization, innovation and creativity end?" "To what extent, if any, does participation in any self-organizing effort become part of an individual's operational style?"

Simon Johnson's recent article in *The Atlantic* entitled "The Quiet Coup" may provide another use of the theory and its application to the study of self-organizations at macro levels. The thrust of Johnson's article is that groups within a country's private sector sometimes organize to form private oligarchies that, in turn, run the country to their benefit: "rather like a profit-seeking company in which they are the controlling shareholders" (Johnson 2009: 48). Johnson sees these organizations as a potential threat to both the host countries and, in many specific instances, the global economy as a whole.

From this book's perspective Johnson's theme and analysis are interesting because they present insights into the operations of organizations with a macro span of influence. The potential threat Johnson outlines seems real enough so that readers are likely to ask themselves how is it these organizations can and are allowed to form, or what can be done to curb their development and subsequent influence, or how might an oligarchy benefit the host nation and not just a group of entrepreneurs?

Clearly answers to these questions, as well as examinations of social conditions of this type and scale, are fodder for complexity and organization theorists. Johnson's oligarchy example follows classic emergence patterns outlined in complexity theory and illustrates potential benefits of this type of analysis on both the cause, design and potential solution for the problem as he defines it. In this instance, then, the theory is taken out of the controlled setting of the lab or college library and is thrust into the dynamic, complicated world of culture or society at its grandest scale.

The times are right for theorists to push our understanding of the inherent processes that define complexity theory and how they might be used in organizations and other social systems to better explain events, operations and, ideally, to speculate on the future. Otherwise another theory will sit on a shelf and another set of opportunities to understand individual and organizational performance may be lost. Indeed, to dramatize the extent of what benefits may be lost or compromised by failing to continue research in this area, consider one final table. It stands alone and simply summarizes what's been discussed in the book regarding organizations, performance, complexity and self-organized behavior. One wonders how it might be used as a checklist to examine organizations in general or as a tool for testing any of the myriad of hypotheses possibly associated with the key points listed in the table.

Table 14.1   What's Been Discussed, Reviewed and/or Learned? A Summary of Key Points Raised Regarding Complexity Theory, Organizational Design and Operational Effectiveness

---

Organizations exist to achieve their vision and mission.

Events are constructed to achieve the organization's vision and mission.

Organizations use structure (e.g., hierarchy, operational practices, policies, procedures) to provide direction and control to achieve vision and mission.

Complexity theory and its components, *emergence* and *self-organization*, are tools for describing, explaining and understanding events and their management.

The *emergence of events* is one type of emergence one can observe.

Events range from routine and planned for to unexpected and unplanned.

Poor management of events can increase risk exposures, threats and vulnerabilities.

Organizations use operational practices as strategies and tactics to get desired behavior.

Organizations embed performance strategies and tactics in operating practices.

Left on their own, people create their own solutions or direction; they self-organize.

An *event management strategy* is a second *emergence* observed in organizations.

Some organizations encourage invention, thinking outside the box, and self-organization.

Table 14.1 (Continued)   What's Been Discussed, Reviewed and/or Learned? A Summary of
Key Points Raised Regarding Complexity Theory, Organizational Design
and Operational Effectiveness

Regardless of an organization's wishes, people sometimes do what they want when faced with
an event.

Simply summarizing results of effort is not a full picture. Products, outcomes and impact are
characteristics of results.

Forecasting or predicting performance in the management of events is possible. Predicting
performance is a function of the organization's performance profile; its strengths and
weaknesses, risks, threats and vulnerabilities, operating practices and competencies given the
events at hand.

Problems, Rationalizations and Performance Management

Rationalization has become such a commonplace alternative to problem-solving that it can be a form of problem behavior in some organizations. For example, Table A.1 presents some common rationalizations heard in the enterprise, the community, groups and teams and the individual contributor organizations. This discussion is presented here, in an appendix, because the topic, while important, seems to stand alone as a special issue associated with self-organization and human behavior, in this case, self-organization vis-à-vis the decision-making process.

Information gathering and planning are strategies designed to counter competitor or environmental challenges one might face, but engaging in them doesn't guarantee the planning or research will be complete, accurate or finished in a timely manner to be of use. Moreover, simply implementing a problem-solving strategy also doesn't guarantee that the results will be communicated to those who need the information. In short, the rationalizations illustrated may be only tangentially related to some "obvious" problem; in fact, the rationalizations may signal troubles resulting from deeper issues within the organization as a whole.

PROBLEM-SOLVING AND INACTION

The four different organizational types do not exist in isolation; their roles are partially defined by their relationships with each other. Because of this inter-relationship, any rationalization about a problem in one dimension affects others in the organization. For example, a team's rationalization about one of its members says something about the organization and/or the individuals who can or do make up the team. The rationalization, "Sure he's a poor leader, but what's our alternative?" may be making a statement about the organization's willingness to deal

Table A.1 Representative Rationalizations used to Avoid Dealing with Problems

ENTERPRISE	"I know our competitors keep coming out with new changes to this year's product but they've got the staff, money and support and we don't. We'll just have to make it up next year." "I know we should have casualty insurance but we can't afford it, not now anyway. We'll just have to make sure everyone is careful." "Sure, it's poor customer service but he's tired. We're all tired. Our customers will just have to understand."
COMMUNITY	"I'm sure he'll fit in over time." "Our mission statement has to be broad enough to reflect the needs of the entire membership." "He's the leader. He cannot do wrong; he is always the leader." "Our culture *does not* have to 'keep up with the times'!"
GROUPS AND TEAMS	"If their team can't handle it we'll just have to let the other teams pick up the slack." "Sure, she's a poor leader but what's our alternative?" "Police brutality? It's a judgment call. I'll bet if you were in that situation you'd do the same thing."
INDIVIDUALS	"I know he's not supposed to eat those foods but he really likes them and it's just a little bit." "They're politicians, what do you expect? There's nothing we can do so just forget about it." "Why go through all the pain of changing? No one can live forever."

with problem managers once they are appointed or the general lack of leadership competencies among individuals in the organization as a whole. The rationalization's apparent target problem, "poor leadership," may indicate that there are bigger problems to be managed.

The same is true for rationalizations used by individuals. They may not reflect a real problem but only a manifestation of a problem or shortcomings of the problem-solver. Moreover, as was the case for the enterprise and group, the use of rationalizations by individuals can be a learned strategy for dodging the problem and its circumstances. As a strategy, rationalizations may be a very economical way to go about addressing problems—at least in the short term. How much time, after all, does it take to "delegate" a problem away?

All strategies require the tactical use of resources (e.g., time, people and money), the development and use of different processes and procedures, and an array of competencies to secure, design and implement the strategies and tactics. For example, strategies for reducing the chances of a heart attack may require quitting smoking (a change process), investment in exercising and exercise equipment (money and time resources) and learning new dietary habits or ways to think about nutrition (competencies). Any one of these tactics can overwhelm an individual and, in turn, lead to the abandonment of a "quitting strategy" and the return to the use of a rationalization ("Everyone has to die sometime").

The same is true within groups or teams. Look at the ways managers handle (or avoid handling) poor or problem team members. After all, what does being a "poor team member" mean? The concept is often ill defined and claims like "I know it when I see it" are not sufficient definitions.

Terminations take time and people to document a problem (resources), they must follow fair and objective policies (process requirements), and the observed problem and termination must be successfully communicated (competency) to the "poor team member," usually as part of a disciplinary program (process). So, again, rationalizations ("That's his way" or "We have to learn to live with all sorts of people") become useful management/avoidance strategies. And, in turn, the problem not only does not go away but others (e.g., lack of confidence in management, lack of consistent policies and procedures, perceptions of favoritism, etc.) can remain or are created.

WHY EXAMINATIONS OF RATIONALIZATIONS ARE IMPORTANT

Taken at face value rationalizations are strategies used to dodge or perhaps delay addressing a problem but this does not mean they are insignificant or trifling strategies. For example, rationalizations also demonstrate another characteristic of problem identification and management and that is the tendency to organize a response regardless of its appropriateness or ability to be effective. In short, rationalizations may be defining a critical, pre-emergent point in a dynamic problem-solving process for the system at hand—whether an enterprise, community, team or individual.

It's natural for those in organizations to prepare a response to problems or problem situations. The documented "fight or flight" response is an illustration. In this instance, deciding to stand and "fight" or to avoid a fight and flee ("flight") reflects the two approaches to problems; one "active," the other "passive." Using "fight or flight" alternatives as an illustration is not meant to imply that rationalizations are a neutral point but rather that they can be a useful strategy in certain situations in at least three ways.

First, the use of rationalizations can provide a deflection point for actions related to politically or emotionally charged situations. For example, a socially desirable response in a politically charged or dangerous situation can help in the management of the situation or communication setting. This strategy may be a necessary first step when, for example, "face saving" is an important part of the solution for a particular problem. Second, rationalizations may provide an unobtrusive or hidden organizing point. In this instance the rationalization is a way for disguising a true response timed to unfold later. Tactically, using rationalizations in this manner helps buy time until, for example, needed information is obtained. Finally, the rationalization may be used as a stall; a response when either an active or passive response is not possible. In this instance the rationalization reframes the problems, perhaps making it more manageable, given the problem-solver's available resources. It's not the final solution but a dodge, a "red herring" or "straw man" argument designed to busy the opponent while a better response is prepared.

What is important about these three uses of rationalization is that they may actually be signaling a very important threshold point—a point that is approached but not crossed and, without being crossed, holds the potential problem-solver in a unique position. He/she knows where he/she is, but others do not or they have a false or unreal impression about the person's position. So, while rationalizing is a commonplace occurrence in the problem-solving and decision-making processes, rationalizations may merit special attention for at least two reasons. First, they can be signals of a deeper problem than one immediately apparent and, second, they serve as a warning system regarding the nature of the decision, and subsequent behavior that may result.

Rationalizations may provide a clue to not only the decisions that may follow but also the magnitude of the response to be generated. If it's possible to use a rationalization sometimes the process can provide a useful type of incubation period. When this happens, the use of rationalizations as delays could lead to the production of decisions or responses that are less predictable, more thoughtful, and perhaps even more appropriate. Rationalizations are not without their risks, however. A rationalization can be perceived as disinterest in the problem, as an insult to injured parties who may feel that insult on top of injury is more than one can tolerate, or as a sign of weaknesses or inability to construct a response because needed resources are not available. If these are the result then "a problem" may turn into "a crisis."

DIRECT PERFORMANCE THROUGH PERFORMANCE MANAGEMENT

Most control mechanisms (e.g., those associated with information and communication management strategies) tend to be designed for wide-scale applications and usually for the entire organization. Individual, team or group "performance management strategies," however, usually are linked to specific individuals or groups.

Table A.2 illustrates how "products," "outcomes" and "impacts" can be used as *performance guidelines* or as part of a larger performance assessment process. In this instance, the *product* is the object produced or service provided. If this material or service meets expectations, one can describe certain "outcomes" associated with the event and the resulting product.

One *outcome* may be that the individual can continue working as planned. This is a positive outcome. Another positive outcome may be an increase in orders or repeat business by the target client, especially after seeing that the product matched expectations. Seeing the finished product also may afford an opportunity to change the design; to make it better. In this case, the change also is positive because it may come *before* any long production runs begin.

Positive *impacts* are possible, too. Seeing the individual or team can perform as expected can influence the type or amount of work assigned. New work may be assigned, or more challenging work may be "the reward." A promotion or a bonus might be an impact of the "product/outcome/impact" sequence as well.

COGNITIVE RESPONSE TRAJECTORY PROCESS AND THE PROCESS OF SELF-ORGANIZATION

When managing individual performance the organization establishes controls (e.g., for new members) or re-establishes controls for existing members when their performance has fallen below expected levels. Whatever the case, the process begins with the stipulation of quantifiable baseline standards associated with the work to be done.

Once these performance levels are established, they are communicated to the individual(s). In this way, communication helps build and define a common understanding of the performance expectations for a particular job or assignment and for a defined period. Usually, too, ramifications for not meeting performance expectations also are communicated to the individual(s) involved. The process continues through the observation period and ends with a final evaluation and communication of the results of the evaluation.

Failure to institute performance management programs can result in several potentially negative effects, one of which is the likelihood that the individual(s) involved will *self-organize* their efforts to meet emerging needs as they see fit. From an organization's point of view, loss of control may result when individuals self-organize and that, in turn, may result in

Table A.2   Controlling Individual Behavior through Performance Management

PRODUCTS	OUTCOMES	IMPACTS	CONSEQUENCES
Products are observable results of one's efforts. They are the things one produces, the way one behaves, actions one takes, decisions one makes, etc. Products can be good/bad, well or poorly done, "as expected" or "less than expected," etc.	Outcomes result from products. It's a classic S–R or causal model. "You did 'x' and 'y' is an outcome." There may be more than one outcome associated with products. Outcomes can be good or bad, desirable or not, etc.	Impacts are the end result of the products and outcomes. Their presence can be long-lasting, can unfold in other areas (i.e., not originally associated with the products or actions taken in the first place). Impacts, good or bad, are the REAL payoff.	Consequences are what emerge as a result of the ENTIRE stream: the POI. Consequences are the "conclusion" for this POI sequence, but not the end of the story.
"Your finished report for project x had these three serious errors."	"Because of these errors three things occurred: 1. the team had to devote a lot of costly rework to the report; time that frankly wasn't planned for. 2. the report was shipped and arrived at the client late. 3. work on other projects and reports is now late."	"Our client needed the report when we agreed to get it to them. The client is dissatisfied with our work on this report. Moreover, an already overworked staff now must work even more to catch up with their other work. This can have ramifications on both individual and team well-being."	"Since you've done this n-times before … so to avoid it from reoccurring we will meet weekly for an update of project progress, issues or concerns. We'll focus on areas where errors occurred and you will 1. outline why they occurred and 2. a plan to assure they won't occur again."
"Over the past month you have been late to team meetings on four occasions, been critical of people and the comments made have been generally disruptive. You have been told about this behavior before: it is rude, inappropriate and must stop immediately."	"Your behavior can intimidate others; it makes it difficult for others to participate."	"Your behavior disrupts meetings and time set aside for team communication. It negatively affects the team and its interaction; it takes time away from projects."	"You demonstrated behavior unsuitable for a person in your position; it must end now. Failure to refrain from the inappropriate behavior noted and for which you have been warned may result in disciplinary action."

the organization not achieving its mission, a change in organization direction, or the formation of divisions within the organization.

Before beginning a discussion of self-organization and performance management strategies as control mechanisms it is beneficial to address the potential for errors. Mistakes in assessments can emerge in a variety of ways. It's natural for people to approach events with some preconceived notions about what may or may not occur, for example, and these preconceptions are a form of bias. So, when one is preparing a performance management plan the potential role of bias needs to be addressed up front to reduce the likelihood of bias compromising the opportunity for a fair assessment.

In performance management plans preconceived notions can emerge as soon as one's behavior comes to the attention of others. First impressions are triggered in the minds of stakeholders who stand to be affected by the effort or are responsible for what is done. We refer to the impression creation associated with the review of products, outcomes and impacts as the cognitive response trajectory process (CRTP). The idea behind the CRTP is that impressions begin forming about performance prior to the performance event. It's as though the evaluator, consciously or unconsciously, is sketching a plan for what might be expected in the event. It's done in anticipation without any real regard for being positive or negative but it remains a form of bias.

Sometimes the bias is clearly positive. Other times it is negative, but there's always an element of bias and it is independent of the nature of the trajectory that unfolds with the performance observed. The bias may be observed at any point during CRTP, even when the process's results turn out to be positive. It's much like the person with a negative bias toward a political candidate. Even after the candidate has demonstrated the capacity to do a good job (e.g., as head of the organization, president of the country, leader of the project team, etc.) the person may still hold on to a negative bias toward the individual.

Both the bias and the trajectory are affected to some extent by the emergence of the product (P), outcome (O) and impact (I) associated with an event's performance management. A positively reviewed product will tend to result in positively reviewed outcomes and impacts. The opposite is true for negatively reviewed products. The organization's management needs to ensure that if the bias looks as though it will interfere with the ultimate evaluation, the person with the bias will be managed. The organization needs *the best solution*, not a biased perspective.

NOTES

CHAPTER 1

1. A quick review of the terms "complexity," "self-organization" and "emergence" in Wikipedia. com illustrates difficulties with the use of these terms. There's a lack of consensus regarding their meaning, the relationship among them, and when and how then can be used in research.

2. There are particular reasons for this focus on behavior versus people or organizations. First, it's an economical approach. It's easier to control for a behavior like "stealing" than it is to try and design a program for 20 different people who might steal (e.g., people with access to the room, new recruits, people with questionable backgrounds, people with motives, etc.). Second, behaviors can be ranked in terms of certain criteria. "Most important," "most valuable," "most likely to occur" are labels used in a variety of situations and, as importantly, have a logical negative referent, for example, "least important," "least valuable" or "least likely to occur." Using criteria helps tailor a behavioral focus in terms of factors like locations, type of event or seasons and this, in turn, helps better utilize resources used to track and manage the targeted behavior.

A third reason to focus on behavior versus people is that behavior is a constant while people constantly change. Good people go bad and bad people go good, smart people can lose their competencies with the introduction of new technology if they do not keep up and hard workers can get tired and become careless. Standards for performance, on the other hand, are relatively fixed, at least for a period of time or for a product, a production run, a customer, or for a job to be done. If performance standards need to be changed this usually can occur quickly. People, on the other hand, don't change in that manner.

Behavior can be measured in time and over time. This is important because it allows for comparisons: one might ask what the quality level was at the beginning of a run, during the run and at the end. Once collected the information can be used in a variety of ways: for example, how is the process working, at what point do workers become fatigued during the process, or what's the wear and tear on equipment and how does that affect quality over time? If there are apparent variances in behavior it is easy to isolate where they're located: just look at the people, processes, material, equipment or culture involved. Focusing on people doesn't allow for the same, straightforward approach. With people there's the list just mentioned and then one can add history, time of day, environmental factors and, of course, home life. Unfortunately, most of these are beyond the control of researchers!

Favoritism or bias is a fifth reason for focusing on behaviors rather than people. Liking one person over others can lead to errors when conducting evaluations, for example. People we like tend to perform better in our eyes than do people we do not like. This is a problem. Issues like favoritism and bias are easier to control when evaluations are based on behaviors. (This doesn't remove the attempt to leverage your decision by the friend who says, "I thought you liked me," but it does offer a response, "I do like you, but your 'behavior' was below what was expected in that event.") There are certain risks associated with the motivation for and use of controls so their use needs to be planned, managed and monitored.

CHAPTER 2

1. Some of the challenges in today's societies have led the leadership of organizations to use and expand the use of controls in ways they wouldn't have considered necessary just ten years ago. Schools have learned to protect their students and staff from "walk-on" or "drive-by" threats and other organizations have found that only paying lip service to matters like discrimination or harassment can lead to serious problems. The issue at all times and in all organizations is *the event* and what the organization does to anticipate, manage or prepare for it.

CHAPTER 3

1. Of course, this then begs the question, which of the other three should occupy the second, third and fourth positions in the organization? The answer is that it depends on the organization. The key point, however, is that it's important that the right sequence be developed. An enterprise like a sporting franchise, for example, must have a strong team segment in the second position if it hopes to be competitive. Likewise a hospital enterprise needs strong team profiles in its surgical and support areas and good doctors, perhaps in the third position, as individual contributors. Neither of these two enterprise examples would probably want their "community" dimension (e.g., glee or fan clubs for the sporting enterprise or hospital auxiliary for the medical facility) ranked higher than the fourth position. That would be the "tail wagging the dog." (Although it's been known to happen. Just ask the college football coach who lost a job because of discontented fans.) Lack of balance or inappropriate makeup of the overall profile can be detrimental.

CHAPTER 5

1. And there had better be an "I" in some teams or there goes your Point Guard who averages 45 points and 15 rebounds a game to a "team" that knows how to spell or, perhaps more appropriately, knows the relative contribution of spelling to their victories!

CHAPTER 10

1. Quality relationships are an important example, especially for community organizations. Good relationships have several distinguishing characteristics. Trust, for example, is a prerequisite for most good relationships, but trust can be defined in a variety of ways and from different perspectives. One person might want to be sure trust results in respect for personal needs, that someone will perform requested tasks with high standards or, most importantly, view all relationship values as important. Another person could easily have another interpretation of what trust means and should look like. Using a consultant or mediator can help resolve and manage potential differences in perspective, especially on important issues.

2. In some instances, however, especially in instances of extreme and unexpected events, training may not be extensive. In these instances, the practices serve as a reference for one to use in building a response where one wasn't anticipated. Again, the collection of operational practices available in a database as a referent serves as an extension of one's own memory, reducing the burden of information one might personally maintain.

REFERENCES

CHAPTER 1

Adam, John. 2003. *Mathematics in Nature: Modeling Patterns in the Natural World*. Princeton: Princeton University Press.

Ashby, W. Ross. 1962. Principles of the Self-Organizing System. In: *Principles of Self-Organization: Transactions of the University of Illinois Symposium*, H. Von Foerster and G.W. Zopf, Jr. (eds.). London: Pergamon Press, pp. 255–278.

Axelrod, Robert. 1984. *The Evolution of Cooperation*. Cambridge, MA: Basic Books.

Camazine, Scott, Jean-Louis Deneubourg, Nigel R. Franks, James Sneyd, Guy Theraulaz and Eric Bonabeau. 2001. *Self-Organization in Biological Systems*. Princeton: Princeton University Press.

Harford, T. 2008. *The Logic of Life*. New York: Random House.

Holland, John. 1998. *Emergence: From Chaos to Order*. Reading, MA: Perseus Books.

Johnson, Steven. 2001. *Emergence: The Connected Lives of Ants, Brains, Cities, and Software*. New York: Scribner.

Krugman, Paul. 1996. *The Self-Organizing Economy*. Malden, MA: Blackwell.

Polanyi, Michael. 1974. *Knowing and Being*. Chicago: University of Chicago Press.

Schrodinger, Erwin. 2006. *What is Life?* Cambridge: Cambridge University Press.

Seeley, T.D. 1985. *Honeybee Ecology*. Princeton: Princeton University Press.

Seeley, T.D. 1989. Social Foraging in Honey Bees: How Nectar Foragers Assess their Colony's Nutritional Status. *Behavioral Ecology and Sociobiology*, 24: 181–199.

Segel, L.A. and J. Jackson. 1972. Dissipative Structure: An Explanation and an Ecological Example. *The Journal of Theoretical Biology*, 37: 545–559.

Sole, Richard V. and Jordi Bascompte. 2006. *Self-Organization in Complex Ecological Systems*. Princeton: Princeton University Press.

CHAPTER 3

Milgram, Stanley. 1969. *Obedience to Authority: An Experimental View*. New York: Harper Colophon Books.

Washington Post. 2005a. Army Files Cite Abuse of Afghans: Special Forces Unit Prompted Senior Officers' Complaints. February 18.

Washington Post. 2005b. Military Court Hears Abu Ghraib Testimony: Witnesses in Graner Case Says Higher-Ups Condoned Abuse. January 11.

Washington Post. 2008. Standard Warfare may be Eclipsed by Nation Building. October 5, p. A16.

CHAPTER 4

Adema, Angela M. 2004. Investigating Space Shuttle Columbia's Accident: A Four Phase Systemic Model of Structure, Technology, Environment, and Transformation. Unpublished Dissertation. University of Alabama.

Beirne, Mike. 2007. The Customer Strikes Back. *Brandweek*, 48(41): 19–22.

Cabbage, Michael. 2003. Final Report by Columbia Board Shows NASA Knew Risks but let Safety Slide. *Tribune Business News*, August 27.

Dimitroff, Robert D., Lu Ann Schmidt and Timothy D. Bond. 2005. Organizational Behavior and Disaster: A Study of Conflict at NASA. *Project Management Journal*, 36(2): 28–38.

Ehrlich, Paul R. 2000. *Human Natures: Genes, Cultures, and the Human Prospect*. Washington, D.C.: Island Press.

Griffiths, Lawn. 2008. Fushek, Second Priest Excommunicated: Founding of Ministry Defied Catholic Church. *Tribune Business News*, December 16.

Jasper, Kelly. 2009a. Bishop Disappointed in Split: St. John's Episcopal Can Rebuild, He Says. *Tribune Business News*, January 6.

Jasper, Kelly. 2009b. St. John's Members Bolt Episcopal Flock. *Tribune Business News*, January 5.

Johnson, Devon S., Fleura Bardhi and Dan T. Dunn. 2008. Understanding how Technology Paradoxes Affect Customer Satisfaction with Self-service Technology: The Role of Performance Ambiguity and Trust in Technology. *Psychology and Marketing*, 25(5): 416.

Nowicki, Sue. 2008. Priest Backs off a bit in Letter to Congregation: Says Views Expressed on Voting, Sin were his Own. *Tribune Business News*, December 23.

Schein, Edgar H. 1985. *Organizational Culture and Leadership: A Dynamic View*. San Francisco: Jossey-Bass.

Tokasz, Jay. 2009. One Group's Leap of Faith. *Tribune Business News*, January 5.

Yim, Chi Kin, David L. Tse and Kimmy Wa Chan. 2008. Strengthening Customer Loyalty Through Intimacy and Passion: Roles of Customer-Firm Affection and Customer-Staff Relationships in Services. *Journal of Marketing Research*, 45(6): 741.

CHAPTER 6

Beverland, Michael, Francis Farrelly and Zeb Woodhatch. 2007. Exploring the Dimensions of Proactivity within Advertising Agency–Client Relationships. *Journal of Advertising*, 36(4): 49–60.

Brown, Garrett. 2008. Perils of a Schizoid Business Model. *ISHN*, 42(9): 34–35.

Industrial Worker. 2008. No Heat at Ohio Textile Shop Sparks Complaint, Workers Win NLRB Ruling. 105(6): 3.

Kever, Jeannie. 2008. College Students Nowadays Choose Action over Protest. *Tribune Business News*, August 10.

Kortelainen, Ketty. 2008. Global Supply Chains and Social Requirements: Case Studies of Labour Condition Auditing in the People's Republic of China. *Business Strategy and the Environment*, 17(7): 431.

Lim, Suk-Jun and Joe Phillips. 2008. Embedding CSR Values: The Global Footwear Industry's Evolving Governance Structure. *Journal of Business Ethics*, 81(1): 143–156.

Meyer, Nick. 2008. Group Rallys against Sweatshop Labor. *The Arab American News*, 24(1169): 22.

Reilly, Peter. 2008. The Benefits of Working Together. *Personnel Today*, August, pp. 26–27.

Rosenbloom, Stephanie. 2008. Wal-Mart to Toughen Standards. *New York Times*, October 22, p. B.1.

Science Letter. 2008. Unite Here: Largest U.S. Military Uniform Manufacturer Settles Charges of Labor Law Violations. October 21, p. 3848.

CHAPTER 7

Bueno de Mesquita, Bruce. 2002. *Predicting Politics*. Columbus: The Ohio State University Press.

Harford, Tim. 2008. *The Logic of Life*. New York: Random House.

Harrison, Neil E. (ed.) 2006. *Complexity in World Politics*. Albany: State University of New York.

Schellenberg, James A. 1982. *The Science of Conflict*. New York: Oxford University Press.

Sole, Richard V. and Jordi Bascompte. 2006. *Self-Organization in Complex Ecological Systems*. Princeton: Princeton University Press.

CHAPTER 8

Krugman, Paul. 1996. *The Self-Organizing Economy*. Malden, MA: Blackwell.

Watts, Duncan J. 2003. *Six Degrees of Freedom*. New York: W.W. Norton & Company.

CHAPTER 9

Arnold, Magda B. 1960. *Emotion and Personality*, Vol. 1. New York: Columbia University Press.

Arnold, Magda B. 1969. Human Emotion and Action. In: *Human Action: Conceptual and Empirical Issues*, Theodore Mischel (ed.). New York: Academic Press, pp. 167–197.

Gilhooly, K.J. 1982. *Thinking: Directed, Undirected and Creative*. New York: Academic Press.

Harford, T. 2008. *The Logic of Life*. New York: Random House.

Morowitz, Harold J. 2002. *The Emergence of Everything*. Oxford: Oxford University Press.

Nonaka, I. and H. Takeuchi. 1995. *The Knowledge-creating Company: How Japanese Companies Create the Dynamics of Innovation*. New York: Oxford University Press.

Von Krogh, Georg, K. Ichijo and I. Nonaka. 2000. *Enabling Knowledge Creating: How to Unlock the Mystery of Tacit Knowledge and Release the Power of Innovation*. New York: Oxford University Press.

PART III

Conlin, Michelle. 2006. Smashing the Clock: No Schedules. No Mandatory Meetings. Inside Best Buy's Radical Reshaping of the Workplace. *Business Week*, December 11.

Conlin, Michelle. 2009. Gap to Employees: Work Wherever, Whenever You Want. *Business Week*, "Management IQ" Blog, September 17.

Ferriss, Timothy. 2007. *The 4-Hour Work Week*. New York: Random House.

Ferriss, Timothy. 2008. No Schedules, No Meetings–Enter Best Buy's ROWE—Part 1. *The Blog of Tim Ferriss: Experiments in Lifestyle Design*. Online, available at: www.fourhourwork-week.com/blog/2008/050210no-schedules-no-meetings-enter-best-buys-rowe-pt-1.

McConnell, Steve. 1996. *Rapid Development: Taming Wild Software Schedules*. Redmond, WA: Microsoft Press.

Tolson, Jay. 2009. Interview, Former Chief Executive Officer of Fisher & Porter, Inc. Used by permission of Jay Tolson.

Wheelwright, Steven C. and Kim B. Clark. 1995. *Leading Product Development: The Senior Manager's Guide to Creating and Shaping the Enterprise*. New York: The Free Press.

CHAPTER 10

Arthur, W. Brian., Steve N. Durlauf and David A. Lane. 1997. Introduction. In: *The Economy as an Evolving Complex System* II, W.B. Arthur, S.N. Durlauf and D.A. Lane (eds.). Reading, MA: Addison-Wesley.

Camazine, Scott, Jean-Louis Deneubourg, Nigel R. Franks, James Sneyd, Guy Theraulaz and Eric Bonabeau. 2001. *Self-Organization in Biological Systems*. Princeton: Princeton University Press.

Conlin, Michelle. 2006. Smashing the Clock: No Schedules. No Mandatory Meetings. Inside Best Buy's Radical Reshaping of the Workplace. *Business Week*, December 11.

Johnson, Stephen. 2001. *Emergence: The Connected Lives of Ants, Brains, Cities, and Software*. New York: Scribner.

Levin, Simon A. 1998. Ecosystems and the Biosphere as Complex Adaptive Systems. *Ecosystems*, 1(5): 431–436.

Miller, John H. and Scott E. Page. 2007. *Complete Adaptive Systems*. Princeton: Princeton University Press.

Sole, Richard V. and Jordi Bascompte. 2006. *Self-Organization in Complex Ecological Systems*. Princeton: Princeton University Press.

Tafoya, Dennis W. 1978. Ethics and Intercultural Communication Research. In: *Ethical Perspectives and Critical Issues in Intercultural Communication*, Nobleza C. Asuncion-Lande (ed.). Falls Church, VA: SCA, pp. 62–68.

Tafoya, Dennis W. 1984. Research and Cultural Phenomena. In: *Methods for Intercultural Communication Research*, William B. Gudykunst and Young Yun Kim (eds.). Beverly Hills: Sage Publications, pp. 47–65.

CHAPTER 12

Anonymous. *Tribune Business News*. 2009. Editorial: Terror Alerts may Fade Out: Color Scale being Reviewed. July 16.

Archer, Todd. 2008. The Dallas Morning News Todd Archer Column: Dallas Cowboys can't Afford to Lose Sense of Urgency. *Tribune Business News*, November 20.

Blumenfeld, David. 2008. TECO Employees Flip for Safety Coins. *Occupational Hazards*, 70(10): 59–60.

Chabot, Hillary. 2008. Terror Alerts Misused, Sen. John Kerry Says. *Tribune Business News*, July 15.

Dean, Ray. 2008. Stand Out—In a Good Way. *Security*, 45(10): 50.

Defense Daily. 2008. Irregular Warfare Official: SSGANA Subs are Navy's Premiere Counterterrorism Tool. Vol. 240, Issue 18. October 27.

Haberman, Clyde. 2007. Mixed Message When Orange is an Agent of Government. *New York Times*, July 13, p. B1.

Hall, Mimi. 2009. Ridge Backpedals on Pressure to Raise Terror Alert Level. *USA Today*, August 31, p. A.5.

James, Frank. 2004. Homeland Security Head Denies Political Motives lay behind Recent Terror Alert. *Tribune Business News*, August 4, p. 1.

Kotter, John P. 1996. *Leading Change*. Boston: Harvard University Press.

Kotter, John P. 2008. *A Sense of Urgency*. Boston: Harvard University Press.

Kremer, Jerry. 2006. Whatever Happened to those Terror Alerts ... *Long Island Business News*, August 4, p. 1.

Shapiro, Jacob N. and Dara Kay Cohen. 2007. Color Bind: Lessons from the Failed Homeland Security Advisory System. *International Security*, 32(2): 121.

US Federal News Service. 2007. University of North Texas Professor Comments on Anniversary of Color-coded Federal Terror Alert System. March 12.

Wyche, Steve. 2008. Cowboys get their Leader Back, Return to Playoff Race with Win. NFL. com, November 19.

CHAPTER 13

Alexander, Mathew and John Bruning. 2008. *How to Break a Terrorist*. New York: Free Press.

Ashby, W. Ross. 1962. Principles of the Self-organizing System. In: *Principles of Self-Organization: Transactions of the University of Illinois Symposium*, H. Von Foerster and G.W. Zopf, Jr. (eds.). London: Pergamon Press, pp. 255–278.

Axelrod, Robert. 1984. *The Evolution of Cooperation*. Cambridge, MA: Basic Books.

Bak, P. 1996. *How Nature Works: The Science of Self-Organized Criticality*. New York: Copernicus Press.

Bak, P. Kan Chen and Michael Crentz. 1989. Self-Organizing Criticality in the Game of Life. *Nature*, 342(6251): 780–782.

Boulding, Kenneth. 1956. General System Theory. *Management Science*, 2(3): 197–208.

Jensen, H. 1998. *Self-Organized Criticality*. Cambridge: Cambridge University Press.

CHAPTER 14

Axelrod, Robert. 1980. Effective Choice in the Prisoner's Dilemma. *Journal of Conflict Resolution*, 24: 3–25.

Axelrod, Robert. 1984. *The Evolution of Cooperation*. Cambridge, MA: Basic Books.

Camazine, Scott, Jean-Louis Deneubourg, Nigel R. Franks, James Sneyd, Guy Theraulaz and Eric Bonabeau. 2001. *Self-Organization in Biological Sciences*. Princeton: Princeton University Press.

Holland, John. 1998. *Emergence: From Chaos to Order*. Reading, MA: Perseus Books.

Johnson, Simon. 2009. The Quiet Coup. *The Atlantic*, 303(4): 46–56.

Johnson, Stephen. 2001. *Emergence: The Connected Lives of Ants, Brains, Cities, and Software*. New York: Scribner.

Kauffman, Stuart. 2000. *Investigations*. Oxford: Oxford University Press.

Krugman, Paul. 1996. *The Self-Organizing Economy*. Malden, MA: Blackwell.

Lieberman, Morton A., Irving D. Yalom and Matthew B. Miles. 1973. *Encounter Groups: First Facts*. New York: Basic Books.

Miller, John H. and Scott E. Page. 2007. *Complex Adaptive Systems*. Princeton: Princeton University Press.

Norton, R., C. Feldman and D. Tafoya. 1974. Risk Parameters across Secrets. *Journal of Counseling Psychology*, 21(5): 450–454.

Rapoport, Anatol. 1970. *Fight, Games and Debates*. Ann Arbor: The University of Michigan Press.

INDEX

Page references to tables are in **bold** print

Conlin, Michelle 176, 183, 275
Connor, Nina xviii
control: community organizations
and the use of 32, **36**, 202;
Complex Adaptive and Competent
Adaptive Systems and 180;
controlling behavior beyond the
organization 49–50, 53;
controlling behavior through
performance management **268**;
enterprise organization 61; events
and control 152; evolutionary and
spontaneous change and 185;
information practices and
191–192; monitoring 57–58;
organizational structure and
40–**41**, 45, 206; organization
control profiles 55; and rule-driven
organizations 49; self-organization
and 16, 134–135; use of vision and
mission as a means for controlling
performance 19
Crentz, Michael 276

Dean, Ray 218, 276
Defense Daily 218, 274, 276
Delaney, Sue xix
Deneubourg, Jean-Louis 273,
275, 277
Dimitroff, Robert D. 66, 274
directional practices: and performance
194; vision and mission defined 6,
29; vision, mission, goals,
objectives as controls 19–20
Dunn, Dan T. 70, 274
Durlauf, Steve N., 275

effectiveness profile: defined in
terms of risks, threats,
vulnerabilities 113
Ehrlich, Paul R. 66, 274
emergence: of behavior **14**, 241–242;
critical element of complexity
theory 121, 124, 240; of a critical
state **127**; defined 4, 7, 181, 253;
emergence process 121; of events
109, 140, 151–154, 170, 179, **187**,
226, **244**; in natural vs. human

social systems **10**; of organization
destabilizers 206; of planned
activities **6**; of risks, threats,
vulnerabilities 114–118, 122–128;
thresholds and **244, 246**
enterprise type organization: defined
32; as an element of other
organizations 38, **39–40**; examples
of 32, **33–34**; make-up of the
enterprise 30, **36, 43**, 200–201;
performance and 200; structure
provides a framework 45; use of
rationalizations within **264**, 265;
see also typology of organizations
ethics: directional management
practices and ethics 194; ethics and
the use of complexity theory to
improve organizational effectiveness
177; ethics as the significant
dimension of credibility 103; as a
learned trait 213; as a stimulus
for growth in non-secular
organizations 63
events: and behavior 153, 156, 157,
170, 172, 177; characteristics of
188; competency and **244, 249**;
phases of **215**; problem
identification 119; problems
organizations face 118; and
resistance to change 213; results of
206; self-organization and **101**;
shaping behavior to manage events
149; slope-clearing events 241;
spectrum of 193, 211, 253;
strategies for managing 218,
221–222; thresholds and 188
evidence tampering as an example of
self-organization 154

false positive identifications 146
Farrelly, Francis 274
Farris, James 219
Feldman, C. 258, 277
FEMA: effect of different political
organizations on FEMA's mission
38; failure to manage Katrina
events as an example of
organization misalignment 38; and

unions: as community organizations
33, 65, 78, 194; as organizations
within organizations xviii; as a
product of self-organization 251;
in response to organizational
risks, threats and vulnerabilities
198; and urgency **212**
urgency: developing a sense of
220–223, 227–229; and event
management 159–162, **160–161**;
as a framework for organizational
effectiveness 209–213, **212**, **234**;
Kotter's principles applied to a
crisis **229**; Kotter's principles for
229; and operational practices
231–235, **234**; and performance
217–220, **223**, **246**; US Fed News
Service 235, 276

value-added: participation 4, **99**,
99–100, 216–219; and urgency
223, 237
vision *see* directional practices

Von Foerster H. 273, 276
Von Krogh, Georg 162, 275
vulnerabilities: controls used to
manage 56; defined 115–116;
illustrations of **133**; by organization
type **36–37**, **39–40**; self-
organization and 133–136

Wa Chan, Kimmy 70, 274
Washington Post 53, 56, 273
Watts, Duncan J. 141, 275
Welsh, Gail xx
Werden, Sara xx
Wheelwright, Steven C. 175, 275
Wikipedia.com 271
Will, Daniel xvii
Woodhatch, Zeb 274
Wyche, Steve 218, 276

Yalom, Irving D. 258, 277
Yim, Chi Kin 70, 274

Zopf Jr., G.W. 273, 276